Simply... Woman!

Hay House Titles of Related Interest

❧✳❧

All of the above are available at your
local bookstore, or may be ordered by visiting:

Hay House USA: **www.hayhouse.com**®
Hay House Australia: **www.hayhouse.com.au**
Hay House UK: **www.hayhouse.co.uk**
Hay House South Africa: **www.hayhouse.co.za**
Hay House India: **www.hayhouse.co.in**

Simply... Woman!

The 12-Week Body * Mind * Soul
Total Transformation Program

CRYSTAL ANDRUS

HAY HOUSE, INC.
Carlsbad, California • New York City
London • Sydney • Johannesburg
Vancouver • Hong Kong • New Delhi

Published and distributed in the United States by: Hay House, Inc.: www.hayhouse.
com • *Published and distributed in Australia by:* Hay House Australia Pty. Ltd.:
www.hayhouse.com.au • *Published and distributed in the United Kingdom by:*
Hay House UK, Ltd.: www.hayhouse.co.uk • *Published and distributed in the
Republic of South Africa by:* Hay House SA (Pty), Ltd.: www.hayhouse.co.za •
Distributed in Canada by: Raincoast: www.raincoast.com • *Published in India
by:* Hay House Publishers India: www.hayhouse.co.in

Interior photos: Korby Banner

Library of Congress Cataloging-in-Publication Data

Andrus, Crystal.
  Simply—woman! : the 12-week body/mind/soul total transformation program /
Crystal Andrus.
      p. cm.
  Includes bibliographical references.
  1. Weight loss. 2. Women—Health and hygiene. 3. Weight loss—Psychological
aspects. I. Title.
  RM222.2.A525 2004
  613.2'5—dc22

                                2004006241

                            ISBN: 978-1-4019-1983-2

                    11 10 09 08   4 3 2 1
                1st printing, revised edition, February 2008

                    Printed in the United States of America

I dedicate this book to my Aunt Sue,
who died of cancer just before its release. . . .

You were and always will be
Simply . . . Woman!

Contents

A Message from Crystal

When I self-published *Simply . . . Woman!* in 2004, I had no idea where this journey would take me. I was a single mother with little money, but I had a dream. I followed my heart, believed in myself, and took a chance. My faith paid off. Within a few months, things started to explode. I was traveling the country, giving talks to full houses, and appearing on television and radio. On December 11 (my birthday), I received a phone call from the president of Hay House with an offer for a book deal. It has been a whirlwind ever since.

It's amazing, really, because although I knew that I had created a profoundly powerful program, I didn't realize just how influential *Simply . . . Woman!* would become for so many real-life women, *just like you and me,* who wanted to empower themselves in body, mind, and spirit. In January 2007, the book was voted as a "Reader's Choice" across Canada, coming in at number 14, and since then it has gone on to touch the lives of thousands of women around the globe.

I am in awe and gratitude.

I've grown so much—not only as a woman and a writer—but as a student of life. I've met the most incredible women because of my fortune, and I've allowed myself to be immersed in their sage wisdom, advice, and love. This rewritten version of *Simply . . . Woman!* is a culmination of all of these new experiences.

So today, as you read this book and apply its principles to your own life, I encourage you to tap into the many resources I can now offer you!

First, be sure to join me on my Website: **www.simplywoman. com**. There you can download FREE meditations and recipes, receive ongoing e-mail support and encouragement (be sure to sign up for my monthly newsletters), join my unbelievably supportive community message forum, and be inspired by the many before-and-after pictures and stories of courage and transcendence.

I also offer a life-changing "12-Week BODY-MIND-SOUL Total Transformation *Tele*Course" that I run three times a year; and I have women of all ages, from all around the world, who call in from the privacy of their own homes to join me for these once-a-week calls. I'm amazed by their testimonials of triumph and discovery. Along with the *Tele*Course, I offer a certification program called "S.W.A.T." (Simply Woman Accredited Trainer) that will help you develop your own personal coaching/training practice.

Last, at the end of this book is a DVD with two workouts on it: The first is called "Tight & Toned," and it is an excellent exercise routine that you can do at home, without any equipment. The second workout is designed for you to do with the beautiful "Simply . . . Woman Total Workout Bench & Crystal Ball." This biomechanically superior apparatus will strengthen, shape, and sculpt your body perfectly and easily! I'm so excited about this machine, as it has been years in the making and the results are astounding!

If you want more information on the "Simply . . . Woman Total Workout Bench & Crystal Ball" or any of the other services available, please visit: **www.simplywoman.com** or call **1-877-SIMPLY9**.

All that I ask of you now is that you commit yourself to this program and watch your life unfold in ways you never imagined possible! You are worth it. You are *Simply . . . Woman!*

Peace be with you,

Preface

Beginning the Journey . . .

Women aren't the same as men; everything about us—from our bodies, hormones, and metabolisms, to our wants and needs—is different. We women are intuitive and sensitive, and most often we respond differently to problems and emotional demands. We're also more likely to be caretakers—we're nurturers and are usually responsible for the needs of others. Generally, we do more of the shopping, cleaning, parenting, nursing, chauffeuring, organizing, cooking, dieting, and (I hate to admit it) complaining than men.

We're also the emotional center of the home. When we're happy, our homes are happy; when we aren't, you can be certain our relationships aren't either. We set the tone. It reminds me of the familiar saying from the South: "When Momma ain't happy, ain't nobody happy!" And isn't it the truth! We're emotionally complicated and hormonal—we're up, we're down; we have good days and bad. We don't need to hear the staggering depression statistics to tell us that we're searching for something more. We know it. We *feel* it.

By and large, men are pretty simple creatures: What you see is what you get. Most men simply do not place the same burden on themselves, or maybe they just believe that looking perfect isn't *that* important. Wrinkles, gray hair, and cellulite are something we gals fight, while most guys view themselves as in better shape than they actually are. When we see an older man who's gained 20 pounds, we often say, "Boy, he must be living the good life now," but when a woman does, the common sentiment is, "She's really let herself go!"

We women are so hard on ourselves and each other, and unless we've done some serious soul-searching, we're extremely competitive and far too critical. We see ourselves through extremely scrutinizing eyes, and we think the world does, too.

Crystal Andrus

According to the American Psychological Association, women are twice as likely as men to suffer from major depression. One in four women is depressed, and antidepressant medication prescriptions are at an all-time high. We're looking to someone, or something, to make us feel better; and we're convinced that if our thighs were thinner or our breasts were firmer, we'd be happier.

The National Women's Health Information Center (NWHIC) claims that women make up more than 90 percent of people with eating disorders. We may be more at risk because of a desire to have the "ideal" figure, which is so often shown in popular media. The female stars of most movies are very beautiful and very young, and we're bombarded with television shows where many women compete for one man's affections or go under the knife for "extreme" plastic surgery in the search for beauty.

Having been a fitness professional, life coach, and advocate for women's health and self-empowerment for nearly 20 years, I know that wanting to look better isn't enough. If wanting *it* was all it took, we'd all have *it.* We'd all eat more healthfully. We'd all have more energy. We'd all stick to an exercise routine, effortlessly. We'd all feel happier, sleep better, and be less stressed. We'd all look and feel our best, but we don't . . . because *wanting is not enough.*

Over the years I've watched as the gyms I've owned or managed fill up with excited new members every January. Ready to take back control of their bodies and lose a few pounds, these people desperately buy into the New Year's–resolution strategy. February 1st would come and half of them were gone; by the 15th, 75 percent were nowhere to be found; and within two months, we'd usually be back down to the same crew of active members who had been there before the Christmas holidays began. Did you know that 90 percent of people who join a gym or start a diet give up after four to six weeks? So if you fall into that category, you're not alone!

Crystal Andrus

The truth is, we all know what to do. We know we need to move our body, we know we need to drink plenty of water, we know we should eat more fruits and vegetables, we know we need more sleep . . . we know, we know, we know. . . . Yet three to four weeks after we start that diet or join the gym, something triggers us to begin self-sabotaging—and within a few more weeks, we're back to our old patterns. We feel defeated, frustrated, and soon the self-punishing begins.

Why is it that only a small percentage of people can actually stick to a healthy lifestyle? What *is* that ever-elusive secret to success? And how do we keep it up for a lifetime?

After working with thousands of women over the years, I've discovered that although we *must* nourish ourselves with the right balance of healthy foods and exercise to look and feel fantastic, until we transform ourselves from within, diets and exercise equipment are futile. We may lose weight, but our problems will just manifest themselves in another way. Therefore, your focus can't *just* be about your body. It can't *only* be about the eating and exercise portion of this program. If it is, then I guarantee that you're setting yourself up for failure because weight gain and weight loss aren't about weight; they're about something much deeper. The body is merely the messenger, sending us warning signs when we're disconnected—and weight gain is just one of them. A heart attack is an extreme warning that things aren't working properly, but small yet significant signs will tell you when something in your life is out of balance, if you will listen.

Simply . . . Woman! is specifically designed to take you deep into your body and to decode its hidden messages, while aligning your body with your mind and soul. Once aligned, you will be empowered to live your most authentic life: *Thin thighs are just a by-product!*

Your Body

Your body is your vehicle for being. In other words, it's like the ship that sails on this "ocean" called life. Your body allows your soul—or the captain of your ship—to float and flow in this physical world.

A healthy body—or an unsinkable ship—is the most important thing you've got, yet sadly, it's not until we face a serious health scare that we realize it. Frantically, we then try to undo the damage we've so haphazardly and unnecessarily done to ourselves! I remember hearing late actor Christopher Reeve remark in one of his last interviews that so many able-bodied people live more paralyzed lives than he. How frustrating it must be for those who are faced with a life-threatening health condition or those living in an undernourished country to watch so many of us totally disrespect our bodies!

The fact remains that your body is your temple and must be treated with love, honor, and respect. Loving your body is very different from self-adoration. Loving your body isn't selfishness; it's fact. It's not shallow or superficial. Your body is the conduit for your soul.

Think of building your temple from the bottom up, like a pyramid: If the foundation isn't strong, you can't build a stable structure. The bricks and mortar are made from the nutrients you put into it, while exercise reinforces the integrity of the structure. You need to make sure that your body is getting the correct balance of foods, in the right combinations and amounts. Our brain, for example, is composed of 50 percent Essential Fatty Acids (EFAs). When given the right nutrients and plenty of oxygen (from exercising), your brain's "circuits" work effectively: Hormones are excreted in the correct amounts. Serotonin (your feel-good hormone) is released and then absorbed into your receptor sites. We feel stable, balanced, and content. Yet, if we don't eat foods high enough in these EFAs *daily,* our brain begins to short-circuit and

Crystal Andrus

soon we feel depressed, foggy, and lethargic. We then blame it on life, when in reality "our computer" has become bogged down and is desperate to be "defragmented."

It's just like the air we breathe: In order to survive, we need 78 percent nitrogen; 21 percent oxygen; and in the remaining 1 percent, a mixture of argon and carbon dioxide—and tiny amounts of neon, helium, krypton, xenon, and other gases. If the balance is even slightly off, we'll die. Similarly, our bodies need to have a perfect formula for optimal health—weight gain, irritable bowels, skin breakouts, heartburn, allergies, and headaches are just a few signals that we're out of balance. And heart disease, diabetes, and cancer—which are all on the rise in North America—are the extreme warning signs that the body isn't being nourished properly.

Simply . . . Woman! will guide you step-by-step, week-by-week, to show you exactly what your body needs to feel balanced, strong, clear, and energized, ready to work in harmony with your mind and soul.

Your Mind

Your mind is merely the navigational tool for your soul (or your captain), who's sailing the ship. Your mind was never intended to direct your life, yet for most of us that's exactly what governs our choices and behaviors (and as we all know, our mind can be our greatest ally or our worst enemy. *For most of us it's the latter!*).

On this journey, you'll come to understand and get better control over your mind. You'll learn to silence that negative voice inside your head so that you can start to hear the whispers of your soul again. You'll learn how to identify self-defeating patterns, raise your "emotional baseline," and alter your self-limiting "core" beliefs.

Core beliefs are different from logical beliefs. (After all, how often do you logically know the right answer or give great advice to others, but can't follow it yourself?) Core beliefs are your deepest, truest views about yourself and life. They're the number one indicator of your success, since your choices will always support your core beliefs not your logical beliefs.

For example, if you believe that men will let you down, they will, because you'll seek out men who will affirm your notions. If you believe that exercising is hard, it will be . . . and even if you began to enjoy an exercise program, you'd end up quitting it. If you believe that you'll never make enough money, you'll always be broke. And, if you believe that you're never going to lose weight, you won't . . . *not permanently!* As silly as it sounds, your mind would rather be right than be happy. You might not consciously realize it, but when you don't truly believe that you'll succeed, you're defeated before you start. When many of us begin to see success happening, we sabotage it because it doesn't line up with what our brain believes will inevitably happen. In other words, we ruin it *before* we can fail.

It's like a self-fulfilling prophecy; one that most people aren't even aware they're making! Perhaps you too truly believe that you're like that helpless ship, being tossed around in the stormy seas and have no control over your destiny. You must know that it's not true. Granted, you cannot change the size of the ocean waves or the way the wind blows, but you can change the way you set your sails.

So what are *your* core beliefs? What do you believe about yourself? What do you believe about life? Do you believe that you're a beautiful, fit, sexy, strong, intelligent, spiritual, grounded, successful, kind, loving, insightful, inspired, and worthy woman? Do you *even* believe that a "good woman" can be beautiful, fit, and sexy? Do you believe that a sexy woman can be spiritual and grounded? Do you believe that a spiritual woman can be strong and successful?

If you want to know what your core beliefs are, all you have to do is look at the circumstances of your life today. It's that simple.

Crystal Andrus

Simply look at what is showing up for you and that will tell you exactly what you believe.

Your core beliefs developed from the time you were a little girl based on what you heard and saw from your parents, siblings, extended family, and teachers. They are primarily driven, however, from the messages you learned about being a woman from your mother. You either rebelled or embraced her role, and you created a whole slew of beliefs based on your experiences (which is why beliefs are never true—they're only perceptions of truth). You learned about men from watching your dad. You learned about money, intimacy, relationships, parenting, and even how to handle stressful situations or deal with confrontation from seeing what your parents did.

So, if your present circumstances aren't what you want *(this is why wanting isn't enough),* then it's time to do the work of shining light on your core beliefs and then rewriting your life script. Until you get honest with yourself, without judgment or shame, you will continue to set yourself up to get exactly what you believe you're worthy of.

Recognizing your "emotional baseline" is also a critical component to changing your self-defeating patterns. Patterns develop in our early years as we learn certain behaviors from our parents. Unknowingly, most of us re-create the same emotional atmosphere in which we grew up. We always regress to our learned behaviors during a crisis, and it is at these times that one can best judge a person. Unsuccessful people lose focus, allowing negative emotions to take over, convincing themselves they didn't really want it in the first place. They often don't even realize that they're self-sabotaging. As a life coach, I see this all the time.

In addition, our body is designed to regulate all our systems within a certain zone. This is called *homeostasis.* And although we often think of this from only a physiological perspective—for example, the way our body tries to maintain a constant blood-sugar level—it also seeks to maintain an "emotional" homeostasis.

If you grew up in an angry home with your emotions "marinating" in anger, your body's emotional baseline would be that of anger. In other words, over time your body would become "addicted"—or maybe better said, "comfortable"—with anger and dysfunction, and as an adult your system would want to re-create that same emotional atmosphere even though your logical mind knows it's not healthy. Remember:

> **Your past will predict your future**
> **unless you can change your self-limiting**
> **core beliefs and shift your emotional**
> **baseline to a higher, happier level.**

Your Soul

Your soul is the mastermind of your life. It was tucked away inside of you at the moment of your conception. It is inspired, joyous, accepting, passionate, courageous, and willing. It believes in you. It believes in life. It knows that what *is* will always find a way and that fighting what *is* is futile. It believes in your dreams, and it never gives up on you. Your soul is your "gut instinct"—your intuition. It is that gentle nudge you feel when something excites you. It is that knowingness you sense when something resonates as truth.

Your soul will be with you long after your "boat" has sunk and your "navigational tools" have rusted away. It is the true essence of who you are. It was created in love, sees the endless possibilities for your life, and always guides you with perfect precision. It is your most trusted and worthy advisor. All you have to do is allow it. . . .

Sadly, few of us do. Instead, we get in the way. We stop listening. We stop allowing. And soon we begin to believe all the negative messages we've heard over our lifetime. We let our mind take

Crystal Andrus

over. We become afraid, and that fear immobilizes us, so we try to numb it . . . run from it . . . escape it. Addictions, eating disorders, bad habits, and depression begin to manifest. We feel inadequate. We feel unsure. We stop trusting. What's more, we're not sure that we can even trust ourselves. We're not sure that we will make the best choices for our *own* lives—for our own bodies, health, joy, passion, and needs—let alone anyone else's.

The truth is that we're taught to override our own instincts from the time we're little girls. We are taught to disregard our own innate wisdom, especially when it comes to anyone in authority: Teachers, doctors, pharmaceutical companies, even "Corporate America" all tell us what to do, how we should look and feel, and what to change about ourselves so that we'll be happier. We listen without questioning, almost like sheep. Then one day, maybe 20, 30, 40, even 50 years later, we wake up, look in the mirror, and barely recognize the woman staring back at us. How did we lose ourselves? Why is our body failing us? Where did those dreams for our lives go? *And who's going to save us?*

Over the next 12 weeks, you'll learn *how to save yourself!* You'll find out how to quickly and effortlessly reconnect with your brilliant "intuitive guide," to take great care of your body, and to get your mind to work for you rather than against you. The rest will unfold perfectly!

❧ ✳ ❧

This 12-Week Body/Mind/Soul Total Transformation Program isn't a new, radical plan filled with ridiculous recipes or unrealistic workouts; instead, it's a process of learning how to listen to your body again by asking yourself "what feels right" and nurturing yourself with life rather than food. The secret is finding out what's right for *you* and creating a harmony of living, loving, moving, eating, giving, and receiving that is uniquely and *Simply . . . Woman!*

Crystal Andrus

Here's what I've discovered and what you will, too, with this program:

- Twelve weeks seems to be just about right for making a lifestyle change. It takes time and effort to travel deep within your soul. You must face your fears, discover your truths, and learn to listen to your body's true needs: to eat when you're hungry, sleep when you're tired, rejoice when you're happy, and grieve when you're sad.

- You'll feel incredible improvements in four weeks, but that's only the beginning. A month isn't long enough to incorporate all the steps necessary to make them lasting. Know that programs that offer radical changes with little effort and in a short time are usually a fraud—anything worth having takes commitment and perseverance.

- After eight weeks, you'll really start to see the transformation happening. You'll say, "Wow, I really didn't think it was possible!" and you'll start to embrace the changes as you experience the incredible difference when you give your body the nutrients it thrives on and your mind the answers it has been searching for.

- Many people will reach their goals in 12 weeks, but this journey is different for everyone. No matter what pace you establish for yourself, you *will* get there. Sometimes you'll make substantial progress, only to be thrown a curveball that might temporarily set you back. *Simply . . . Woman!* gives you the tools that will teach you how to let setbacks empower you and catapult you forward. With honesty and resolution, you can make extraordinary improvements in all areas of your life.

Keep Your Focus

At times you may feel frustrated because you'll want changes to happen immediately. Taking control of your body (or any area of your life) requires patience, focus, and effort. I'll often refer to this process as taking "baby steps," yet it's the small and often seemingly insignificant daily decisions that will have the most impact on your future. *Focus is everything.*

Too many people say that they want to achieve success, but then they don't stay focused long enough to accomplish it. They're great on the good days, but they give in on the hard days. Yet if you were to spend a week with the most successful person you know, you'd discover that it's not that they necessarily work harder than an average person; it's that they're consistently focused on their objective. Each day they do the small but significant things that will bring about success. Their focus and daily choices determine where their lives are headed. They don't *hope* everything will work out—they stay focused until it does. They always have a "Plan B."

We all know what "Plan A" is: It's the diet we're supposed to be on—and are on when everything is running smoothly in our lives. Plan A is exercising every day, eating perfectly, loving our lives, and having willpower. But what happens when Plan A fails?

Plan B is your backup plan, or your real-life plan of action. It's how you maintain your effort and keep your focus when everything in your life isn't falling perfectly into place. For example, it's what you do when your child gets the chicken pox and you can't leave the house for a week, or how you cope when your boyfriend breaks up with you. *Simply . . . Woman!* will give you the real-life tools you need to create your own Plan B.

Challenge is a part of all success, but it's up to you to develop staying power and accountability for your reactions when challenged. Since you're probably already overwhelmed with life, the last thing you need is a confusing, belittling program that leaves you feeling even worse about yourself when it fails. I've discovered one of the most valuable secrets to guaranteed success:

> **Decide what you want.**
> **Form the right plan of action.**
> **Stay focused until you achieve it.**

I developed *Simply . . . Woman!: The 12-Week Body/Mind/Soul Total Transformation Program* over the past seven years, but it initially came from my own journals and the process of taking back my own body, and subsequently my life. I then created a 230-page manual that I used with my own personal-training clients, and eventually I created a customized system to teach my philosophy and techniques to an entire team of Simply . . . Woman Accredited Trainers (S.W.A.T.).

Many of our clients made incredible life changes, and some even decided to become certified personal trainers themselves. So, motivated and inspired by their success, I now have a team of extraordinary women who are living endorsements for my system. I've created a transformation plan that is helping countless women look and feel their best ever. And now you can have it, too.

Interwoven among the important nutrition and training secrets are many of our illuminating and inspiring stories. All my clients have shared a small part in this plan, and I'm so honored and thrilled to be a part of this journey with you.

〜〜〜 〜〜〜

Introduction

My Journey . . .

Like many people, I stumbled upon success, never having planned to design a life-management program or write a weight-loss book. In my early 20s, I managed a chain of health clubs, competed in fitness shows such as "Ms. Galaxy," appeared in magazines and on television, and taught aerobics. By most standards, I had a great life. With long blonde hair, a great physique, and a growing career, I *appeared* to be successful and happy . . . but I always felt as if something was missing. I was always striving for the next goal, never enjoying or even acknowledging the one I'd just accomplished.

My looks were critical for my chosen profession, and although I loved the attention, I resented the constant pressure. Deep down, I believed that wanting to be beautiful was superficial and shallow. I thought I craved attention and recognition, but I really yearned for something more—without having any clear idea of what it was or how to find it.

Being fit was all about the outside image, and I was hard on myself. For years I had 9 to 11 percent body fat (the average range for women is between 20 and 24 percent), yet I never thought I was lean enough. I didn't understand at the time that health and fitness should improve one's quality of life; instead, I put myself on insanely strict diet-and-exercise regimens for a few months, and then once I was in shape, I'd eat whatever I wanted and stop exercising. When I started to gain a few pounds, I'd start my cycle all over again. There was absolutely no balance in my life—nevertheless, I was disciplined when I had to be.

After a few years, I grew increasingly frustrated with the exploitation I experienced on the fitness circuit. I decided that maybe marriage and babies would make me happier, and I fantasized about the "white picket fence" life. I did everything with fierce determination, and within no time at all, I was in fact married and pregnant with my first daughter. I was sure that this "new life" would make me happy.

Pregnancy was tough, but I was both thrilled and relieved. I began enjoying food more than I ever had in my life. This was my perfect excuse to eat what I wanted and gain weight without anybody judging me. I craved McDonald's cheeseburgers and ate them almost every day (I convinced myself it was probably for the iron). My weight started to climb, but I didn't care—I was sick of being so "body beautiful."

Eventually, I quit my job and gave up exercising. No longer a career woman, I intended to be the perfect homemaker. With immaculate floors and homemade bread, I was adamant about doing this job impeccably.

Weighing close to 200 pounds when my first daughter was born, I never imagined that gaining weight could so profoundly affect my life. I'd never lived as a heavy person before or experienced the world through this larger body. I loved my baby, and I tried to convince myself that it no longer mattered how I looked—that was the old, superficial me. Beauty was all a façade anyway. I had a perfect child, and that was enough.

Within a year, I was pregnant again with my second daughter. Caught up in a whirlwind of nursing, changing diapers, cooking, shopping, decorating, gardening, doing laundry, and mopping up spills, I was "Super Mom," fast turning into "Crazy Mom." I could not, *or would not,* show anyone my weakness; this was the hardest job I'd ever done.

With two healthy daughters, a committed husband, and a beautiful home, I should have been happy. Although I was indeed ecstatic with many parts of my life, all I could focus on was my weight . . . and I was ashamed and embarrassed to admit it to anyone. I couldn't fit into any of my old clothes, and a shopping spree was out of the question, as I'd given up my career and had no money of my own. My husband was a workaholic and obsessive bodybuilder who couldn't deal with little babies, especially

Crystal Andrus

the crying kind. I avoided people from my old life. I was tired, lonely, and searching for something more, so I ate comfort food and watched *Oprah*. It was 1996 and as Oprah was getting smaller, I was growing larger. How ironic that only two years earlier I'd believed that I could help *her!*

Crystal before having kids!

Crystal less than a year later.

I remember one evening stopping for a consoling dough- nut after an argument with my husband. As I pulled up at the drive-through this particular night, the young employee hastily glanced down at me. Barely sliding open the window, he grabbed my money, quickly handed me my doughnut, and tossed some change back at me. Without speaking a word or giving me a smile (or even a second glance), he pulled the window shut. I knew he was just a thoughtless kid looking at—but not seeing—an over- weight housewife, but I felt like crying as I drove off. I realized that I'd never experienced this lack of attention before. Were most heavy people treated this way?

It may sound shallow or trivial, but I learned firsthand that life is incredibly different when you're not thin and beautiful. I finally understood the anxiety so many people have when facing the things I'd always taken for granted, such as joining a gym or getting undressed in a public fitting room. I couldn't believe this was happening to me. I couldn't believe I was *letting this happen* to me.

My breaking point finally came one night as I sat curled up in my rocking chair nursing my baby. I was probably suffering from the winter blues, a little postpartum depression, and complete exhaustion, but it was also much more. I realized that I didn't even know who I was or what I wanted for my life. Sobbing as I looked down at my daughter, I realized that I'd made so many life-altering decisions based on pleasing others or to ease my temporary boredom or discontentment.

The truth is, I was always discontent about something, even though to the outside world I was happy-go-lucky. It was my emotional baseline: I came from parents who were never content with what "was" and who always needed more, better, bigger. And so I was always in a race for the next thing, never feeling happy with what I had either. I lived in a constant state of wanting. I wanted to be married. So within a year I was engaged and married. I wanted babies. I got pregnant the first month of trying. I wanted a beautiful house. I got it. I wanted lots of things: money, status, jewelry, cars, businesses. Whatever I wanted, I got. I was still in so much pain. None of the distractions kept me distracted long enough. Eventually I'd feel my discontentment all over again. Then, on that night, nearly 12 years ago, the reality of *what was* revealed itself to me . . . and I cried.

I cried for all the pain I'd so neatly tucked away and for all my nearly lost dreams—the ones I'd convinced myself were selfish and superficial. I cried for my own little girl—the one nestled deep inside of me that longed to be loved. But mostly, I cried for my own children. Looking down at my precious baby and thinking of my two-year-old sleeping in the other room, I realized that I was cheating them. I was no longer that dynamic, positive woman

Crystal Andrus

I'd once been. It was time I treated myself with more respect and showed my girls that life was all about choices.

The motivation to change often comes through inspiration or desperation—in my case, it was the latter. Sitting in that chair, I had an "Aha" moment. I realized:

**I was solely and exclusively accountable for my life.
My unhappiness and weight gain
weren't really about cookies or chocolate—
that was just the way they had manifested themselves.
I didn't want to just lose the weight:
I wanted to lose my *preoccupation* with the weight.
And I needed to make peace with myself.**

The next morning, I dragged myself out of bed and headed out while everyone else slept. The freezing wind whipped into my face, burning my ears and lungs. I stopped several times, gasping for breath. Shocked at just how out of shape I was, I turned around halfway down the road and walked back.

At home, I sat down and began to write, not realizing at the time that I was beginning a life-changing journey. I questioned:

- Why did I want to get back into shape?

- What did the extra weight represent?

- Why did I care so much what people thought about me, and why did I want everyone to like me?

- When did I feel happiest?

- What was I most afraid of, and what were those fears costing me?

- How did I want to live the rest of my life?

- Was I willing to do what it took to take back my life?

Many things were revealed to me that day. I'd spent nearly 30 years searching for love, validation, and worth, never realizing until that moment that I was the only one who could give it to me, and until I did, nothing or no one else would make me happy in the long run. I knew that I only had one life to live, and I deserved more than this. We all do. . . .

The next morning, I stuffed cotton balls into my ears, bundled up warmly, and set out again. This time I walked briskly and coached myself every step of the way: "Stick with it, you can do it! Come on, girl, you're tough—and when the going gets tough, the tough get going."

Morning after morning, I went out, jogging a few minutes more each day. I wanted my old body back, but this time I wanted to do it right. Eventually, I could run for an entire 30 minutes. I talked to God as I jogged along; and the fresh, crisp morning air filled my lungs. The birds chirped, and the glorious world awakened around me (or maybe *I* was awakening to the glorious world).

Two and a half months later, I stepped onto the scale, and I was more than 30 pounds lighter. I felt fabulous! My four-mile run gradually increased to ten, five or six days a week (don't worry, I won't ask you to do this). My weight continued to drop until I finally weighed in at 121 pounds. Only six months earlier, I'd been close to 200 pounds. This was the lightest I'd been since I was a teenager.

I discovered that I could eat a little bit of anything as long as I exercised. I began demanding more for my life and refused to find comfort in a bag of potato chips. Instead of waiting for permission to live, I did what I loved without compromising my values or beliefs.

Perhaps you're not quite as desperate as I was, but I'm sure that you're more than ready to make peace with your body and

Crystal Andrus

to become the woman you were always meant to be. Although my expertise is in health and fitness, I've learned that looking and feeling great is about so much more than counting calories or doing leg lifts. We all have fears that hold us back, but in spite of everything, we still have those nearly forgotten dreams buried somewhere inside us.

Getting in shape is certainly not the only step to achieving peace and contentment, but I believe it's one of the first in a journey toward self-discovery and fulfillment. How can we claim to love ourselves when we can't stand to look at ourselves naked in a full-length mirror? In his wonderful book *Make the Connection*, personal trainer Bob Greene says that when you look into a mirror, you can say, "This is where I am in my life today. I could be better. I could be worse. This represents my life." The point is not to beat yourself up, but to be honest about how you look, and even more important, how you *feel*. The mirror, says Greene, doesn't just reflect your eating and exercise habits—it reflects your life.

Not everyone who looks great is happy, that's for sure. I've met many miserable skinny women, and I know firsthand that being thin doesn't guarantee happiness. I discovered that it's not looking good, but rather the process of taking care of yourself, being comfortable in your own skin, and demanding more from your life that opens the door to joy. Living with passion and following your life path is the most effective weight-loss aid available to humankind.

I sometimes wonder if my message to women is even about weight loss at all. Yet all I know is that if I can help just one woman discover that she's a beautiful swan rather than an ugly duckling, and if I can help her soar, then I've done what I was put here to do.

Finally, I'm happy to say that although I could be better, I could be worse. I am *Simply . . . Woman!*

Now it's your turn! Let's get started. . . .

അഛ ഛഛ

Crystal Andrus

There's nothing I want more than for you to achieve all your dreams and goals with *Simply . . . Woman!* Telling yourself, "I hate my body!" or "I want to look better" isn't enough to keep you motivated for a lifetime—or even 12 weeks! Although you may want to skip ahead to Week One, the following section will give you the tools that will help you stay focused along this journey. For busy women, this can seem like too much effort, so you may just want to get on with the diet and fitness routines; but for true change, you must do some thinking, writing, and record taking.

Gather What You Need

You don't have to go out and buy a great deal of equipment for this program. In fact, you may already have much of what you need at home.

A Journal

A crucial part of your plan of action is the written exercises that I'll ask you to do in the coming weeks, so the first thing you'll have to get is a journal. (If you want, you can purchase the *Simply . . . Woman! Journal* online at: **www.simplywoman.com**.) Over the course of this 12-week program, I'd love for you to try to write in your journal each night before you go to bed. Use it to write letters to yourself or others (don't worry—you'll never send them); or as a diary to record your feelings, worries, and fears. Ask yourself the tough questions you wish you could ask a counselor, and then answer them as if you were one. *This is your special book, which will help you discover the woman you were meant to be.* Your journal is going to be with you long after its pages have been filled. This may be your first written point of reference, and it will serve many purposes along this journey.

Running Shoes

For the exercise portion of your program, get some good running shoes. Take a pair of your old shoes to the store with you and let the salesperson look at them. A specialist can see if your feet pronate or supinate (roll in or out), and recommend a pair of shoes for you. Your shoes are the support for your entire body—your joints, ankles, knees, and back—as well as for cushioning your feet, so they're a worthwhile investment.

Strength-Training Equipment

You'll need some hand weights to do the first workout on the *Simply . . . Woman! Tight & Toned Workout* DVD located in the back of this book. I recommend getting a pair of three-pound dumbbells for your shoulders and triceps exercises, and a pair of eight-pound dumbbells for your back and biceps routines. If you don't have hand weights, get started using two 28-fluid-ounce cans of tomatoes or filled 16-ounce water bottles. As you progress, you might need heavier weights. (For the floor work, you may also want to buy an exercise mat to lie on.)

The second workout on the DVD uses the *Simply . . . Woman Total Workout Bench & Crystal Ball.* This bench/ball combination works your body in hundreds of different ways using applied resistance via the bands. Biomechanically sound, it will train your muscles at the perfect angle, which will get you in shape faster, easier, and with little chance of injury. Different band lengths create different weight loads, and the various attachments make training each muscle group simple and efficient. The *Simply . . . Woman Total Workout Bench & Crystal Ball* has been proven to effectively shape and sculpt your body with perfect precision. If you haven't purchased the *Simply . . . Woman Total Workout Bench & Crystal Ball* yet, visit: **www.simplywoman.com.**

Equipment to Check Your Progress

Most women cringe at this part, but I'd love you to get some of the basics so you can assess your results: a cloth measuring tape like a tailor uses, a scale (you don't have to weigh yourself if you really don't want to, but it does help if your goal is weight loss), a watch with a second hand (to check your heart rate), a full-length mirror, and a camera.

Record Everything You Eat for Three Days

In order to make the necessary changes, you have to know exactly where your strengths and weaknesses lie, what you've been doing and feeling, and why you eat the way you do. So for three consecutive days, I want you to become a meticulous record keeper—in other words, I want you to write down what you eat and when you eat it throughout the day. Don't worry, you won't have to measure and record everything you eat for the next 12 weeks, but please give me these few days. Aim for one day on the weekend and two weekdays. Don't kid yourself into thinking that you'll remember without writing anything down—you won't.

I once had a client who assured me that all she needed was a new exercise plan. She claimed that her diet was excellent and had nothing to do with the extra ten pounds she couldn't lose. Yet after I persuaded her to keep a food diary, analyze it, and make small changes, she lost the weight in only three weeks. These three days of recording will be one of your most important reference points. This is where many of your eating discoveries will come from.

When recording your food entrees, pay particular attention to detail. Writing "a tuna sandwich" doesn't reveal what kind of bread you ate. Did you use mayonnaise? If so, was it low fat or regular, and did you have one tablespoon or three? Did you eat the whole can of tuna or half of it? Don't feel embarrassed or guilty about what you're eating—it's my job to help get you on the right track over the coming weeks. Don't be judgmental, but don't be self-deceptive either.

I also want you to become aware of your eating patterns. Notice if you can detect the true feeling of hunger, or do you always eat before your body reaches that point? What about feeling full—can you stop before you're stuffed, even when you love what you're eating? Do you ever finish a meal and feel sick because you've had too much? What role does food play in your life: Do you use it to deal with unpleasant situations?

Record what time you got up in the morning and when you went to bed. Did you get tired during the day? How did you feel before and after you ate? Make a note of all this; you'll refer to it in the coming weeks as you begin to understand yourself and the choices you make.

Measure Where You Are Now

Conjure up the courage and get a close friend to snap a few photos of you, preferably in a two-piece bathing suit. Develop them, and put them away somewhere safe. (If you have a digital camera, you can store the images on your computer.) You never need to show these pictures to anyone, but I promise you that they'll become some of your biggest motivators as you work through the program. Even if your goal isn't to lose weight, you'll see how far you've come and will have a concrete reminder of where you once were in your life.

The next reference points are your body measurements, dress size, and weight, along with your current level of fitness, which you'll record on the "Success Tracker I" at the end of this chapter. This is incredibly important for those times when you feel like giving up and think, *Oh, I don't think I look any different. What's the point?* Well, *here's* the point: If you've charted your progress, then you'll see that you're on track. Perhaps your weight hasn't dropped as fast as you'd hoped, but your measurements might have changed. You may discover that your resting heart rate is lower, or you can do more sit-ups. As with your photographs, you don't need to show this to anyone, but it's vital for you to do this evaluation before you get started on the program.

Even before you start your assessment, I want you to answer the following questions to be sure you don't have any conditions that may present a physical problem while exercising. If you do, see your doctor for approval before starting the program. Even if you're young and healthy, you might consider getting a physical before starting. This way you'll have documentation and an amazing testimonial of the changes that will happen in this program. And 12 weeks from now, I'd love to hear from you!

Health History

Have you had, or do you have, any of the following (circle the answer):

1. A history of heart problems, chest pains, or stroke?
   Yes   No

2. Increased blood pressure?
   Yes   No

3. Increased blood cholesterol?
   Yes   No

4. Any chronic illness or condition?
   Yes   No

5. Recent surgery (within the last 12 months)?
    Yes   No

6. Pregnancy (now or within the last 3 months)?
    Yes   No

7. A history of breathing or lung problems?
    Yes   No

8. A muscle, joint, or back disorder, or any previous injury still affecting you?
    Yes   No

9. A diabetes or thyroid condition?
    Yes   No

10. A history of heart problems in your immediate family?
    Yes   No

Do not start this program if you had any <u>yes</u> answers without getting approval from your doctor. Please explain any <u>yes</u> answers and take them to your doctor before continuing with this program.

Great, you're still with me . . . so let's get on with your assessment. You're going to need your measuring tape, scale, and watch now. Get changed into something comfortable and wear running shoes because we're going to be checking many aspects of your success, from your resting heart rate (a huge indicator of your cardiovascular health) to your muscular strength and measurements. The optimal time for the most accurate figures is in the morning. As you do each test or measurement, enter the results on your Success Tracker I in the Week One column.

Resting Heart Rate

This test will tell you how many times your heart beats in a minute. Just like the engine in a car, the fewer miles or less wear and tear you put on your heart, the better.

Sit down with your watch and relax for a few minutes. Now take your pointer and middle fingers (never your thumb) and find your radial pulse at your wrist or your carotid pulse on the side of your neck. Once you find it, feel the rhythm, and then count the beats for 30 seconds starting at zero. Multiply that number by 2. This will give you your number of heartbeats per minute. Do this twice to find an average.

If your resting heart rate (RHR) is greater than 100 beats/minute, *do not proceed with the rest of this program without your doctor's approval.* Also, be sure to get your blood pressure checked.

RHR 1 _____ beats/minute RHR 2 _____ beats/minute

Score

<65 beats/minute = excellent
65–75 beats/minute = good
75–85 beats/minute = average
>85 beats/minute = poor

*Your RHR score =*_____

Weight

Weigh yourself. The best time for the most accurate figure is in the morning. Either weigh yourself nude, or remember what clothes you're wearing and put them on for future weigh-ins. (Never weigh in more than once a week.)

Your Current Weight = _____ lbs.

Push-Up Test

The purpose of the push-up test is to evaluate endurance and the muscular strength of your upper body, including your triceps, shoulders, and chest. Although men use the standard position with only the hands and toes in contact with the floor, you can use the modified position with bent knees. You've completed one full push-up when your nose has touched the floor and you've returned to the starting position with your arms fully extended. Exhale on the way up, pushing away from the floor. Count the total number of push-ups you complete before reaching exhaustion. You can rest between push-ups, but *only* in the up position.

Many beginners have a difficult time doing even one full push-up off the floor, so if you're just getting back to exercising, or have more than 30 pounds to lose, you may want to do a standing push-up off the wall.

Number of Push-Ups You Completed: _____

Curl-Up Test

The purpose of the bent-knee curl-up test is to evaluate your abdominal muscle strength and endurance. (To eliminate the potential of lower-back strain, the curl-up was modified from the original sit-up test.) Lie on the floor with your knees bent, palms of your hands down on the floor by your sides. When you're ready, flatten your lower back into the floor and curl your upper spine and head, sliding your hands along the floor until they reach your heels; but don't lock your feet under anything, as that will take the focus from your stomach to your hips and thighs. Curl back down. Perform as many curl-ups as you can.

If you're a beginner and this is too difficult to do from the floor, you can do your curl-ups on your bed.

Number of Curl-Ups You Completed: _____

Measurements

With your measuring tape, record the inches at each of the sites indicated on the Success Tracker I. Find the largest spot at each location on your body, and indicate how many inches up or down from your belly button you've marked. Write this down so that in a month, you'll measure yourself at exactly the same spot. For example, for your lower abs, look in a mirror from all sides; find the widest spot, measure how far down it is from your belly button. Write the number of inches down on the chart, and then each month that you do your measurements, measure the same way and then record.

Always measure yourself at the widest part. Don't pull on the measuring tape, as it should be tight enough to keep it in position without causing an indentation in the skin. (You'll be glad you didn't pull it tight when you take your measurements again in a month.) Also, don't hold your breath.

At the end of the measurement section on the Success Tracker I is a "Total Inches" column. Add up all your inches so that you'll be able to see how many overall inches you're losing.

Average Clothing Size

Go to your closet and look at the size of the four pairs of pants you wear most often. Do the same with the four tops you wear most often. Take the average size and record it on the Success Tracker I.

Body-Fat Percentage

The biggest problem when you use weight loss as a goal is that muscle weighs two and a half times more than fat. Decreasing body fat is far more important than weight. As you're losing fat, you'll be toning your body and thus gaining muscle. So your weight loss on this program won't be as significant as if you were only dieting. On many diets, the majority of the weight loss actually comes from water and muscle, and is a very inaccurate indicator of actual fat loss.

I once had a client who only lost 22 pounds on the scale, but she completely transformed her body and looked as if she'd lost at least 40. Because I had a body-fat tester, we could see that she'd actually lost close to 35 pounds of fat and gained nearly 13 pounds of lean muscle. In the first couple weeks, she actually gained weight, but her clothes were fitting looser and she was losing inches. Her body-fat percentages were dropping drastically, and by the end of the 12 weeks, she went from a size 10/12 to a 3/4.

There are a number of ways to check your body fat. There are scales that measure it, as well as your total body weight. You could also have your body fat measured with special calipers or an electronic device (many gyms perform this service). If you have access to any of these body-fat testers, record the results on your Success Tracker I.

There are also some Websites where they'll calculate your body fat for you. There's one on the site of the National Institutes of Health: **www.nhlbisupport.com/bmi/bmicalc.htm.** The results are much less accurate than having a personal measurement, but can give you a rough idea of where you are. According to the site, if your body fat is:

- below 18.5 percent, you're underweight
- between 18.5 and 24.9 percent, you're in a healthy, normal range for women

- between 25 and 29.9 percent, you're overweight
- over 30 percent, you're clinically obese

Sign Your Own Contract

In my initial years of working with women, I think that I sometimes wanted their results more than they did. I'd pour myself into my clients' lives, and take on all the dramas of their day-to-day existence. Driving to their homes to pick them up in the morning to ensure that they'd get to the gym, or calling in the evening to find out what they'd eaten that day, I soon learned some tough personal lessons. I was so passionate about helping my clients that I took ownership of their problems. I was a "fixer" who believed I could help anyone. I've now discovered after so many letdowns that my job is to provide information, inspiration, and motivation—but it's your job to do the work. I'll be here to hold your hand along the way (and our trainers are only a phone call away), but in truth, success will only come when you take complete ownership over your own life—*that means the good times and the bad.*

The funny thing about this step is that it's the reason why so many of us have gotten into the very boat we're in: *We haven't become accountable for ourselves.* Before I took back my life, I used every excuse in the world for my failures and frustrations: I didn't have a car, we lived in the country, it was cold outside, I didn't have the time, I had two small babies and no family to help me, my husband was a workaholic . . . my list went on and on. It wasn't until I finally said, "This is my life, so I better start living it," that lasting changes finally started to happen for me. It doesn't mean that the conditions I complained about didn't exist—they did. But when I accepted responsibility and realized that I'd created my life to get what I thought I deserved from it, I was able to take the blame away from others, accept that these were my patterns, and learn how to make better choices. You see, we can never change our outcome while we're blaming others for our circumstances. I was tired of waiting for someone to come and save me. It was time I saved myself.

So, before you get started on Week One, you need to sign a contract with yourself. That written commitment means you can't blame anyone else for your shortcomings—and it also means that you'll *own your success!*

Your contract can outline specific goals, such as: "I will exercise a minimum of three times per week, or for any sessions missed due to unavoidable reasons, I will plan to make up the missed session by [specify] _____." It should also detail some type of commitment to your mind and soul, such as, "I promise to write in my journal every evening, and spend at least one hour a week doing something I really love." These commitments should be realistically achievable to promote success.

You can use the following as a guide to create your own self-contract—and be sure to write it in your journal! Remember as you create your self-contract that it's about and for *you!*

Self-Contract

I,_____,
agree to commit to the development and enhancement of my body and my life. I promise to love and respect myself and to take the time each day to honor that commitment by following all the steps outlined in this 12-Week Body/Mind/Soul Total Transformation Program.

I promise to hold myself totally and completely accountable for all my choices, every emotion and reaction, both negative and positive, and I won't blame anyone for my shortcomings or failures. I know that life may sometimes get in the way and that I may encounter people who don't agree with or appreciate my needs or desires, but I've made this commitment to myself—body, mind, and soul. I know that life will only give me what I demand of it, so it's up to me to make my dreams come true.

I commit to exercising a minimum of three times per week, and for any sessions missed due to unavoidable reasons, I will plan to make up the missed session by [specify] _____.

I know that if I keep doing what I've been doing I'll keep getting what I'm getting. I'm ready, willing and able to make my dreams come true. The time is now. . . .

_____   _____

Signed   **Date**

Make the Most Out of This Program!

As you prepare to get started on your plan of action, here are a few tips to help ensure success:

- Read "Beginning the Journey" entirely before starting the program.

- Read "Week One" from beginning to end before you start implementing the program. Sometime during that first week, read the next chapter, "Week Two," so you'll be ready to go with it. Repeat this process throughout the 12 weeks.

- Don't skip ahead more than one week—after all, the program is laid out over 12 weeks for a reason. You didn't develop bad habits in a few days, and you can't possibly change them all at once. Little steps make the biggest difference over time, and incorporating them weekly makes it much easier to stay on track. Doing this week by week also enables you to see which steps are working for you.

- Continue to build on what you've learned each week. I won't repeat the steps in Week Four that I asked you to begin incorporating in Weeks One, Two, and Three. Each week lays the foundation for the next, so if you didn't understand the information, reread it. It's very important to comprehend why you're doing each step.

- Don't get discouraged if things don't happen immediately because your body may desperately try to fight what's happening and hold on to your stored fat. Everybody wants an overnight solution, yet we all put on and lose weight differently. Nevertheless, I promise that you'll look and feel better with each passing week.

- Go on our online message forum at: **www.simply woman.com** to develop a positive support system and get to know some other women who are just like you. Support is essential when you're feeling discouraged.

- Stay focused—after all, success is 10 percent perspiration, 20 percent inspiration, and 70 percent determination.

Success Tracker I

For the next 3 months, record your progress at the bottom of each month.
Take your measurements and then total the number of inches lost at the bottom of each "difference" column.

DATE : _____	WEEK 1	DIFFERENCE	END OF WEEK 4	DIFFERENCE	END OF WEEK 8	DIFFERENCE	END OF WEEK 12
Resting Heart Rate							
Blood Pressure (if possible)							
Weight lbs/kg							
Push-ups							
Curl-ups							
Measurements:							
Neck							
Chest							
Upper Abs # of inches above B.B.							
Waist @ B.B.							
Lower Abs # of inches below B.B.							
Hips (at widest part)							
Thighs-Upper							
Thighs-Lower							
Knee							
Calf # of inches up from floor							
Arm # of inches in from elbow -Relaxed							
-Flexed							
Total Inches =							
"Average" Dress Size							
Body Fat % (if possible)							

Week One: *Awareness*

Your journey is about to begin, and I'm truly so excited for you! If you embrace this program in its entirety, *Simply . . . Woman!* will be one of the most enriching and life-changing experiences you'll ever undertake.

It's unfortunate that some women take weeks to realize that this isn't another diet, but rather an illuminating excavation of themselves. Yes, you'll lose weight and look better, but most important, you'll discover who you are—that is, why you eat what you do, how to change your patterns and release your issues and hang-ups, and how to find new passion and excitement for life. You must do the written exercises for this program to work to its full capacity, and you must ask yourself the difficult questions that you may want to avoid emotionally. Push yourself to dig deep for the answers—after all, that's the only way lasting and profound change will come. . . .

Step 1: Figure Out What You Crave

Many women complain to me that they eat well and/or exercise but still can't seem to lose their bulge. Haven't we all known someone who works out for hours every day but never looks any different? Or someone who's constantly on a diet but has yet to lose a pound? It's not about working *hard;* it's about working *smart.* In other words, it's about understanding what your body needs to excel at optimal levels.

In order to discover the right formula for your body, you must become conscious of your current eating habits and coping skills. Are there certain times of day when you feel tired, or are there types of food you always seem to crave? By answering the following questions, you may be able to identify some of your food weaknesses and start making healthy changes in your diet. Try to choose an answer that best represents your most common selection.

1. When you go to the movies, you prefer:

   a. candy, chocolate, or popcorn

   b. nuts or beef jerky

   c. an alcoholic drink before or after the movie

2. A late-night treat might include:

   a. cookies, chocolate, cake, ice cream, chips, cereal, popcorn, crackers, toast, or French fries

   b. chicken wings, cheese, cold cuts, yogurt, or nuts

   c. a nightcap

3. If you rushed into the house hungry and grabbed something quick, you'd pick:

   a. a piece of fruit, a glass of juice, a soda, a cookie or candy bar, bread, crackers, a muffin, a bagel, or some chips

   b. cheese, meat, yogurt, or peanuts

   c. a beer or a glass of wine

4. Your favorite part of a traditional Thanksgiving or Christmas dinner is the:

   a. cakes, pies, or cookies; and potatoes, pasta, yams, or stuffing

   b. turkey, ham, roast beef, or gravy

   c. toasts you make with family and friends

Crystal Andrus

5. Which would be the hardest for you to give up completely for one month?

    a. comfort foods such as ice cream, cake, chocolate, cookies, soda, candies, fruit, pasta, rice, bread, potatoes, crackers, cereal, or chips

    b. seafood, red meat, pork, poultry, eggs, cheese, or luncheon meat

    c. alcohol

Scoring

— If you had predominantly **a** answers, you crave carbohydrates. Although vegetables, grains, and fruits should be the staple of a healthy diet (since that is where all our vitamins and fiber come from) too many of us are eating an exorbitant amount of carbohydrates, with far too much coming from refined sugars. Refined sugars, such as those found in candy, soda, chocolate, sauces, dressings, condiments, and cookies, aren't nutritious, have no fiber, are high in calories, and are easily stored as fat; similarly, white bread, white rice, and white potatoes are high in starch and are also easily stored as fat. This applies even if the product is labeled "no- or low-fat." There are more fat people eating fat-free foods—and gaining weight—than ever before.

— If you had mostly **b** answers, you crave protein. Eating protein is an essential component of this program, for it speeds the metabolism and has little effect on insulin production. It's digested by the body and converted into amino acids: the building blocks for lean, toned muscles. Although protein isn't easily stored as fat, the *saturated fat* in many dark meats and milk products is. Here, "no- or low-fat" choices are vital.

— If you had mostly **c** answers, you crave alcohol. Alcohol slows your metabolism and is a depressant. It also has nearly twice the calories of carbohydrates and protein—one glass of wine a day could put on ten pounds a year! Although the incidence of heart disease is lower in people who have a glass of red wine each day, recent studies have shown that drinking alcohol can increase a woman's risk of breast cancer. Additionally, too much drinking is related to alcoholism, liver disease, and cancer of the mouth, throat, and liver. The ideal way to lower your risk of heart disease is through your diet, physical activity, and weight control, *not by drinking alcohol.*

In addition, alcohol is extremely dehydrating—it can make your eyes, face, and hands appear puffy and give your skin a squishy, bumpy-looking, fat appearance. Alcohol also lowers will-power: Your day of healthy eating can be ruined when, after a few drinks, you suddenly get the urge for pizza or ice cream. (If you're worried about the amount of alcohol you're drinking, or you feel the need to drink whenever you're in an unpleasant situation, please seek help. Talk to your family doctor or contact Alcoholics Anonymous.)

— Finally, if you didn't fall into any one category consistently but are within 15 pounds of your ideal weight, you need to make some simple yet effective changes to your diet and exercise routine. You're fairly balanced in your food choices, and you'll be looking and feeling your best in no time. If you have more than 15 pounds to lose, then you're most likely overeating and/or consuming too much of the wrong types of food.

In the coming weeks, we'll discuss each of the above categories in detail. As we do, please pay extra attention to your area of weakness. By consistently incorporating each step of this program, you'll come to understand your coping skills and make smarter food choices. By first recognizing your cravings and then developing more positive ways of dealing with them, you'll start to make the lasting changes necessary to take control of your body.

Step 2: Become Aware of Your Eating Patterns

The key to rebuilding a stronger, leaner, healthier you comes from understanding the relationship you have with yourself. Before you can begin to manifest positive changes, you must first figure out where you are right now and how you got there. This is called *self-awareness,* and it's the first step toward discovering if, perhaps, food plays more of a role in your life than to feed your hungry tummy.

Maybe you can relate to this scenario: It's Friday night and you're alone. You had a stressful week, and your boyfriend said that he'd come by with a movie three hours ago. As you wait, your worry turns into anger, which escalates into loneliness, insecurity, jealousy, and eventually self-pity. You deserve more than this. You head for the kitchen, swing open the refrigerator

Simply . . . Tips!

- At 3 P.M., when you're craving a cup of coffee and a Danish, ask yourself, "Am I hungry or tired?" Try lying down for 10 minutes (don't forget to set your alarm clock!). A recent study at Flinders University in Australia found that a 10-minute rest in the afternoon will give you more energy than sleeping for 30 minutes or more, which can leave you feeling groggy. When you wake up, have some sort of low-fat protein or a cup of green tea.

- Don't keep junk food in the house. When you crave certain things late at night, such as chips and dip or chocolate-chip cookies, you wouldn't be tempted if they weren't conveniently sitting in your cupboard and refrigerator.

- Be organized. For example, bake 12 chicken breasts (see

recipe on page 315), pack them individually in sandwich bags, and throw them into the freezer. Each morning, pull out one or two, toss them into a plastic container along with two handfuls of prepackaged salad dressed with cider vinegar, and *voilà!*—a perfect lunch with no inconvenience.

- Take food to go. If you eat fast food or junk when driving in the car during the day, pack healthy snacks and lunch in a small cooler the night before and have food with you during the day. Or supplement with a low-carb, low-fat protein shake—simply carry around a dry powder protein mix like **proteins+** in a sealed cup, add water, and shake.

- Avoid it until you can resist it. If you have morning coffee at your favorite café and always accompany it with a muffin or doughnut, make coffee at home and resist the café until you feel strong enough to say no to the pastry.

- Cut back on portions. Eat to the point where you're *satisfied,* not *stuffed.* If you're desperately craving a Big Mac, get one—but throw half of it away.

door, and stare inside, blindly searching for something that tastes good. Ice cream . . . *yes!* Maybe you'll even add some chocolate sauce. You cut up a banana, add some whipped cream, and smile as you take that first bite. It tastes so good. "Forget him," you say to yourself as you wash the creamy confection down with your first of many glasses of wine. "I don't care about him anyway!" Sound familiar?

I'll give you lots of questions to get you thinking about your eating patterns. Start by taking a look back at the three days of eating that you meticulously logged before you started the program. I want you to check for any consistencies in your eating habits.

Crystal Andrus

- Do you eat breakfast daily?

- Do you eat within two to three hours of bedtime?

- How long do you go between meals?

- Do you eat foods simply out of habit?

- Do you crave junk food at certain times of the day?

- Do you feel that specific foods go hand in hand with certain events, such as movies and popcorn, or beer and baseball games?

- Are you an emotional eater?

- Do you eat out of boredom?

- Does food provide you comfort when you're upset or stressed out?

- Do you feel tired a lot, especially by 2 or 3 in the afternoon?

- Do you have a bowel movement daily (without the aid of laxatives or suppositories)?

- Do you take heartburn medication such as Tums?

- Do you feel bloated by the time evening comes?

- Do you experience PMS?

- Does alcohol make the good times better and the bad times better?

Now think back to your childhood or teen years and look at your family. See if your choices now simply continue those patterns and support those beliefs:

- Was dinner a celebration, a time to come together each night around the table, where you bonded with your family and ate healthy meals?

- Was it first-come, first-served, and could you eat whatever you wanted?

- What was the emotional atmosphere like in your home as a young child?

- How did your parents comfort themselves when they were upset or stressed out? How did they comfort *you?* And how did you comfort yourself?

- Was fast food a staple of your diet?

- Did holidays and family reunions revolve around eating?

- Did you learn poor eating habits from your mom or dad?

- Did your parents exercise? Were they in shape?

- What do you remember being told about your body?

- Was your mother or sister overweight?

- Did you eat out of boredom?

Crystal Andrus

- When did you begin to struggle with your weight or body image?

- Did you have a rough childhood or teenage life?

Please don't get me wrong here . . . I don't want to suggest that every person out there who has some body fat to lose has deep emotional issues, or that anyone who eats a bowl of ice cream or sips a glass of wine is repressed and on the verge of a breakdown. Sometimes you just wake up and feel rotten for no particular reason, be it thanks to a lack of sleep, PMS, a virus, or an extra workload. You just need to accept that you periodically feel blue—it isn't a life-shattering event. A hot cup of coffee and chocolate bar can occasionally work wonders, and even a super-sized hamburger meal or banana split isn't the end of the world, but I want you to consider the possibility that food may play more of a role in your life than you realized.

Ask yourself the following:

- Do you eat when you really need sleep?

- Is it harder to stay on track at night when you're tired and physically drained?

- Do you binge when you're on your period, or mid-month when you're ovulating?

- Do you feel a lack of self-restraint when faced with a decadent meal?

- Are you an "all or nothing" kind of person—that is, strict on your diet, then after one night of too much food or alcohol, you give it up completely?

- If you love the taste of something, do you continue eating even after you're full?

- How do you feel an hour after eating too much or when you've gone too long without eating?

- Do you listen to your body's true desires?

- Do you know how much food you need to feel full?

As you begin to delve deeper into these issues, you'll quickly discover that just like anorexia nervosa (not eating enough) and bulimia nervosa (bingeing followed by vomiting), overeating—more specifically, compulsive overeating—is a disorder. It's not as deadly as anorexia, but mentally, it's comparable. Eating food when you feel pain or powerless over a situation is actually quite similar to how someone with anorexia copes. We overeat to numb. They starve to numb. It's all a form of escapism.

Now ask yourself the following:

- Do you often use food or alcohol to pamper, console, or relax yourself?

- Do you feel a sense of safety and nurturing from eating?

- Do you feel like you deserve a "treat" after you've been "good"—that is, after sticking to a strict diet or exercise regimen?

- Do you feel angry or disappointed with yourself after eating?

- Does your busy career cause you to miss time at home?

Crystal Andrus

- Does being at home cause you to crave the interaction and excitement of the outside world?

- Are you bored and feel as if you're in a rut?

- Do you feel fulfilled in your life?

- Are you in a wonderful, loving relationship?

- Do you feel guilty for wanting more?

- Are you living with purpose?

- Are you pursuing your dreams?

Many people have adopted ways of dealing with life's stresses and worries by snacking, munching, and even bingeing. For most overweight people, food is comfort. It's the thing they look forward to at the end of a stressful day; it's their relaxation; it's a silent friend or late-night companion; it's their fun, their entertainment—eating is a huge part of their life. While for others who struggle to slay slim, food is the enemy, and it's viewed with fear. It isn't a life-giving celebration, but rather an adversary that can force these individuals back to a place to which they never want to return.

Both of the above scenarios are self-defeating and self-sabotaging. Whenever you feel as though something outside of yourself has a hold over you, you're oppressed by it. Too often you diminish your sense of power with statements such as "I can't live without it." The realization and ultimate acceptance that you *can* and *will* live . . . as long as you have yourself . . . is empowering.

In retrospect, temporary abstinence from *anything* is actually liberating, even though it's tough at the time. You'll discover how strong you really are. The thing you thought you couldn't live without is now just an occasional want, not a need. Once you relinquish any dependency—whether on chocolate, mashed potatoes, wine, or even sex—you can then begin to truly enjoy it.

When Did It Start?

Please understand that I'm not suggesting that overweight people have more problems or deep-seated emotional issues than those who are thin. Of course, everyone has struggles within themselves and in life, but each of us handles these challenges differently.

Look back to when you first started gaining weight. What was going on?

As is the case with almost 90 percent of my clients, a dramatic weight gain happened during or just after an emotional upheaval or transitional period: splitting up with a significant other, leaving for college, relocating to a new city, recovering from illness or injury, starting a new job, getting married, and so forth. Even the beginning of a new relationship—when we eat out constantly or order late-night pizza in bed—can cause weight gain. For others, it can happen during pregnancy, after the birth of a child, or following a traumatic event such as the death of a loved one.

Is it possible that you adopted poor eating habits during an overwhelming period in your life? Perhaps your eating habits changed, and over the next year or two the weight began creeping onto your hips and tummy. Weight gain is sometimes immediate, but most often, three years will pass and you'll realize that you're 20, 30, maybe 50 pounds heavier. You may have worked through the tough time in your life, but now you've acquired a bad habit of eating when you aren't really hungry, or munching on unhealthy food that's causing you to gain weight.

I have some clients who, when they first start this program, truly believe that they just love food, and they'll even argue that they have no personal issues that may be causing them to self-sabotage. They honestly believe that their weight gain is due to a lack of exercise and willpower; or to age and metabolism, having children, going through menopause, or simply enjoying the good life. Although those factors can certainly be part of it, most often something else is also going on. Look back a year before you noticed your weight gain. What was happening?

Perhaps you don't have any severe stress in your life. Maybe you're just very busy or eat out too much; maybe over the years you've adopted poor eating habits and haven't exercised enough. If that's where you are, then thank your lucky stars, because with a little adjustment to your lifestyle, you can become a leaner, healthier *Simply . . . Woman!*

If you have healthy and positive ways of coping with life's stress, and overeating isn't one of them, congratulations—you've already won half the battle! Just by following the workout and nutritional portion of this program, you'll love the way you look and feel in no time.

Check your three-day log and see how healthy your food choices are:

Simply . . . Inspirational

When Jane and I began training together, she informed me that she didn't need to journal because she wouldn't be doing the "emotional crap." According to her, that part of the program was for unhappy housewives and people with low self-esteem. She was a successful, ambitious, single woman who, at 260 pounds, had no trouble getting men. All she needed was a good diet-and-exercise regimen.

Three weeks into our training, Jane had a breakthrough. She was telling me about her friend who shopped beyond her means and was going into severe debt. Jane was so frustrated with this woman, and she couldn't understand why someone would so senselessly ruin her life.

This was my opening to enlighten Jane about how that "emotional stuff" plays itself out in our lives. I gently pointed out that many of us unwittingly self-sabotage in different ways—we

Crystal Andrus

miss important meetings that could have catapulted our careers. We avoid stressful phone calls or let bills pile up. Some of us push aside confrontation at all costs, even when it's beneficial. We ruin wonderful relationships and can't figure out why we keep doing it. We go on a drinking binge the night before an important event, or we eat and eat and eat . . . even though we hate what we're doing to our bodies.

Lightbulbs went on in Jane's eyes, and she immediately sat down. I joined her, abandoning our weight-training session, for something far more powerful was happening. Jane's "tough" exterior began to dissolve, and she started to cry. She stared into the mirror in front of us, realizing that the stretch marks she'd always dismissed as no big deal were suddenly so apparent. "Scars," she said. *Self-hatred,* I

thought. This wasn't love Jane was giving herself, it was abuse. Her 260 pounds didn't come from celebrating life. It came from running from it. . . .

Even with all the confidence she claimed to have, Jane was filled with a great deal of fear, and the weight was her security. She wanted so much out of life, but she was holding herself back from it. She needed to discover what she was truly afraid of, because once she faced that, she'd no longer need to hide behind her body.

Jane knew that it was time to look within, so that night she went home and began to write in her journal. In the following 12 weeks, she lost more than 40 pounds and 50 inches, and she's continued on this journey, still discovering the woman she was meant to be.

- Do you eat whole-grain carbohydrates, or refined, processed ones?

- Do you have lean protein at every meal?

- Do you eat or cook with oil, margarine, or butter?

- Do you regularly eat dessert?

- Do you eat prepackaged or processed food?

- Do you have junk food—such as chips, chocolate, cookies, or soda—available in your home?

- Do you eat junk food or fast food regularly?

- Do you eat cheese, cream cheese, butter, margarine, mayonnaise, or peanut butter often?

- Does a meal not seem complete without bread, potatoes, pasta, or rice?

- Do you drink soda, sugared drinks, or sweetened iced tea?

- Do you drink some type of alcohol each day or consume more than seven drinks in a week?

- Do you drink plenty of water on a daily basis?

Don't get me wrong—good food is amazing. Taste is one of the most incredible senses we have, and a delicious dinner is certainly one of life's greatest pleasures. Eating can also ease an aching soul, entertain us when we're bored, or satisfy a craving. And that's okay occasionally, but we have to be aware if it becomes our habitual "temporary" fix. Is it our crutch?

Step 3: Eliminate Sugar

What you eat, and how much you eat, is even more important for weight-loss success than how much you exercise. Some foods will speed up your metabolism and help you burn body fat, while others will impede your success. In the coming weeks, you'll learn how each of these different nutrients metabolize—but this week, we're going to focus on carbohydrates.

Carbohydrates are all sugars (naturally occurring or refined) and starches: fruits, vegetables, cookies, candies, chocolate, juice, beverages, power or granola bars, soup, bread, pasta, rice, potatoes, cereal, crackers, popcorn, chips, muffins, bagels—it's quite an extensive list. Even many foods we think of as proteins or fats are actually loaded with carbs, too. For example, beans and lentils are high in carbohydrates, as are ice cream, milk, yogurt, salad dressing, and preserves. All carbohydrates break down into sugar once in your bloodstream.

Look back at your three days of eating, and examine all your choices. Roughly what percentage of your foods are carbs: 50, 70, or 90 percent? Although carbohydrates are your body's main source of energy (you couldn't live or work without them), the majority of women who struggle with their weight have a diet that consists of at least 80 percent carbohydrates, many of them refined or processed. Refined sugar isn't the only "evil carb" (there are many others, and we'll tackle them in coming weeks), but sugar (sucrose and high-fructose corn syrup) is the first that has to go. It's non-nutritious, loaded with empty calories, and is the main ingredient of so many of the packaged foods we eat. Worse, eating sugar puts you on the roller coaster of a high blood-sugar level, followed by a dip or crash, also known as hypoglycemia or "sugar blues."

When you eat high-glycemic foods (carbohydrates such as sugar that digest quickly), you experience a surge in blood sugar; this is the peak of the roller-coaster hill. Your body wants to maintain metabolic homeostasis, so it sends out a hormone called *insulin* to remove the excess sugar from your bloodstream and stores it in your cells; thus, the dip. Your trusted machine doesn't like the dip either, so it sends out the signal to eat again. Hunger pains, cravings, headaches, fatigue, moodiness, depression—you name it—your body will do whatever it takes to keep your baseline steady. It also quickly resorts to Plan B—"self-preservation mode"—and begins squeezing stored sugar from your liver. We experience the ups and downs of blood-sugar levels as a roller-coaster ride, and our mood

Crystal Andrus

and behavior go up and down accordingly. And then we wonder why we're so moody! In short, sugar is a drug.

When my weight was at its peak, I realized that 80 percent of my diet consisted of carbs. My kitchen cupboards were full of rice cakes, soda pop, chewy candies, licorice, fat-free cookies, granola bars, and "diet" power bars. Lots of fat-free, though! I was a sugar junkie on the carbohydrate roller coaster. By midmorning I'd feel so tired that I'd need a pick-me-up . . . and I'd need another by midafternoon. Yet once I started eating more protein, legumes, and fresh fibrous vegetables, I had way more energy and totally diminished cravings for sweets. I started losing fat like crazy and didn't feel those overwhelming highs and lows each day.

Simply . . . Tips!

- Read labels. Avoid packaged foods that list sugar, including glucose, sucrose, corn syrup, or high-fructose corn syrup—this includes sugared drinks, candy, chocolate, cookies, cakes, sauces, and salad dressings (be aware that most of the fat-free ones replace the fat with extra sugar).

- Stick to the outside aisles of the grocery store, where the fresh produce, meat, and dairy cases are. The inner aisles are where the fatty, preservative-laden, high-glycemic foods are kept.

- Brush your teeth immediately after eating, as this will help you resist eating dessert and will prevent munching in between meals or late at night.

Sugar cravings are very much like nicotine cravings: Once you get off the roller coaster, you won't want them as much. But, just like quitting smoking, it takes a little willpower and time. You'll be amazed by how different you'll look and feel within one week with this single step alone.

> **Fat-Burning Secret #1:**
> Eliminate sugar and get off the carbohydrate roller coaster.

You'll find out more about how sugar and other high-glycemic carbs work in your body in the coming weeks.

Step 4: Eat Breakfast

I know we've all heard it since we were children, but the truth is that breakfast really *is* the most important meal of the day. Studies have shown that those who lose weight and keep it off eat breakfast daily, as this meal elevates metabolism and helps burn body fat. It's like throwing dry kindling on a campfire that's been smoldering all night. In other words, if you try to restrict calories by not eating breakfast, you stand to slow your metabolic rate. Your body is a brilliant machine that will adapt to calorie reduction and, therefore, conserve fat. When you miss meals and don't exercise, it's like you're throwing a big wet log on your campfire.

The secret is to eat the right foods first thing in the morning: those that crank your metabolism; are low in sugar and saturated fat; and are high in protein, vitamins, and fiber. For example, have an egg-white omelette (see recipe on page 315) with a slice of pumpernickel bread (no butter) or half a cup of oatmeal. If you're in a rush, try drinking a protein shake blended with ice and berries. Yum!

> **Fat-Burning Secret #2:**
> Crank up your metabolism with a high-protein, low-fat breakfast.

If you exercise first thing in the morning, eat immediately after you shower. On the days that you aren't exercising, eat as soon as you get up.

Step 5: Drink Water

Water . . . water . . . water. I either have clients tell me that they drink lots of it or they drink none at all—either way, most aren't drinking enough. Our bodies are composed of approximately 70 percent water, so drinking it is essential. Even our muscles and bones contain water!

Research shows that not drinking enough water may increase fat deposits because the liver can't function properly. Water will fill your stomach, making you feel less hungry; it will also improve your complexion, flush toxins, and help you metabolize food better—along with providing many more great benefits. If you haven't been drinking enough, you may find that for the first week on this program you're going to the bathroom all the time. But eventually you'll get used to it and will soon notice when you're dehydrated. You may even start to crave water.

The type of water you drink is essential. Just as we shouldn't eat fruits covered in pesticides, we need water that's clean and pure. Chlorine by-products used in our public tap water are hazardous chemicals. In addition to chlorine, many water supplies have significant levels of other chemicals, which, even in small doses, aren't good for us. Why do you think babies should never be given drinking water straight from the tap without it being boiled first? These chemicals and nitrates that our government supplements our drinking water with have caused "baby blue syndrome," which can kill.

The trouble is, without these chemicals, parasites and bacteria can be even deadlier. In May 2000, seven people died in the small town of Walkerton, Ontario, because the deadly E. coli bacteria contaminated the town's water supplies. Hundreds, even thousands, were incredibly sick. If you drink tap water, run it for a few minutes before filling your glass, and never drink or cook with hot water from your hot-water tank, which is full of impurities and dissolves more lead than cold water.

Whenever possible, drink reverse-osmosis water. Indulging in your own reverse-osmosis system in your kitchen is well worth the money. Bear in mind that there *is* a loss of essential minerals, such as fluoride, with this process, so be sure to take your daily vitamin/mineral supplement! If you don't have access to reverse-osmosis, I'd choose spring water as your second choice, then mineral water, followed by tap water. I'd avoid "bottled water," as it is no better than tap water. In fact, many major bottled-water manufacturers start with municipal tap water! And bottled water isn't as highly regulated as municipal tap water systems. Some studies have shown that bottled water can contain more harmful bacteria than tap water.

As far as distilled water is concerned, there are two schools of thought: For years I promoted drinking eight to ten glasses of distilled water daily, and many of the world's leading health gurus also believed this was the superior choice. I now recommend it only when detoxing or working to heal a serious health challenge. Dr. Zoltan Rona, the former president of the Canadian Holistic Medical Association, agrees: "Distillation is the process in which water is boiled, evaporated, and the vapor condensed. Distilled water is free of dissolved minerals and, because of this, has the special property of being able to actively absorb toxic substances from the body and eliminate them. Studies validate the benefits of drinking distilled water when one is seeking to cleanse or detoxify the system for short periods of time [a few weeks at a time]."

The concern with long-term distilled water consumption is that it may contribute to high blood pressure and other cardiovascular problems because distilled water is an active absorber, and when it comes into contact with air, it absorbs carbon dioxide, making it acidic. The more distilled water a person drinks, the higher the body's acidity becomes. The most toxic commercial beverages that people consume (that is, cola beverages and other soft drinks) are made from distilled water. Studies have consistently shown that heavy consumers of soft drinks (with or without sugar) spill huge amounts of calcium, magnesium, and other trace minerals into the urine. The more mineral loss, the greater the risk for osteoporosis, osteoarthritis, hypothyroidism, coronary artery disease, high blood pressure, and a long list of degenerative diseases generally associated with premature aging.

Whatever water source you choose—reverse-osmosis, spring, or mineral—choose one! It really is the fountain of youth. Ideally, I would eliminate all other drinks from your diet! Water and herbal tea should be all you consume. Other drinks—even healthy fruit juices—are too high in calories (and diet drinks are loaded with artificial sweetener).

Be sure to drink two to three glasses of water during the morning, another three to four in the afternoon, and another one after dinner. (Substitute sparkling water for two of your eight glasses if you want.)

> **Fat-Burning Secret #3:**
> Drinking eight glasses of water each day will help burn fat, fill your stomach, and suppress your appetite.

Hydrate yourself, nourish your cells, and get drinking water from a clean source. Just by incorporating this one step, you'll lose weight and feel better—guaranteed.

Step 6: Get Walking

This week I want you to try to go for at least three 20-minute *brisk* walks. If you prefer, find another form of aerobic exercise that you can keep up for at least 20 minutes: This could include martial arts, skiing, or racquetball. Aerobic exercise is any activity that uses large muscles and requires the presence of oxygen for sustained energy production. In simple terms, it's any activity that makes you breathe heavily, raises your heart rate, and uses body fat for energy. But I highly recommend brisk walking or jogging as the number one way to burn fat.

Try to walk first thing in the morning. If this isn't possible, then exercise as early in the day as you can manage; if you go later in the day, try to do so on an empty stomach. (And make sure that you wear shoes that are designed for this exercise.) Head out for ten minutes, then turn around and take the same route home. This guarantees 20 minutes and prevents you from finding yourself stuck somewhere miles from home.

If you have a treadmill, program the timer for 20 minutes at a pace between 3.7 and 4.2 miles per hour. If you're already doing cardio at this pace or higher, push yourself up to a level where you could talk if you had to, but it's not really comfortable to do so.

Focus on how you feel as you walk: Could you easily carry on a conversation, or is the activity requiring all your energy? Over the next few weeks, we'll discuss intensity level, caloric expenditures, and many other important aspects of your fitness regimen, but for now I want you to try to walk at a pace as if you were late for an important appointment. Your heart should be beating quickly, and you should be breathing heavily and perspiring lightly. This higher intensity level is essential to taking the weight off and keeping it off.

I originally started exercising in the morning because with a four-month-old and a two-year-old, I could never fit it in once my day began. Every day I'd crawl out of bed, and before even brushing my hair or teeth I'd pull on my sweats, take a swig of water, and creep out the front door. By accident, I discovered a key to weight loss: exercising on an empty stomach. And the pounds started to drop off me!

You also want to get your metabolism elevated as soon as you climb out of bed. Your metabolic rates naturally begin to decline in the evening as

---

Fat-Burning Secret #4:
By exercising first thing in the morning on an empty stomach, your body will use stored fat for energy because you have no food or glycogen to give you the required fuel to exercise.

Crystal Andrus

you prepare for sleep; and by morning, they're completely slowed right down. By exercising at this time, you'll kick your metabolism into gear and burn more fat all day. (On the other hand, if you exercise in the evening, your body won't be ready to slow down for a good night's sleep—and there's nothing worse than coming in from the gym at 10 P.M. . . . and lying awake until 3 A.M.)

By the next morning, your metabolic rate will be returning to normal levels, but you'll be ready to speed it up again. Think of your metabolism as an oil-burning furnace: When you turn up the thermostat in the cold winter months, you burn more oil; but when you turn it off in the summer, the oil in the tank just sits there until next fall. By exercising, you're cranking your thermostat and burning your oil (your fat). You can't possibly expect to burn fat when your furnace is turned off.

I also feel that morning is the optimal time of day to exercise because then it's done and out of the way. You don't have to re-shower or try to fit it in as your day gets busy. Once you get used to early-morning activity, it will become as normal as brushing your teeth, having coffee, and showering . . . I promise. You may have to get up a little earlier, but within a week or two your body will adapt to the new

> **Fat-Burning Secret #5:**
> Aerobic exercise elevates your metabolic rate, burns lots of fat, and suppresses your appetite.

time and you won't feel any more tired than getting up at your regular time. It's the perfect way to start your day.

Exercise is nature's Prozac. A recent study showed that jogging three times a week was as effective for mild depression and other mood-altering disorders as taking antidepressants. Moving your body will have a profound effect on your temperament.

I know that I'm 99 percent more likely to miss a workout if I plan to do it later. I also find that if I start my day with a run, I eat better for the rest of the day. Psychologically, I'm more motivated to stay on track.

If you really can't exercise first thing in the morning, don't worry: Doing it at *any* time of the day is going to make massive changes to your body and fitness level. This is a lifestyle, so it has to fit yours. Now, instead of thinking of exercise as a chore, try to think of what you're doing for yourself. The point is that you need to burn calories and increase your metabolic rate.

You decide what works for you, but get started. I truly hope that you'll take my advice and begin a walking/jogging program first thing in the morning.

Your Walking/Jogging Program

1. Warm up before each walking session:

    *   Begin by walking slowly or marching in place. Gradually increase your speed over a few minutes.

    *   Then stop and gently stretch your muscles, using the stretches outlined at the end of the book (Appendix 3). Don't stretch your muscles before walking for a while, as they'll be cold and you could strain or pull them. Stretching will increase blood supply and nutrients to joint structures, thus helping with any degenerative processes. It also helps to improve muscular imbalance and postural awareness, and it decreases the risk of lower-back pain. To get any lasting benefit, and to increase your flexibility, take your stretch to a point where you definitely feel some tension; hold the position for 20 to 30 seconds, but don't bounce or jerk. Stretching is one of those areas most people overlook, but increased flexibility is an extremely important component of your physical fitness.

Crystal Andrus

- After stretching, begin with a low-level exercise to gradually increase your heart rate. Give yourself another few minutes of building up your pace.

2. Once you've completed this warm-up process, pick up the pace for 15 minutes of brisk walking (or other form of cardiovascular exercise if you choose something other than walking).

3. For the last five minutes, slow your pace back down, but don't stop completely until you feel your heart rate lowering and your breathing slowing down. Stopping suddenly may stress your heart. This is your cooldown.

4. At the end of your cooldown, take five minutes to stretch your leg muscles again. Stretching after a workout can help reduce delayed-onset muscle soreness (that pain we get a day or two after we exercise). It also reduces stress and ends your exercise session on a gratifying and positive note. When stretching, focus on your breathing and try to relax your body, preparing yourself mentally for a great day ahead. You could try the cooldown section at the end of the *Simply . . . Woman! Tight & Toned Workout* DVD for stretching and relaxation.

꾜✻꾜

Summary of Week One: *Awareness*

Don't worry if you're thinking, *I haven't made enough changes to get any results.* To stick to this or anything in life, you need to make small changes every day to work toward your goals. If you become overwhelmed at the prospect of doing too much, you may end up doing nothing at all. The biggest fault with many of the most accurate and informative weight-loss books out there is that they're simply too difficult to follow. What I've learned is that just like the cliché "Rome wasn't built in a day," you've got to make simple yet effective changes each day in order to bring your dreams into reality. I know that you may be tempted to jump ahead, but I strongly recommend that you keep following along week by week.

Let's take a quick look back at the steps in Week One:

Body:

- Go for three 20-minute brisk walks or do three cardio sessions, preferably first thing in the morning or on an empty stomach.

- Focus on eliminating sugar.

- Drink eight to ten glasses of water daily.

Mind:

- Use your journal to become aware of your eating patterns and figure out what you crave.

Soul:

- Look back to when you first started gaining weight. What was going on in your life?

Week Two: *Passion*

Last week, the focus was on becoming aware of yourself and what you eat—discoveries that will be extremely important for you. One day you'll suddenly be conscious that you're listening intuitively to your body's needs and true desires; at that point, food will become a pleasure and will no longer control or threaten you.

Step 7: Discover Your Path

You may feel as if you have no idea what your passion is or even how to find it. Have you ever heard the saying "You can't see the forest for the trees"? Well, many of us have wandered down a path that led us so deep into the forest that we feel lost and unsure. We've completely lost our bearings and don't even know where we are anymore.

Passion isn't to be confused with obsession or unbridled intensity, nor is it about sexuality or being a hot-blooded woman (although many passionate women are just that). To live with passion is to "move to the beat of your own drum"—to face fear and do it anyway!

Discovering and following your own way can feel frightening; and you may feel guilty, afraid, or even too proud to admit that you're on the wrong path. Fear holds most of us back—but conquering it appears harder than it actually is. Simply facing what frightens you is the biggest step. The alternative is to live a life not fully lived, leaving you feeling stuck, helpless, waiting, and wondering. I'll often tell my clients to "fake it till you make it." Imagine someone you admire and ask yourself what choice she'd make in your same situation. If you do the same, one day you'll find yourself living the life you dreamed of, and you'll realize that your fear no longer has a hold over you.

I want you to get out your journal. Relax in a quiet spot without distractions (no telephone, television, computer, or children). The first thing I want you to think about is *how* you want to feel. I know that thought can almost be overwhelming if you're feeling really "lost in the forest" right now, so all I want you to do is look over the following words and write down whichever ones intrigue you. Without judgment or justification, simply notice the words that most inspire, soothe, fascinate, or excite you:

Abundance, acceptance, accomplishment, achievement, acknowledgment, adoration, adventure, affection, affluence, ambition, appreciation, approachability, assertiveness, attractiveness, awareness, awe, balance, beauty, belonging, bliss, boldness, bravery, brilliance, calmness, celebrity, charm, cheerfulness, clarity, cleanliness, clear-mindedness, cleverness, closeness, comfort, commitment, compassion, confidence, connection, consciousness, consistency, contentment, contribution, conviction, coolness, courage, creativity, curiosity, daring, dependability, desire, determination, devotion, devoutness, dignity, directness, discipline, discovery, discretion, diversity, dreaming, dynamism, eagerness, ecstasy, education, effectiveness, efficiency, elation, elegance, eloquence, empathy, encouragement, endurance, energy, enjoyment, entertainment, enthusiasm, excellence, excitement, exhilaration, experience, expertise, exploration, expressiveness, extravagance, faith, fame, family, fashion, fearlessness, feistiness, ferocity, fidelity, fierceness, financial independence, firmness, fitness, flexibility, flow, fluency, focus, fortitude, frankness, freedom, friendliness, fun, generosity, gentility, giving, grace, gratitude, gregariousness, growth, guidance, happiness, harmony, health, heart, helpfulness, heroism, holiness, honesty, honor, hopefulness, humility, humor, imagination, independence, ingenuity, inquisitiveness, insightfulness, inspiration, integrity, intelligence, intensity, intimacy, intuition, intuitiveness, inventiveness, joy, justice, keenness, kindness, knowledge, leadership, learning, liberation, liberty, liveliness, logic, longevity, love, loyalty, majesty, making a difference, mastery, maturity, mindfulness, modesty, motivation, mysteriousness, neatness, nerve, open-mindedness, openness, optimism, order, organization, originality, outlandishness, outrageousness, passion, peace, perceptiveness, perfection, perkiness, perseverance, persistence, persuasiveness, philanthropy, piety, playfulness, pleasantness, pleasure, poise, polish, popularity, potency, power, practicality, precision, preparedness, presence, privacy, proactivity, professionalism, prosperity, prudence, punctuality, purity, realism, reason, reasonableness, recognition, recreation, refinement, reflection, relaxation, reliability, religiousness, resilience, resolution, resolve, resourcefulness, respect, rest, restraint, reverence, richness, rigor, sacredness, sacrifice, sagacity, saintliness, satisfaction, security, self-control, selflessness, self-reliance, sensitivity, sensuality, serenity, service, sexuality, sharing, shrewdness, significance, silence, silliness, simplicity, sincerity, skillfulness, solidarity, solitude, soundness, speed, spirit, spirituality, spontaneity, spunk, stability, stillness, strength, success, support, synergy, temperance, thankfulness, thoroughness, thoughtfulness, timeliness, tranquility, transcendence, trust, trustworthiness, truth, understanding, uniqueness, unity, usefulness, valor, victory, vigor, virtue, vision, vitality, vivacity, warmth, watchfulness, wealth, willingness, winning, wisdom, wittiness, wonder, youthfulness, zeal.

As you look over your list of words, say out loud, "I want to feel _____" and say each word in your list and see if your body speaks back to you. Ask yourself, "Does that really light me up? Is that specific emotion really important to me?" And then compare the words on your list one last time and narrow it down to your top ten words—these should be the words that most captivate you.

Good job! You now have your first insight as to who you really are, what lights you up, and what your soul needs in order to feel alive and nourished. Isn't that exciting?!

You don't have to do anything else with these words for now except to embrace them, without judgment or justification. You may wonder how knowing what words you love most is going to help you discover your passion; nevertheless, it's the first step toward making your life fierce with reality!

For many years I stressed myself out, wanting to know what I should do with my life. I wanted to know the "exact path" I needed to take. I've subsequently learned that it's not *how you're going to get there* that's important; it's *why* you want to get there and *how you want to feel*. Why do you want to take that course, buy that car, or get married to that man? Why would you say yes to one option and no to another? Once you discover *how you want to feel,* it makes figuring out what choices you need to make that much easier!

I also want you to ponder the following questions, which will further help you figure out what makes you tick. If you're hesitant to answer them honestly because someone might read what you've written, hide your journal somewhere safe or join our "On-line Journal" on our free Message Forum at **www.crystalandrus. com**. Journaling in this way provides you with a safe, private, and confidential medium to share your feelings. If your name is Betty, you can sign up as Suzy. And no one can access it from your home unless you share your password. In order to get benefits from journaling, you must feel absolutely secure that you can write whatever you feel. Don't think too much—just write the first thoughts that jump into your head after you consider the following questions:

- When you think back over your adult life, when were you happiest?

- What made you feel great about yourself when you were a kid?

- What hobbies or activities did you love?

- What did you want to be when you grew up?

- What was the emotional atmosphere like in your home growing up? Do you often go back to that emotional baseline now as an adult?

- When do you feel true joy?

- If you could be anything—and if education, money, children, parents, and whatever you are in your life today didn't matter—what would you be?

- Will getting in better shape make you happier? Why haven't you done it before now?

- Why do you want to be in better shape? List every possible reason.

- What are you most afraid of in life? What has that fear cost you?

When you've finished, read your answers over a few times and really digest them. It's essential that you live your life true to *you*. Based on your answers, I want you to think about *why you're doing this program*. I call these reasons your "List of Burning Desires," and they should be for and about *you*. Your List of Burning Desires could include things such as: "I want to feel sexy and confident. I want more energy or to feel proud of myself. I want security and well-being. I want to live a long and healthy life," and so on. Your burning desires are different from your goals—they're the reasons *why* you want to accomplish something, so they strengthen the intensity of your focus. These burning desires must be written down. Once you've done so, make a photocopy of your list and tape it up where you'll see it every day, such as beside the toilet-paper holder or on your bathroom mirror. Read it daily, or any-time you're feeling discouraged or disheartened.

Now that you know *how you want to feel*, you need to create some goals that will help you achieve this. In 1953, Yale University polled its graduating class to see how many people had written down goals, and only a minuscule 3 percent had done so. Twenty years later, Yale went back and followed up with this same class—unbelievably, the same 3 percent who had written down their goals had accumulated more money and assets than the other 97 percent combined. Wow!

Your goals don't have to just be about health and weight loss; they might also involve other areas of your life. For example, are you married or in a serious relationship? How is that going? Where would you like to see it three months from now? How about your friendships? When was the last time you met your closest friend for a cup of coffee, just the two of you? How about your financial situation? Do you have a retirement plan or a little savings stashed away? How much money would you like to save in just the next 12 weeks (multiply that number by four to discover how much you could save over the next year). Is there a course you've wanted to take or a career change you've been thinking about? What steps

Crystal Andrus

could you take to make that happen? Are there countries you've always wanted to visit, or new things you want to try?

Think of goal setting as following a road map. If you wanted to get to a specific destination, you wouldn't just get in your car and start to drive aimlessly, hoping that you'd have enough gas and would figure out the route as you went along. No, you'd devise the smartest and easiest route and figure out how many hours or days the trip was going to take. You'd make sure that you had enough money and gas, that your car was working properly, and that you had a clear map. With a plan on how to get there, you'd be able to relax and enjoy the journey. If a little detour occurred, no sweat—you'd deal with it and continue on, always checking your map and staying on course.

Likewise, if you simply decided to take one step each day to make your goals a reality, think about where you'd be one year from now. Imagine if you made that important call you've been putting off or signed up for that course you've been talking about. What if you decided to throw away all the junk food in your cupboards and began to work out each morning? Without purpose, most goals seem too hard to achieve. It's a strong, burning desire that gives us the drive to succeed.

The same principle applies to any area of your life: Having a written goal helps you create an effective plan of action because it creates just the right amount of pressure needed to actually accomplish that aim! Goal setting requires thought, keeps you on track, and helps you stay focused. Although life is full of unexpected detours, without direction you'll simply coast along, wondering what you should be doing with your life.

The truth is, eventually you'll get to a place where goal setting will seem redundant since your life will be falling into place perfectly and you'll trust and abide by what is showing up for you, but for now, goal setting is vitally important to setting your life into motion and getting the ball moving!

✢✻✢

You may find that the idea of looking so far down the road is too overwhelming, so just begin with three months from today. Your goals for the next 12 weeks should be challenging but attainable. (If you already know some of your longer-term goals, then by all means, jot them down, too.) Remember that this is a program designed to integrate the body, mind, *and* soul, so don't just set goals for your appearance. But if you're going to set goals for your body, set realistic ones. For weight loss, don't necessarily go by life-insurance charts, which don't take into account your lean body mass, your muscles, bones, organs, and fat mass. (I've worked with many 130-pound women who are considered obese by these tables but are actually in amazing shape.) Body-fat percentage is the true indicator of how much fat you need to lose. Bearing this in mind, a realistic weight-loss goal on this program is to average two to three pounds a week.

Another goal could be to lower your resting heart rate (RHR). If you could reduce it by 10 beats a minute, then each day you'd save approximately 15,000 beats.

Whatever your goals, be clear and specific. Believe that you *will* attain them, because the strength of your beliefs is one of the most important indicators of whether you'll succeed or not. Focus on your dreams with a burning desire. Visualize your new self: How will you look and feel? What will this success bring you? Stay consistent in your actions and persevere, even when you feel frustrated or unsure. Fear of success is one of the primary reasons for self-sabotage, but remember that it's as easy to prosper as it is to fail. It's all in your daily choices.

**Written goals,
combined with a burning desire,
help you knock down your mental roadblocks
and accomplish anything!**

The following goal-setting workshop is an important tool for your long-term success. Think about your bad habits or patterns of action that could impede your success—for example, procrastinating or sleeping in. Come up with ideas that will help keep you on track—in other words, create your Plan B.

Goal-Setting Workshop I

Over the next three months, your body, mind, and spirit will undergo some huge changes. The potency of these changes is directly proportionate to the strength and power of your focus.

Based on your burning desires, choose three precise goals that you want to see happen over the next 12 weeks. Follow the S.M.A.R.T. formula for goal setting:

Specific

Measurable

Attainable

Realistic

Time-Bound

Over the next 12 weeks, one goal I really want to accomplish is:

_____

_____

_____

Three of my bad habits or mental roadblocks that could hold me back from reaching that goal are:

1. _____

2. _____

3. _____

Three things I can do to help keep me on track are:

1. _____

2. _____

3. _____

For my second goal, I'd like to:

_____

_____

_____

Three of my self-sabotaging behaviors that could hold me back from reaching that goal are:

1. _____

2. _____

3. _____

Three things I can do to avoid these behaviors are:

1. _____

2. _____

3. _____

The third goal I'd like to accomplish by the end of this 12-week program is:

_____

_____

_____

Crystal Andrus

Three things that could hold me back from reaching that goal are:

1. _____

2. _____

3. _____

Three things that can help me reach that goal are:

1. _____

2. _____

3. _____

Internally Motivated Desire

I often hear women say things such as "I have to lose weight because I want to look good for my husband" or "If I looked better, I know my parents would accept me," but the truth is, you'll never make lasting lifestyle changes for someone else. You have to do this for *you*. If you're confused about whether or not you're internally motivated—in other words, motivated to change for yourself—or you're doing it for reasons outside yourself, consider this scenario (many women will be familiar with it!):

> *Joe Blow has been single all his life. A good-looking "man's man," he parties a lot and dates many women. One day a special lady comes into his life who has all the qualities he wants in a partner, but she won't put up with his shenanigans. He convinces her that he can change and become the man she wants him to be. He gives up the crazy nightlife, but he misses the good old days. He wants to please her, but he still wants his single life, too. Before long, he's back out with his buddies, partying all night and disrespecting the woman he wanted to*

be with so badly. His changes didn't last <u>because they were for someone else</u>.

Now let's use this same scenario, with one significant difference . . .

> *Joe Blow is a good-looking "man's man" who parties a lot and dates many women. He's beginning to feel the emptiness of his lifestyle and wants to find someone special with whom he can build a wonderful life. He knows that he needs to make changes in his life because his former ways are getting old and meaningless. He wants to be a better man. One day this wonderful woman comes into his life who has the qualities he wants in a partner. He knows he's finally found the right one, and he's ready to make the necessary changes to create the life of his dreams. His dream woman didn't make him change—he changed for himself.*

A quote from Margaret Young in Sarah Ban Breathnach's wonderful book *Simple Abundance* helped me begin the process of understanding who *I* really was and what I needed: "Often people attempt to live their lives backwards: They try to have more things, or more money, in order to do more of what they want so that they will be happier. The way it actually works is the reverse. You must first *be* who you really are, then, *do* what you need to do, in order to *have* what you want!"

Your Internal "Audiotapes"

I'd like you to forget about the negative for a moment and think about the positive qualities you admire in yourself. Imagine yourself to be the balance sheet of a corporation's financial statement: Your positive qualities are your assets, your negative points are your liabilities, and your net worth is your assets minus liabilities. If you spend all your time centered on your so-called liabilities by trying to fix yourself, your net worth may increase slightly. If, however, you take the focus off your inadequacies and put all your energy into building on what you're really good at, then your net worth can increase by a factor of ten.

> **Fat-Burning Secret #6:**
> Internally motivated desire is critical for losing weight or for accomplishing any goal.

We all have things about ourselves that we want to change. These negative thoughts and self-defeating internal messages often came from the people closest to us—maybe our parents, siblings, mates, friends, or perhaps even a teacher—those who see us as we once were or when we were at our worst. (Not many of us were wonderful teenagers, but hopefully we've grown up.) Ingrained into our psyche, these negative messages continue to pull us back to who we once were, even after we've grown up or changed, and often the people in our lives remind us of our past habits whenever we try to elevate ourselves.

You must work really hard to erase these messages and focus on your positive attributes (your assets). It's important to realize that everyone struggles with their self-image at times—it doesn't matter how beautiful or successful someone appears . . . they too have moments of insecurity and self-doubt. However, your purpose in life is to seize your potential and maximize it, and you can never do that if you're constantly bringing attention to your shortcomings. Think about all your best qualities and stay focused on them: Are you thoughtful or organized? Do you cook well or garden? Do you have beautiful, long eyelashes or straight, white teeth? You must start seeing your assets and believe in yourself! These positive messages will eventually override your old beliefs, and one day, very soon, you'll find yourself feeling confident and on top of the world.

This approach works in most areas of your life. Your attitude about a particular situation is often the determining factor in its outcome. This may sound too simplistic, but the fact is that your perception of yourself is a reflection of your self-esteem. By concentrating on your positive attributes, you'll essentially begin to erase the programmed audiotapes that you began recording in childhood. These are the ones you replay over and over in your mind—the ones that make you doubt yourself, question situations, and crave the approval of others.

These negative internal messages can be triggered by a simple comment or even the way someone looks at you. You instantly hit the "play" button and begin reaffirming the transmissions that you've been recording from birth, believing that you're fat, ugly, shy, stupid, selfish, or somehow just not quite right.

While I was training her on the set of one of her movies, an absolutely gorgeous actress once told me that she couldn't shake the awful image she had of herself at age 12. And although that certainly isn't the reflection the world sees, this was her taped internal message. Until we all stop pressing "play," we'll continue to self-sabotage and experience inaccurate perceptions of ourselves.

But it's not enough to just hit your "stop" button—you must also erase the tapes and begin to create a new internal dialogue. It can take time, effort, and even a little discomfort, but until you change your belief system, absolutely nothing in your life will change!

※

The brilliant author Deepak Chopra believes that your view of yourself at this moment directly affects what you are, right down to the cellular level. By changing your vision today, you can alter what you'll be tomorrow—and for the rest of your life!

Begin by writing down a positive statement about yourself. This is *not* a list of what you want to change, like a New Year's resolution; instead, it's a description of you when you're at your very best. Focus on all your assets, and write a small paragraph describing yourself at your greatest. I know that if you're feeling rotten about yourself, this process may seem almost impossible, so you may need to begin by creating the fantasy of the "life you lust after" and the woman you know you can be. This is what I call your "Self-Proclaiming Declaration," and you should write it as if you already are that person. *And don't just think about doing this exercise—you must write it down.*

Be conscious of the way you speak about yourself when you're alone and publicly. Stop every time you begin to chastise yourself! No more "I'm chubby, boring, flabby, ugly," or whatever—and say nothing negative about your hair, clothes, face, nose, body, breasts, butt, stretch marks, cooking, parenting, personality . . . even if you're desperately feeling it! Simply stop!

You'll quickly realize just how often you're putting yourself down, reinforcing your weaknesses, and bringing constant attention to your insecurities. This gets old fast. Even if no one else puts you on a pedestal, it's time you put yourself on one. We've all met that woman who can walk it, talk it, and make everyone else think that she's all that. Then there are those who have so much going for themselves, but they walk feebly, talk in an unsure manner, and can't take a compliment—they don't believe in themselves, so no one else ever believes in them either.

Sometimes we self-sabotage and don't follow our path as far as it could take us. I believe that we all have a natural set point for life, just like the metabolic set point that scientists have theorized about. You see, our brain has a mechanism in it like a thermostat that keeps us regulated. This tiny gland, called the *hypothalamus,* stimulates us to keep our body within a certain zone. We eat a certain amount to keep our weight roughly the same. It dictates how much sleep we need, which is why we all require different amounts to function—and we each have varying sexual appetites and desires for love or attention.

These same set points apply to everything we do and believe: We'll make only enough money as we believe we're worth, or find a mate whom we feel is worthy of us. We'd rather stay with that comfortable old friend then venture out into a new-but-scary world. Most of us never force ourselves past our threshold and go through life demanding just enough to meet those needs. These are mental roadblocks, and once you knock them down, you'll zoom out of your restricting comfort zone and begin to speed down your path.

This recalls a story in the amazing book *Think & Grow Rich* by Napoleon Hill. It seems that one day a man hears a dog moaning and groaning as he lies on his master's front porch. After hours of hearing this dog whimpering, the man finally walks over, looks at the dog and then over at the dog's master, a farmer, and asks, "I've been listening to your dog moaning and groaning all day. What's wrong with him?"

"Oh, don't worry about him," the old farmer nonchalantly replies. "He's just layin' on a nail."

"Laying on a nail?" the man asks, bewildered. "Well, why doesn't he move?"

"Well," the old farmer answered, "it don't hurt enough. . . ."

It don't hurt enough. Hmm . . . just think about how many times you've been just like that dog: moaning and groaning, complaining about your life or body but unwilling to get up.

Only you can decide that you're going to step out of your comfort zone (or rather, discomfort zone) and do something about it.

Think of all the reasons to get on your own path, which outweigh the reasons to stay stuck where you are. Motivate yourself to push past your set point and live the life you desire.

Crystal Andrus

Step 8: Start Eating Green Light Carbohydrates

This week I want you to get out your recorded three days of eating and refer to the Traffic Light Carbohydrate Charts located at the end of this book (Appendix 1). Use red, yellow, and green markers to identify your carbohydrate choices: What type are you eating most?

When you eat any carb, it's broken down into a smaller molecule called *glucose*. Your stomach isn't discriminating, so it doesn't differentiate between cotton candy and an apple. Once in your small intestine, the only difference is that one (the apple, of course) contains fiber and nutrients.

For many years, carbohydrates were believed to belong to one of two categories: simple or complex. Simple carbohydrates were sugars such as fruits and candy, while complex consisted of starches such as bread and pasta. Scientists believed that because of their smaller molecular structure,

Simply . . . Tips!

1. Write in your journal every night. Become conscious of your eating habits and your coping skills.

2. Try behavior modification. If you snack on junk food while watching TV, give up the boob tube for a while. Try other activities not associated with food: Call a friend, read a book, go for a walk, clean your house, play with your kids, write in your journal, stretch, do some gardening, listen to music, try yoga . . . whatever.

3. Eat only at the table. Don't get distracted from what you're eating by reading, talking on the phone, or watching TV. Enjoy your food—don't just stuff it mindlessly into your mouth.

4. Don't self-sabotage. If you mess up, get right back on track. You won't always eat perfectly, but don't punish yourself by making it worse. This is a lifestyle, not a diet.

5. Reward yourself. If you tend to overeat or drink after a long stressful day, reward yourself with some relaxing

pleasure other than food or alcohol: Take a bath, paint your nails, meditate, or dance. Use food for its true purpose: to nourish a hungry body.

6. Don't eat late at night. If you struggle with this one, eat more healthy food throughout the earlier part of the day. Try drinking herbal teas at night rather than eating food. And head to bed an hour earlier—you could probably use the sleep.

simple carbohydrates would digest faster than starches, thus raising blood-sugar levels too quickly, and should be avoided; however, complex carbohydrates were thought to be better for sustained energy and weight loss. Yet newer research has revealed that the starch in foods such as white bread, white potatoes, and many types of rice is actually digested and absorbed more quickly than most sugars!

Other factors that affect the speed of carbohydrate digestion are how much you eat at one time, the fiber content, how it's cooked, if it's combined with protein and/or fat (as both tend to cause a delay in stomach emptying, thereby slowing the rate of carbohydrate digestion), and if vinegar or lemon juice is added. The term *glycemic index* was introduced, and largely replaced the old distinctions between simple and complex carbs: Some foods absorb quickly (they have a high-glycemic response), while others take longer (they have a low-glycemic response).

As you know from our discussion of sugar last week, the body doesn't like glycemic highs and lows, so it always wants to maintain balance. When there's a rise in blood sugar, the body needs to bring its levels back to normal. The secret to maintaining a healthy balance is to eat carbs that have that low-glycemic response and break down in the bloodstream at a decelerated rate. With this slow release of sugar, the blood doesn't feel the surge; thus, very little insulin is released, meaning that you don't get the crash that usually follows. Your blood sugar, endorphins, and serotonin levels rise at a nice, constant rate and begin declining at the same gentle pace, so you'll feel content for at least three to four hours. This helps avoid the cravings you feel after eating high-glycemic carbs.

The glycemic index rates carbohydrates on a 1 to 100 value, using glucose as the baseline. High-glycemic foods are those that rate upwards of 70 on the index; medium falls between 55 and 69; and those listed 54 and down are low glycemic.

Don't worry about trying to understand how this index measures glycemic response; just know that it rates *only* carbohydrates. Fat and protein are broken down into different macronutrients and don't affect blood-sugar levels. In fact, to make this simple for you, I've developed a list of Red Light, Yellow Light, and Green Light carbohydrates. They're based on high-, medium-, and low-glycemic carbs, as well as other important nutritional components such as fiber content, fat content, glycemic load, preservatives, and processing.

- **Red Light** carbohydrates are often processed or refined, meaning that they often come out of a package or can. Often light in color, Red Light carbs include white bread, white potatoes, and white sugar, and they're tough to eliminate initially because they're often comfort foods. Mashed potatoes on a cold winter's night or crusty French bread warm from the oven can temporarily cure the blues on a tough day or when you're PMS-ing—but remember, although eating Red Light carbs is occasionally necessary for your soul, too many of them will be stored as fat, and that's not comforting at all!

- **Yellow Light** carbohydrates are foods that you'll still want to avoid, but you can have small amounts of them once in a while. These include foods such as nuts and avocados, which, while filled with nutrients, are also quite high in calories and fats.

- **Green Light** carbohydrates are unrefined and unprocessed. Most often dark in color, they're filled with antioxidants, phytochemicals, vitamins, and fiber; and they'll speed up your metabolism. In other words, they're *Go, Go, Go Foods!* They enter your system at a slow, gentle rate, and sustain your appetite longer.

You'll find my charts of Red, Yellow, and Green Light carbs in the Traffic Light Food Section in the Appendix. Beside each listed food in the charts, you'll notice a number from 1 to 100. This is the *speed of digestion,* not the calories or grams of carbohydrates. Most of the Red Light carbs will have numbers above 70, the Yellow Light will have numbers between 50 and 70, and the Green Light will be mostly under 49. This week, just begin to eliminate Red Light carbohydrates and start eating more from the Green Light list, but *don't worry yet about your serving sizes of Green Light foods.*

As you're cutting back on Red Light and eating more Green Light carbs, you must also include palm-size portions of low-fat protein with every meal. Choices include chicken or turkey breast, water-packed tuna, sole, egg whites, low-fat tofu and tempeh, protein shakes, and dairy products such as fat-free yogurt and fat-free cottage cheese. (You'll learn about protein and fat in the coming weeks.)

Step 9: Eat Every Three to Four Hours

Avoid going too long between meals—instead, eat by the clock and not by your hunger pangs (or for that matter, your cravings). By eating three small meals and two snacks spaced out every three to four hours, you'll eliminate the ravenous feeling that can suddenly occur when hunger hits after you've gone too long without nourishment. Your "perfect-calorie day" can be ruined by 5:30 P.M. if you ate lunch at noon and suddenly you feel too hungry to wait until 7:00 for a healthy dinner. More important, eating every few

> **Fat-Burning Secret #7:**
> Eat Green Light carbohydrates, and eliminate Red Light carbs.

hours keeps your metabolism burning fat all day long. Believe it or not, you have to eat to lose body fat. You'll learn more about exactly what to eat in the weeks that follow, but in the meantime, here's what an ideal day should look like.

AN IDEAL DAY

TIME		Calories	Protein	Carbs	Fat	8 oz Water
6:00 a.m.	30 minutes of intense Cardio & Stretch					✔✔
6:45 a.m.	2 cups of mixed berries (Wait 20 minutes before breakfast to let the fruit digest and do an "internal cleansing")	100	1	20	0	✔
7:15 a.m.	Breakfast 4 egg whites scrambled with ½ cup fat-free cottage cheese (salsa, mushrooms, green peppers) (1 pc. fat-free cheese melted on top—optional) 1 piece of pumpernickel toast green tea	68 100 20 30 80 0	14 15 0 5 3 0	0 7 5 3 15 0	0 0 0 0 0 0	✔
10:00 a.m.	Snack Any low-glycemic fruit (apple)	40	0	10	0	✔
1:00 p.m.	Lunch open-face tuna sandwich on one piece of pumpernickel bread 1 can of tuna in water with fat-free mayonnaise and lettuce or sprouts (like alfalfa) large salad: romaine lettuce, Boston lettuce, with tomato, cucumber, red onion, etc… 3 tbsp apple cider vinegar and ½ tbsp of olive oil large Perrier	80 160 100 60 0	3 40 5 0 0	15 .5 20 0 0	1 0 0 7 0	✔
3:30 p.m.	Snack fat-free/sugar-free yogurt with ¼ cup of nonfat cottage cheese	50 50	5 7	8 3.5	0 0	✔
7:00 p.m.	Dinner 6 oz grilled, baked, or broiled sole ½ cup baked or boiled yam (sweet potato) 3 cups of broccoli and cauliflower steamed with garlic sautéed in 1 tbsp of extra virgin olive oil	200 80 50 4 120	31 1 8 0 0	0 18 14 1 0	2 0 0 0 14	
10:00 p.m.	herbal tea (non-caffeinated)					✔
11:00 p.m.	BEDTIME!					
	TOTAL (approximately)	1400	140	140	25	8 waters

·Extra healthy fat coming from essential fatty acids would also be supplemented into the diet.

Crystal Andrus

Step 10: Exercise in the Zone

One of the reasons why I created this program was because I'd watched so many women work out with weights, climb on those stair machines, and do aerobics classes consistently for months, even years, without making any real progress. In the '80s, we were told to train hard: "No pain, no gain" was the mantra. Then all those high-impact aerobics classes were suddenly gone, and the fat-burning workout became popular. Apparently, to burn fat more efficiently, we needed to exercise at a lower intensity for a longer period of time.

Many fitness professionals have promoted the notion that exercising at a lower intensity actually burns a greater amount of fat than higher-intensity exercise. For years, many people have believed that when we exercise at a lower intensity level, say 50 to 60 percent of our maximum heart rate (MHR), we use more stored body fat as energy than if we train at 80 percent of our MHR.

Clients would ask me about that mysterious "fat-burning zone," as they were afraid they might not be working in it. Unfortunately, just like the fat-free diet myth, the fat-burning workout is also fiction. Factually, lower-intensity exercise does use more fat as its main source of energy than higher-intensity exercise, but the total fat calories consumed are greater when exercising at a more difficult level. For example, walking uses about 60 percent of your fat as energy, while only about 40 percent comes from carbohydrates (or glycogen).

As your intensity levels increase—say, going from a walk into a jog, the percentage of fat being used begins to decrease as your body begins to pull more energy from stored carbs. However, this is the key: Although walking uses 60 percent of its calories from fat and jogging only uses 40 percent, you're burning *far more total calories* when jogging than walking. This is important, because to lose one pound of fat, you'll need to burn 3,500 calories.

In September 1999, an article in the *American College of Sports Medicine Health and Fitness Journal* stated that in order to burn the highest levels of fat, you'll need to exercise at an intensity level of 80 percent of your MHR. So low and slow has to go! You'll begin training at 50 to 60 percent of your MHR, but by the end of 12 weeks, you should be able to reach a goal of an intensity of 70 to 80 percent. Remember, these are only guidelines and should be used as a rule of thumb.

If your resting heart rate is higher than 85 beats per minute, never train higher than 60 percent of your MHR until you lower it to under 80. If you've had a heart condition or are obese, you should begin by keeping your heart rate at the lowest level of your zone, or even at 40 to 50 percent of your MHR.

So how do you figure out your maximum heart rate? Many fitness professionals use the simple formula of 220 minus your age to determine MHR; however, I believe that your resting heart rate is also very important to incorporate into this equation. So, first subtract your age from 220, and then subtract your resting heart rate that you entered on your Success Tracker I. This gives you a baseline to find your Target Training Zone. For example, if you're 40 years old with a resting heart rate of 80, this would be your equation: $220 - 40 = 180 - 80 = 100$. This is your baseline rate.

To determine your Target Training Zone for losing weight, you want to exercise between 60 percent and 80 percent of your MHR. Using this same example, take your baseline rate of 100 and multiply it by 0.6 and then *add back your resting heart rate*. So 60 percent would be $100 \times 0.6 = 60 + 80 = 140$. And 80 percent would be $100 \times 0.8 = 80 + 80 = 160$.

Crystal Andrus

So your Target Training Zone's low end would be approximately 140 beats per minute, and the most your heart should beat in a minute is 160. You need to do this equation for yourself, based on your own age and heart rate.

The other way to put yourself in the right zone is exercising at a pace where you could talk if you had to, but it would be a lot of effort to carry on a conversation. Personal trainers call this the "talk test." Whenever I see someone effortlessly gabbing away as they walk on the treadmill or pedal on the bike, I think, *What a waste of time!* These are generally the same people who've been working out for years without getting anywhere.

Make your exercise sessions count: 20 to 30 minutes at a high intensity will begin to take the fat off and keep it off. Take a watch with you, and every five to ten minutes take your heart rate for six seconds and add a zero. Are you exercising between 60 and 80 percent of your MHR? To increase or decrease your heart rate to get yourself in your Target Training Zone, simply speed up your pace if your heart rate is lower than your 60 percent or slow down if it's faster than your 80 percent training heart rate zone.

If you're currently exercising and are doing more than 30 minutes but can't seem to lose a pound of fat, you're not exercising hard enough (and are eating too many Red Light carbs). Pick up your pace. If you find that brisk walking or jogging bothers your joints, then perhaps swimming or cycling would be better choices for you—but again, the key is to take your pulse to make sure that you're in your training zone.

So this week you need to increase the intensity level of the walks you started last week. As you're briskly walking, you need to constantly be aware of your pace. Could you easily carry on a conversation? If so, then pick it up: Try a slow jog for 30 seconds to one minute, then go back to a walk for three minutes. Continue these jog/walk intervals for the full 20 minutes if you can. And don't worry if it seems difficult; the first 10 minutes are always the toughest.

Step 11: Strength Train

It's time to get out your *Simply . . . Woman! Workout* DVD located at the back of your book. If you have the *Simply . . . Woman Total Workout Bench & Crystal Ball,* you'll want to use it two times this week. You'll need to do an overall workout, working each muscle group in your entire body. There are so many different exercises you can do with this machine, so don't allow yourself to get overwhelmed with the options. Have fun with it! You can download different workout routines at: **www.simplywoman.com** to accommodate a beginner-to-advanced fitness level.

If you don't have the *Simply . . . Woman Total Workout Bench & Crystal Ball,* you'll need to do the *Tight & Toned* workout twice this week: It's an overall body workout, and it's surprisingly tough, so go at your own pace. Focus on form, and don't get caught up in how you look or how many repetitions you do of any specific exercise on the DVD. Take a break when you need to.

We'll be concentrating on core body-strength exercises using muscular contractions, as contracting a muscle forces it to tighten and tone. You don't want to just get smaller—you want to get firmer, too! Remember that muscle by its very existence is going to speed up your metabolism, burn calories and fat, and tighten and tone your body.

We know that close to 90 percent of people who join a gym or buy exercise equipment quit within 60 days. I think a big part of that is because they're working hard, sweating, training, and feeling sore and tired . . . and then they step on that scale and their

Crystal Andrus

weight hasn't dropped. Their beliefs that they won't succeed are being confirmed by the scale, and their choices then begin to support those beliefs.

If you're using the scale as your only indicator of your fat loss, you can get quite discouraged because muscle weighs more than fat. Imagine holding a full ten-ounce water bottle in one hand and an empty quart water bottle in the other: Which would be heavier? Of course, the smaller, full bottle. Do you really care what you weigh if you're smaller and leaner? I mean, do you want to be light but bigger? Exactly!

Don't keep weighing yourself, especially for the first four weeks. Pay attention to how your clothes fit and how you feel. You may start dropping weight quickly and easily, but you might not do so right away. Don't cause yourself unnecessary stress: Your body will respond, and with each passing day you'll look and feel better. In about two to three weeks, everything is going to start coming together. You'll begin feeling different, and people are going to start noticing changes in you.

Do your workout video on alternate days from your walks, and try to do it in the morning as well. If that doesn't work for you, do it whenever it fits your schedule, but choose the days in advance and schedule them in, as though these workouts are as important as any appointment you might have. Stay focused on your goals, and let nothing deter you from your path. Together, we'll get you into the best shape of your life.

> **Fat-Burning Secret #9:**
> Resistance training burns calories, speeds up your metabolism, and shapes your body in all the right places!

※ ✳ ※

Summary of Week Two: *Passion*

Body:

- Choose natural, "dark-colored" fibrous fruits and vegetables such as berries and salads; and avoid "white-colored" carbohydrates such as white potatoes, white bread, white rice, white sugar, and white pasta.

- Try to eat three healthy meals and two snacks every day.

- Work in the zone to burn more fat.

- Start tightening and toning your muscles with your *Simply . . . Woman! Tight & Toned Workout* DVD.

Mind:

- Create your list of Burning Desires and your Self-Proclaiming Declaration, and refuse to bring attention to your weaknesses.

- Do your Goal-Setting Workshop.

Soul:

- Discover your path. Begin by figuring what revs you up, without judgment or justification. You don't need to know *how* you're going to get there yet. First you need to know where *there* is. . . .

෴ ෴

Crystal Andrus

Week Three: *Acceptance*

Week Three: Wow we're moving fast! By the end of this week, you'll be a quarter of the way through! But just remember . . . baby steps.

Step 12: Get Real

Feeling fit and healthy is certainly not the only step to achieving contentment, but it *is* one of the first. It's usually fair to say that how you look and feel is symbolic of what's going on in your life. Although thin thighs are absolutely no guarantee of happiness, I've yet to meet a woman who hates her body but loves her life. That doesn't mean that all women with great bodies have perfect lives, but it's next to impossible to feel joyful when you despise what you see in the mirror.

Are you content with your reflection, or are you being too hard on yourself? The truth is that most of us see ourselves as much fatter and less attractive than the rest of the world does. Yet how can we blame ourselves when we have anorexic-looking actresses and models plastered all over TV, the movies, and on the covers of fashion magazines? What used to be considered too skinny is now sexy by Hollywood standards, and what used to be sexy is now thought of as fat. Many of today's stars don't even appear to have any muscle tone at all—they literally look like skin and bones!

Dr. Anne Becker of Harvard Medical School interviewed 63 girls from Fiji in 1995—only 3 percent of them reported using induced vomiting to lose weight. Coincidentally, this was also the same year that television was introduced to this island. By 1998, that number had risen to 15 percent, and many of the girls had embraced the Western ideal of thinness that was featured on shows such as *Melrose Place*. How can we mere mortals look in the mirror and see our beauty rather than the lumps of lard we have on our hips and thighs?

Photographer Holly Sasnett had her project *Body Revisited: Photographs from the Body Image Project* on exhibit as part of Atlanta, Georgia's "Eating Disorder Awareness Week" in 2000. She's been photographing women with eating disorders and distorted body image for years. Although no faces were shown, the entire exhibit consisted of nude photographs. Work like hers is important because it shows us that there is beauty in every woman. These types of images help us accept that we come in all shapes and sizes, and that we're all much more alike than we realize. *Playboy* centerfold pictures aren't real, and it's a shame that we compare ourselves to images that have been computer enhanced and manipulated to appear perfect. We're all far too self-conscious and hard on ourselves, and it's time to see the true beauty that we all possess.

※※※

I have personal experience when it comes to this very topic. Because I have a lot of muscle on my already athletic frame, I struggled with the numbers I saw on the scale. I know that muscle weighs more than fat, but it bothered me that I weighed so much. Even after I'd lost all my extra body fat, there were times I still felt huge. No matter how good I looked, I wondered if I could be better. Then I started looking at women my own age who had a few kids, and I realized that this ridiculous ideal of what I was supposed to look like kept me captive to a need for perfection. We women aren't Barbie dolls—so, although I loved looking at my 121-pound body, it wasn't healthy, normal, or realistic to maintain. And trying to do so was self-defeating.

One thing that helped me with my distorted body image after I'd lost all my extra weight was a trip to the beach with my family. While we were planning the outing, my mind was racing. I imagined gorgeous, firm, little bodies in string bikinis all over the sand. But the reality couldn't have been further from the truth. Sure, there were the typical perky 20-year-olds, but I saw normal women,

Crystal Andrus

too—most of whom had cellulite and rounded hips; and many of whom sported stretch marks, loose skin, and sagging breasts. I realized that I'd been comparing myself with ridiculous ideals. The girls of *Baywatch* aren't on our beaches. I'd been comparing myself to undernourished teenage models and retouched pictures that elongate legs, shadow in cleavage, and airbrush out cellulite.

I do think that positive and healthy role models are great for us when we need a little inspiration or motivation. Nothing gives me a kick in the butt like a picture of Vanessa Williams or Madonna, and sometimes even seeing a great picture of myself will remind me of how I can look when I make the extra effort. So start looking through magazines targeted at women your own age—of course most of the women featured will still be unusually beautiful and thin, but you may start to see some more attainable role models as well.

We all see different versions of our bodies throughout our lives; however, in our quest to accept and even honor ourselves, we must now begin to see ourselves for who we are. When we change our focus from being *the* best to being *our* best, we can rejoice that we'll never look like anyone else. Why would we want to?

A healthy way to determine a realistic weight for you is the lowest weight that you've been since you were over the age of 25 (when you were eating sensibly and exercising reasonably), which you were able to maintain for a minimum of two years. If you've never been at a weight you were happy with, then ask yourself if you're being irrational and are expecting to be thinner than you should be. Or is it because you've never made an effort in your adult life to eat healthfully, exercise, and take care of your body?

Stop this cycle of self-loathing now: Stop beating yourself up and putting yourself down by saying aloud (even just to yourself) that you hate your thighs, rear end, or anything else about yourself. When a pessimistic thought jumps into your head, refuse it. Pick out your attributes and focus on them. And if you're a mother of a daughter, make sure that she knows that you feel happy living inside a woman's body—if you don't, for her sake, fake it.

Exercise and eat healthfully so that you'll look and feel your best, but throw away the notion that there's a better or more perfect you. She's already there, just waiting for you to discover her!

Simply . . . Inspirational!

"It's been almost ten years now since my doctor said I'd never work again. With COPD [Chronic Obstructive Pulmonary Disorder] and fibromyalgia, I had trouble breathing and lived daily with joint pain and severe fatigue. My lungs worked at less than 40 percent of their normal capacity, and most days all I could do was manage to shower and get dressed. My weight ballooned to 206 pounds. I wheezed constantly and struggled with everyday activities. If I had energy to go out, I'd just end up on the couch for days to recuperate. Eventually I withdrew from my family, my friends, and my life—I was tired of trying. I took so many painkillers to get me through the day that they no longer had any effect on me. I kept promising my family that by next year I'd get better, and our lives would return to normal. But next year never came. . . . I felt helpless and outraged. I lost my spirit and drive to go on and became a prisoner in my own body.

"Here I was, 37 years old, the mother of three great kids but too tired to enjoy them, and too sick to ever get better. It seemed that no matter what I tried, or how positive I thought, nothing changed. I developed what I now call a 'patient mentality.' One day after many prayers and requests for help, my sister-in-law encouraged me to make a change. I began searching for a program that could help me find the answers and started reading different diet books. That's when I found *Simply . . . Woman!*

"One baby step at a time, I started to exercise from my couch. With no money for fancy weights or a gym membership, my coffee table was my weight bench. I sat up from the couch and lifted soup cans, water bottles, and bags of apples. I had to take many rests during and after my workouts, but I didn't let this get in the way of finishing. Eventually, I started to walk; each day, I'd pass an extra house or block depending on my strength. I was tired, but as time went on I became stronger. I began to realize that no matter where you are in life you can always move forward.

"I heard somewhere that *God's gift to you is your body. What you do with it is your gift back to Him.* Well, I wasn't doing much with my body, yet He sent me Crystal. I no longer lie on the couch in pain all day—I don't take a minute of my new life for granted. I now feel like a child in a wonderland of opportunity!"

— **Mary Kim Harper,** Whitby, Ontario

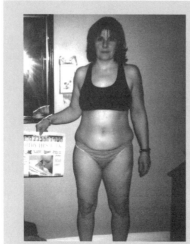

Mary Kim just before starting
the Simply... Woman program.

After 12 weeks on the
program.

Step 13: Surround Yourself with
Supportive, Loving, Positive People

How the people around you respond to your desire to lose weight and take back control of your life is very crucial to your success. So look at the people you spend the most amount of time with: Have they helped you in the past to accomplish your goals? Do they achieve their own aims? Are they positive, or do they complain about their lives? Are they possessive or jealous of your time? Will they support you? Such individuals will have a greater influence on your accomplishments than just about any other external factor, so, ideally, they should be goal oriented, success driven, spiritually enlightened individuals who inspire you and make you want to be a better person.

Countless clients have told me that once they began to lose weight and look good, their friends or family members started to

Crystal Andrus

make negative comments or pull away. If you find that every time you start to follow a diet your husband brings home chocolate, you need to ask yourself why. Better yet, you need to ask *him* why! Sadly, we live in a world where many people are uncomfortable with success and determination, especially if it's a physical or financial improvement, because it subconsciously forces them to look at themselves.

It's very difficult not to care what people think, especially if they're the ones who matter the most. If those around you continually try to knock you down, you just may fall. You probably won't notice any of these changes with family or friends right away, if you do at all, but once you start to really look and feel great, they may start treating you differently. They may tell you that you've changed—and guess what? You have! You've taken control of your life and body.

❋

After I lost all my weight, my marriage initially flourished because I was so much happier with myself. But after a period of time, I began to feel frustrated with life again. Feeling held back, I continued to avoid advances in my career for fear that my marriage couldn't survive it. I felt afraid to tell my husband what I really wanted, and I didn't know how to ask for it. His lack of support frustrated me because I was still looking to him to validate my self-worth.

Before long, I started to sabotage my marriage. In my own personal journey I learned that until I faced my fears and discovered my own truths, I'd continue to undermine different aspects of my life. Although I felt happier with what I saw in the mirror each day, I was just beginning to discover my true authenticity.

If you start sensing that the people you love are becoming different or distant with you, try to remember that it's really just what they're feeling about *themselves,* not you. Their emotions aren't always based on reality but rather their perception of it. Don't own their issues or allow yourself to be pressured.

Let's say that your mate begins to act jealously and starts saying things such as "You're always at the gym," "You never make time for me anymore," or "Why do you want to look better?" What he really means is: "I'm afraid," "I feel insecure," "You aren't paying as much attention to me now," "Am I losing you?" "Once you start looking really good, will you still want me?" "I don't want to be alone," or "Don't leave me."

You can reassure him, but in the end he's responsible for his own fears, as well as his own successes. Sometimes, however, fear is grounded in fact, so you need to honestly assess whether you *have* become neglectful or selfish, disrespectful, or inconsiderate.

On the other hand, should you start to experience unreasonable demands from those around you, you have some choices to make, as this relates to setting your own boundaries. Are you going to quit if your mate doesn't like your new eating plan? Will you give up when your friends think you aren't as much fun now? You need to explain to them that it doesn't matter if you've tried a million diets but never stuck to them before—if they love you, they must support you this time. Tell them you need every bit of encouragement along the way—you don't need to be criticized. There will be times when you feel like giving up, and you'll need to hear them say, "Keep going, I believe in you!"

I'm not suggesting that you toss your loved ones' needs out the window in search of self, but by letting them all know that you'll be a better wife, mother, daughter, and friend once you begin to take better care of yourself, everyone should feel safe. If they don't, this could become one of your biggest obstacles. Deal with it now and don't let guilt stop you from honoring yourself! Many of us believe that we're selfish or thoughtless if we take care of our own needs—yet I've seen so many women eventually become so fed up and resentful because they haven't taken care of themselves that they leave their marriages in order to start making themselves happy. I guarantee that if you take the focus off of your relationship, your mate, your friends, your kids, or your boss and put it on your dreams and needs, you'll become a happier woman—which will result in a happier life. You're not going to lose all your friends, although you may become more selective about whom you choose to spend time with.

Too often, we hold on to old relationships with people we know aren't good for us. They may be fun, or they've simply been around for so long that it seems cruel to dissociate ourselves from them. But the fact remains that folks we surround ourselves with have the biggest external influence on our future than any other factor. As Oprah has said, "No one can take your power from you— only you can give it away." Don't give insecure or negative people power over your life. You own your life, so let them own theirs.

Make a list of the five people closest to you: Are they successful, kind, and loving? Do they truly look out for your best interests? Are they content and happy in their own lives? And do they have a positive influence on you? Start to eliminate the negative energy drainers in your life, and surround yourself with supportive influences. The saying "Birds of a feather flock together" isn't far from the truth . . . who are you flocking with?

Step 14: Monitor Your Glycemic Load

How's your eating going? Do you still crave refined sugar? In the attempt to get you off the carbohydrate roller coaster, this week I want you to not only switch from high-glycemic Red Light carbs to nutritious Green Light carbs, but now I'd like you to monitor the amount you have at each meal.

Low-glycemic Green Light eating isn't enough to prevent carbohydrates from being stored as fat—the amount you consume at each meal is also important. This is referred to as the *glycemic load,* a term that researchers at Harvard University came up with to predict the blood-glucose response of a meal. The glycemic load is determined by multiplying the glycemic index (GI) value of a food by the amount of carbohydrate per serving divided by 100.

Don't worry about trying to understand this equation. Simply be aware that even Green Light foods that are low-glycemic but high in grams of carbs can still negatively affect your blood-sugar level and be stored as fat. A perfect example of this is brown rice: Although brown rice is a Green Light carb, *1 cup* has the same amount of carbohydrates per serving as *20 cups* of broccoli. Using the glycemic-load equation, a cup of cooked brown rice has a glycemic load of 20, and a cup of broccoli has a glycemic load of 0. (A low glycemic load would be less than 10.)

The secret is to limit the amount of highly dense carbohydrates you eat at one time, as most of them are starchy foods such as bread, pasta, and rice. Another example is a sweet potato—although it's low on the glycemic index with a rating of only 44, one cup contains 56 grams of carbohydrates and 224 calories. Let's compare that to green grapes: One cup has a glycemic rating similar to the sweet potato at 48, but the grapes contain only 15 grams of carbohydrates and just 60 calories.

Therefore, the glycemic load of one cup of sweet potatoes (which is actually lower on the GI than the grapes) is 25 (44 x 56 ÷ 100 = 25), whereas one cup of grapes only has a glycemic load of 7 (48 x 15 ÷ 100 = 7). The speeds of digestion are similar; however, you'd be able to eat far more grapes than sweet potatoes before you'd begin storing them as fat.

In simple terms, you want to choose foods that are low on the GI and monitor how many carbs you eat in one sitting. On the Green Light carbohydrate charts, you'll see asterisks (*) beside the foods that generally have a high glycemic load—if you're going to eat these foods, watch how much you consume at one time. Keep your portions small.

How Much Should You Be Eating?

You'll notice that you tend to eat the same foods over the course of a week: You'll routinely have the same breakfast, lunch, and dinner; and you've got your favorite snacks. By weighing and recording your food consumption in your journal and then looking up the nutritional content from your Traffic Light Food Charts located at the end of this book, you can see exactly where you need to make changes. (You don't need to do this forever, but do it for a few days until you get the picture.)

It's easy to determine the amount of carbs in packaged food by looking at the "Nutrition Facts" listed on the side of every box or can. For food that's in its natural state, such as an apple or potato, look it up in the Traffic Light Food Charts. Two other fabulous books that every nutritionally conscious person should own are Corinne T. Netzer's *The Complete Book of Food Counts,* 6th edition, which lists the calorie, protein, carbohydrate, and fat grams of most foods; and *The New Glucose Revolution* by Jennie Brand-Miller, Thomas M.S. Wolever, Kaye Foster-Powell, and Stephen Colagiuri, which gives you the glycemic load and index of virtually every food available. When in doubt, look up what you're about to eat and make a smart choice.

Here are some basic guidelines or equations you can use to determine how much you should be eating each day. You may need to play around with these amounts to figure out what works best for you. Although I don't want you to become fixated on your weight, using it as a guideline will help you determine what the right amounts of carbs you should aim to consume each day are. (We'll talk about protein and fats very soon.)

To maintain your current weight, multiply your body weight in pounds by 12 to determine the daily calories you need to consume. If, for example, you're 160 pounds, a daily caloric intake of approximately 1920 calories would maintain that weight (160 x 12 = 1920). If you exercise and continue to eat this amount, you'll gradually lose weight simply because you're expending calories. One pound of fat is equal to 3,500 calories, so in order to get rid of it, you'd need to decrease your caloric intake and increase your caloric expenditure.

Some weight-loss plans often set your caloric intake at only five times your current body weight. This is way too low. You'll initially lose a lot, but most of it will come from lean muscle and water—and more important, you're slowing down your metabolism, causing worse problems for yourself down the road.

To "guesstimate" the daily caloric intake you need to lose weight, determine how much you're eating right now and how much you're currently exercising (it's important to note, however, that you should *never* drop your daily caloric intake below 1,100):

- If you've been eating a fair amount and/or haven't been exercising prior to starting this program, but you do plan to follow the exercise portion of *Simply . . . Woman!*, multiply your current weight by 10 to determine your daily caloric intake. At 160 pounds, you'll need to consume roughly 1,600 calories per day to lose two to three pounds per week.

- If you aren't overeating and/or are already very active but simply can't seem to lose a pound, multiply your current weight by 9 to determine your daily caloric intake. At 160 pounds, you'll need to consume roughly 1,440 calories per day to lose two to three pounds per week.

- If you struggle with exercise and will only do the nutritional part of this program, multiply your current weight by 8 to determine your daily caloric intake. At 160 pounds, you'll need to consume 1,280 calories per day to lose two to three pounds per week.

Nevertheless, I strongly urge you to try doing the basic exercise requirements.

As you continue with this program, you can adjust your intake. Eventually, you'll end up at your maintenance caloric intake (your weight multiplied by 12). Using the equation in this step, calculate how many calories you should be eating.

So how many of these calories should be carbohydrates? Let's start by getting you on track by consuming 40 percent of your total calories from Green Light carbs. If you've calculated that you need 1,440 calories per day, that means you should have 576 calories from carbohydrates (1,440 x 40 percent = 576). This is essential for body-fat loss. The rest of your calories will come from protein and fat.

> **Fat-Burning Secret #10:**
> Monitor the glycemic load of your carbs. Even Green Light carbs in excess will be stored as fat. Your daily carbohydrate intake should be approximately 40 percent of your total daily calories.

There are four calories in one gram of carbohydrates (excluding alcohol, which has seven calories in every gram). So your daily intake of carbs is 144 grams (576 ÷ 4). Divide that roughly into three meals and two snacks each day, and then refer to the Traffic Light Food Charts to find Green Light carbs.

Step 15: Take Vitamin and Mineral Supplements

In the 19th century, the earth's soil was rich in nutrients and minerals, so plants were full of vitamins. Over the years, crops were planted, tilled, and harvested, and nothing was added back in; consequently, the soil became depleted of its riches. Today,

Carbohydrate Metabolism

(This analogy will make the glycemic load simple and easy to understand.)

Think of your body as a four-story hotel, with 12 rooms on each floor. The rooms, which represent your cells, are for carbohydrates only on the first and second floor (so there are 24 rooms altogether). The rooms on the third floor are for fat, and the rooms on the fourth (the penthouse) floors are reserved for protein. The hallways represent your blood, which carries the food to the different rooms. Get a mental picture of this hotel!

Carbs are necessary, and any diet that completely restricts them is starving you of the most incredibly healthy foods that come from our planet—tomatoes, strawberries, broccoli, oatmeal, oranges, lettuce, roots, sprouts, squash, sweet potatoes, brown rice, blueberries, green peas—so many tasty and life-giving foods. However, one of the most important formulas for weight loss and achieving optimal health is to understand how your body metabolizes these different carbohydrates, *and how much your body actually needs (even the healthy Green Light ones!).*

All carbs break down into glucose (sugar), and your body requires one teaspoon (five grams) of glucose every hour to perform efficiently. So imagine one carbohydrate guest (for instance half a cup of strawberries or broccoli) checking into your hotel every hour. Within a 24-hour span, all the rooms on your first two floors would be filled. By the next morning they'd all be checking out, leaving some vacant rooms for new carbohydrate guests to check in. Perfect!

Now imagine a whole busload of people—say 30 carbohydrate guests (or three cups of pasta)—checking in all at once. The first two floors would fill up quickly, and the extra carbohydrate guests would have to find somewhere else to go. They'd desperately beg the front-desk manager for a key to a room on the third floor. That key is insulin . . . and this is where your pancreas comes in. This tiny organ excretes insulin that carries the sugar out of the blood and "unlocks the doors" to your cells, allowing the glucose to enter.

The extra carbs scoot down the hallway via your blood and head up to the third floor. They slide the insulin key into the door of the fat rooms and *voilà,* they've got lots more space to rest. You see, fat cells *love* to have visitors. In fact, fat cells can hold up to 1,000 times their size, so they're quite happy to convert and store carbs as fat.

Carbohydrates never need to get to the fourth floor, for the

the protein rooms are reserved for very discriminating guests, and those insulin keys won't even unlock their doors. Protein says, "Humph! No, you go back down there and stay in with the fat guests. We don't want you here!"

Fat cells, however, will continue to take extra visitors. The other trouble about these guests is that not only can they expand, but they can multiply easily—and once they're on your body, they *never* go away, even after you lose weight. Yes, they shrink, but they're always hanging around, ready for you to fill them back up. This is one of the most important reasons to not let your children put on excess weight: If you do, you're setting them up for a lifelong battle.

But now you've created an even bigger problem by eating more carbs than your body can handle: You've produced excess insulin, and over time this creates a whole slew of health problems. Excess insulin is a primary cause of aging; distorts your other hormonal systems; and is the precursor for Type II diabetes, obesity, and cardiovascular disease. Excess insulin forces the body to produce increasing amounts of the stress hormone *cortisol,* which speeds up bone loss (osteoporosis), promotes the formation of visceral fat that builds up around your internal organs, and is

the fastest way to lose muscle and gain excess weight.

Muscle by its very existence burns body fat, so if you were to put on 5 pounds of muscle, you could lose up to 25 pounds of fat in one year! This also means that if you lose 5 pounds of muscle, you can gain 25 pounds of fat in one year.

So, getting back to your hotel— if you eat more carbs than your body requires, you'll store it as fat, even if that carbohydrate is healthy and fat free. According to Dr. Barry Sears, creator of "The Zone" diet, the average North American consumes the equivalent in carbs of two cups of sugar a day, and carries a minimum of 100,000 calories of stored body fat on their bodies at any one time.

"But that's okay," you say, as you gobble down your bagels and fat-free potatoes. "I'll just exercise and burn off that fat."

Well, there's a problem with that theory. Stored carbs (the guests on the first two floors of your hotel) are your most readily available form of energy. When you start exercising and require fuel, you'll begin to use up energy, or calories, from those first two floors. You'll burn the stored carbs, and before you can get to the third floor where the fat is stored, you've finished your workout. Hungry, you grab something to eat, filling up those vacant carbohydrate rooms again (and maybe you even eat a little too much, which gets stored again in the fat rooms). This is the reason why you should exercise on an empty stomach.

Through the night, your body uses up the stored carbs, and it's like they've checked out. So if you can exercise first thing in the morning, you'll begin to draw energy from the only available source left—fat!

pesticides, fungicides, herbicides, and acid rain pour down on our crops; and we're completely unaware that we're being deprived of rich bioenergetic foods. Organic fruits and vegetables are still regarded as frivolous by many—and it's often these same people who refuse to believe that supplementation is necessary.

Now, before you go out and spend lots of money on vitamins, first make the commitment to eating healthfully and drinking two quarts of pure water daily. Supplements won't compensate for a poor diet. However, even many healthy people who eat well still suffer from deficiencies or imbalances due to stress, lifestyle, and the occasional bug. I recommend that everyone take a good-quality multivitamin daily, which you should consume with meals for better absorption. If you're unsure about supplementation, schedule a visit to your local naturopath or consult a nutritionist to have a proper assessment done.

I know that many people have a difficult time affording supplements, but I want you to consider the incredible importance they have in maintaining your health. Vitamins seem ineffective to some—they'll take one for a week or so and expect to see or feel radical changes in their health, but that's simply not the way they work. Baby steps over time create huge leaps and bounds, and I truly believe that along with an ideal diet and pure water, vitamin supplementation is like a health-insurance policy. I urge you to look at your monthly expenses and create a budget that will allow you to purchase these powerful health healers. And remember that all vitamins are not created equally—talk to a trained expert at your local health-food store or to your local naturopath.

Following is a list of the ideal supplements that I recommend you take each day.

- **A basic high-quality multivitamin/mineral.** This will contain all your essential minerals and vitamins in standard amounts.

- **Three 1,000-mg capsules of enteric-coated essential fatty acids,** preferably from toxin-free fish such as sardines, mackerel, and anchovies. (We'll talk more about these in Week Five.) In short, if you had to choose one supplement to take every day, over and above your multivitamin/mineral, it would be this. The benefits are extensive, aiding in almost every system in your body: cardiovascular, endocrine, digestive, neurological, structural/muscular, reproductive, etc. Simply put, they are *essential* and your body cannot produce them on its own.

- **A B-complex vitamin** (50 to 75 mg is ideal), which is essential for those suffering from stress, fatigue, depression, PMS, and irritability.

- **500 to 1,000 mg of vitamin C.** This water-soluble vitamin is a powerful antioxidant whose benefits are too numerous to mention. If you're taking prescription drugs, smoking, drinking more than a moderate amount of alcohol, eating processed or refined foods, or are exposed to chemicals, you can increase your intake to 1,500 mg daily.

- **400 IU of vitamin E.** There's strong evidence that this vitamin may play a role in the prevention of heart disease; and it's especially needed for those with

Crystal Andrus

an underactive liver/gallbladder, diabetes, celiac disease, nerve damage, or muscle weakness.

- **500 mg of calcium with 300 mg of magnesium** (take twice a day). Calcium must be absorbed, so taking a digestive enzyme with HC1 (see below) can help correct a calcium deficiency. Calcium is especially important for those suffering from osteoporosis, brittle nails, muscle cramps, insomnia, and an irregular heartbeat, while magnesium is vital for those who drink coffee or alcohol or take prescription drugs.

- **A digestive enzyme with HC1** (taken with meals), as proper digestion is where it all begins. If you can't properly metabolize your foods, you won't absorb the vitamins and minerals from them, nor will you effectively digest them. (We'll talk more about these in Week Six when I explain food combining.)

- **A high-quality green drink** to provide energy and antioxidant support, and to help alleviate a lot of your food cravings.

Step 16: Start Interval Cardio Training

Your cardio level should be improving each time you exercise. Keep on track with your brisk walks, but now let's begin to incorporate some serious fat-burning intervals.

As you're picking up the pace, try to think about your form and technique. *Posture is everything:* Your body should be tall, as if you're walking proud. Imagine a string attached to your head, lifting you up. You should have a slight forward lean (avoid leaning backward.) Relax your shoulders, jaw, and hands. As you walk

Your Walking/Jogging Program

- You're aiming for four to five 20-minute cardio sessions this week, but do at least three. (Since fitness is relative, do the best you can.)

- Warm up with two minutes of regular walking to get your blood flowing and to gently raise your heart rate.

- After you warm up, pick up the pace to a walk where you could carry on a conversation but it would take effort. If you're new at this, your pace should be about 2.5 on a treadmill; however, if you're in great cardiovascular shape, begin this first interval at 3.5. Walk at this pace for one minute.

- For the second minute, increase your speed to a pace that you could maintain for ten minutes if you had to—up to 3.0 for beginners and 4.5 for the more advanced.

- The third one-minute interval should feel quite difficult. It should be at a pace that takes concentration and effort.

or jog, imagine that there are two potato chips in each hand that can't be broken—this is how loose and relaxed you should stay. Hands are one of the first things to tighten up when you feel tense, so in any stressful or difficult situation, focus on keeping your hands relaxed. Envision two separate ropes attached to each of your hips, pulling you forward into a pelvic tilt. This will allow your body to fall into the correct posture, keeping your pelvis in neutral alignment.

Step 17: Add an Additional Strength-Training Workout

Getting fit takes a combination of five components: muscular strength, muscular endurance, flexibility, cardiovascular training, and nutrition. Put energy and focus into each area as you do your *Simply . . . Woman!* workout with either the *Tight & Toned Workout DVD* or the *Simply . . . Woman Total Workout Bench & Crystal Ball.* Don't fear gaining muscle: You won't look like one of those female body-builders you've seen in magazines—it's impossible for you to do so without lifting heavy weights and taking muscle-building supplements. Unless you want the same exact shape you have right now, just smaller, you'll have to sculpt your body by contracting your muscles and toning your core body. Do your strength-training workout three times—in the morning if possible. And train hard—it does work.

❋❋❋

If you've never exercised before, please monitor your heart rate and keep it at 60 percent of your maximum heart rate. Beginners will be at about 3.5; if you're a seasoned runner, kick it right up for this third interval.

- The last interval of your four-minute cycle should be all out: At a pace that you wouldn't be able to maintain for more than one minute (beginners will be at about 4.5, and experienced runners at about 9.5).

- Take it back down to a comfortable walk and begin the cycle again. Do this a total of four times.

- Cool down after your intervals by slowing down the last few minutes to a stroll.

- Spend 10 to 15 minutes doing the stretches at the end of the book, or use the last 10 minutes of the workout DVD.

Summary of Week Three: *Acceptance*

Body:

- Understand and monitor your glycemic load.

- Supplement your diet with a high-quality multi-vitamin/mineral and consume a green drink daily.

- Try interval cardio training, and do your *Simply . . . Woman! Tight & Toned Workout* or use your *Simply . . . Woman Total Workout Bench & Crystal Ball* two to three times.

Mind:

- Find some realistic and healthy role models.

Soul:

- Don't give your personal power away to negative people in your life. Take notice of who you surround yourself with; and choose supportive, loving, and positive individuals.

Crystal Andrus

Week Four: *Courage*

Courage is one of the most powerful words in the English language, and it is the most important ingredient needed in order to set your life into motion. It takes courage to honor yourself. It takes courage to believe in yourself, to value yourself, and to take care of yourself. It takes courage to speak your truth, to follow your dreams, and to reach for the stars.

Just like building a muscle, taking small *and large* acts of personal courage is what builds your own strength. Courage opens you up to the endless possibilities in your life. Courage opens the floodgates to your soul.

Are you willing to step into a life of courage now that you're entering your fourth week? It's so important that you do, as this is often when people begin to self-sabotage. Their fears, frustrations, and doubts begin to whisper louder and louder in their ears. And it is here that you will separate yourself from those who talk about it with those who do it!

Have you ever heard the saying "If you keep doing what you're doing, you'll keep getting what you're getting"?

What is it that causes some of us to stay on that "dreaded treadmill of life"—wishing, hoping, and praying that something will suddenly get better? Are we suckers for punishment? Do we enjoy running ourselves ragged? Or do we truly believe that this is "our destiny," so we must live it, sacrifice, and simply allow it to take its course? Do we really believe that if we give enough to everybody they'll finally wake up and see how wonderful we are? Maybe, as long as we're taking care of everyone else, we don't have to focus on our own hopes and dreams (what a noble-sounding excuse for not stepping it up for ourselves!). Maybe it's just a deep need to be in control—to think we can change *what is* and make it be what we want it to be? Perhaps it's merely the natural fear of the unknown. Maybe not enough belief in ourselves or faith that

God will take care of us? Could it be that we've been victims of circumstance for so long that we've forgotten that we're still the captains of our own ship . . . ?

It reminds me of a conversation I was having with a good friend. I was complaining, feeling so frustrated and unsure of what road to take, almost forgetting that I even had "roads," when my friend boldly yet lovingly told me, "Crystal, don't be a victim. Be in charge! Even against overwhelming odds, CHARGE! Better to die in charge than die the thousand deaths of a victim. You are still the boss of your own life!"

His words woke me up that day. Funny, I hadn't even realized how asleep I'd been until I'd gotten that huge bucket of cold water tossed in my face!

I hadn't realized that I'd even stepped back on "that treadmill"— running on the same spot, yet feeling frustrated that I wasn't getting anywhere (at least not where I wanted to go!). I felt like my life—my future . . . my choices—was resting in others' hands, and I was merely a puppet hoping they'd come through and make it all better for me. Each day I'd hope for an answer: a sign, a vote of encouragement, a reason to keep on fighting. But in doing that, I'd almost become a bystander in my own life, like I was waiting for some "coach" to give me a chance to go back in the game and score the winning goal.

How many of us do that, though? We wait patiently, hoping that if we work hard enough, do our best, make a difference, give it our all, do more, give more, sleep less, and try harder, that someone will notice and reward us. But when it doesn't happen we feel sad, maybe angry. We cry, pray, and then cry some more. We bitch, complain, blame, and vent, hoping that, somehow, someone will take notice of all the drama we're creating. *We're in pain—doesn't anyone see that?!*

**It takes a lot of work to put on a
full-blown self-pity party, *doesn't it?*
It takes a lot of work to be a victim!**

When we give away our power to whatever or whomever we're waiting on to come and save us, we diminish our own light. We fade. We stop shining bright. We stop attracting abundance. And within no time we feel defeated. Frustrated. Helpless. Stuck. Unsure. Tired. Alone. Fed up. Afraid. You name it, we feel it. *Sound familiar?*

So where do we go from here?

Well, if you're ready to step off the treadmill . . . to stop being tossed around in the storm . . . and to become the master of your own ship again, then you must first accept that no one is coming to save you. *I know that's a hard one to face!* But once you wake up, accept what *is,* face your fears, look them square in the eye, grieve your so-called losses (which may, in fact, really be a brilliant gift), and then get fired up enough to decide that you matter, that your needs matter, that your life matters . . . then YOUR REALITY WILL CHANGE!

This will be one of the most important decisions you'll ever make: to have the courage to honor your spirit. But when you do, it's like you're telling the Universe that you're back in the game again. It is here that you'll feel your power coming back, your energy shifting, your sense of self growing, and your fearlessness taking over!

As you step off your "self-defined treadmill," be willing to look at your life through different lenses and ask yourself, "What would courage have me do, change, or say (even if it scares me) in order to move me out of feeling helpless and disempowered and into feeling free, hopeful, and inspired? What would courage ask me to hang on to while I ride out the storm? And what would it ask me to throw overboard?"

The truth is, it takes courage to honor you—your life, dreams, needs, body, faith, health, vision, and desires—but in the end, it is only courage that can turn your boat around and put you back in the flow! As my dear friend told me, "You go *with* the current, Crystal, but not *because* of it!"

If you're struggling, please have the courage to contact us toll-free at 1-877-SIMPLY9 or visit us at: **www.simplywoman.com.** We're here to help! We also offer additional motivational support tools that can often be the extra boost you need. Many women love my *Simply . . . Woman! Listening Collection,* which includes eight 30- to 45-minute CDs that they can listen to each week, or you can sign up for one-on-one telephone coaching or our life-changing 12-Week BODY-MIND-SOUL Total Transformation *Tele-*Course. Do whatever it takes to stay focused!

Step 18: Take a Reality Check

There's no point in going any further with this 12-week program if you aren't being honest with yourself. You will only get out of this what you put into it. If you haven't lost one pound, it's time to make a list of your foods again for three days and get really serious with yourself: Are you eating junk food—even just little bits here and there? Are you sneaking the odd cookie or munching on chips? Have you conquered sugar and begun eating Green Light carbohydrates? Are you eating low-fat protein at every meal and having salad every day? What are you having for breakfast? How much water are you drinking?

Obviously, I'm not able to watch your every move. I can give you information and guide and inspire you, but if you're not sticking to this program, you're fooling no one but yourself. You've spent money, bought the book, invested in equipment, taken a "before" picture, and made a commitment that you're going to get into the best shape of your life, haven't you? Are you reading each week's steps and following them closely? Are you working out with the DVD at an intense level? If not, go back and reread the previous weeks' steps and get with the program. An analogy I use with some of my clients is comparing this program to the birth-control pill: It won't work if you use it *most* of the time. Daily effort plus daily choices equal success. It's time to get serious.

> **The "Seven C's" for Total Transformation**
>
> 1. Cardio exercise
> 2. Carbohydrate management
> 3. Contracting your muscles
> 4. Core body-strength training
> 5. Calories
> 6. Cleansing
> 7. Consistency

Step 19: Relinquish the Need for Approval

We all want to be liked, valued, and appreciated; and when we aren't, we feel rotten. In fact, we often care too much about what people think: We live our lives in a "pleasing mode," trying to impress our in-laws, amaze our boss, keep the perfect house, and do our children's school projects. We worry more about what others believe about us than what we know to be true. We blow off those who snub us, and embrace those who like us, so we become mirror reflections instead of independent thinkers. Of course, we need to be politically correct at times and gracious at others— and occasionally, grin and bear it diplomatically, such as when our mother-in-law corrects our parenting. However, we certainly don't have to be quite so fragile and sensitive. The fact remains that we'll never please everyone. And in trying to please everyone else, we most often always let ourselves down. It takes courage to relinquish the need for approval!

Crystal Andrus

I spent so much of my 20s trying to be perfect. I thought that if I bought the ideal gift or had a flawless dinner party, I'd be admired. If my house was immaculate and my children were well behaved, I'd be looked upon as an amazing mother and wife. If I had a perfect body and long blonde hair, everyone would think I was beautiful. I felt great if my world was picture-perfect, but if someone was cruel or thought ill of me, I got very upset. External things and other people's approval determined my self-worth. I now look back and see so clearly where that need originated from, but at the time all I knew was that I hated it when someone was upset with me. I wanted to be loved—and I needed to feel valued and respected so much that it dictated my life.

I know now that making "love-driven" choices are very different from making "guilt-driven" choices. We women have a very difficult time separating the two. Love-driven choices leave you feeling full, satisfied, joyous, and calm. Guilt-driven choices leave you feeling empty, discontent, resentful, and frenetic. When we do things because we feel guilty we disempower ourselves and end up robbing the people in our lives from ever knowing the real us. We teach them that just *being* isn't enough. Guilt-driven choices develop because deep in our core we don't feel that others will like us *just for us*. We assume that if we *do* enough, we'll eventually *feel* enough. It rarely happens, though. Instead, we end up feeling frustrated and exhausted—poisonous energy for any relationship!

This need for approval starts when we're children, when we look to our parents for validation. Recently I spent some time with my ten-month-old nephew. Every time he did something funny or brave, we all cheered and smiled, so he'd laugh and try harder to impress us. I was intrigued by this phenomenon, and I realized that searching for approval is part of our natural makeup.

We all hold on to the past to varying degrees. We're a culmination of our past experiences: The significant relationships we've had over our lives make us who we are, yet many of us pretend that they have nothing to do with the way we feel about ourselves.

Ask yourself how your past affects you: Do you have a hard time maintaining meaningful, committed, long-term relationships? Do you feel hurt when someone doesn't like you or disapproves of your choices? Do you feel the need to convince them of your point of view? How about in your career . . . do you feel that you've been held back financially? Do you make enough money? Do you like your job? Are you happy physically? Do you have the willpower to take better care of yourself? Have you ever felt beautiful? Have you ever felt truly loved?

The first thing you need to do is determine what's holding you back in your life and find out when you made the decision that you, alone, were not enough. When did you make the inaccurate assumption that if you gave up yourself, others would give you more? Where did you learn that from? Mom? Grandma? Aunts? What did your father teach you about your lovableness? Did he adore you, spend time with you, and treat you like his princess—regardless of your grades, accomplishments, or social status?

Get out your journal and take a look back in time. It's time to shine a light on patterns you learned and beliefs you developed during your childhood or teen years. Begin by making a list of what (or who) you believe limited you in your life and how. What pivotal moments changed your life? What did you hear, see, or feel on a daily basis while you were growing up? How did this make you feel about yourself, and how has it held you back?

Before we go on, you must accept that this step isn't intended to make you feel like a victim or to blame your parents for your unhappiness—but if you do have issues that you know are directly related to your childhood, don't feel ashamed to admit it, even if it's just to yourself. Too many of us feel ridiculous about bringing up our childhoods for fear that we'll sound like someone on a *Jerry Springer* episode; however, every one of us has had critical moments in our childhood that we'll always remember. These experiences become embedded in our psyche, causing us to form beliefs that stay with us and dictate our choices as adults.

Don't continue reading until you've done this exercise. I don't want to influence your answers.

Looking at your list, ask yourself if you feel that your life would be better if others had treated you better. Do you believe that most of your disappointments and failures have been out of your control? Was one or both of your parents held back in their own life? What messages regarding opportunity and expectation did you learn from them? Did you see a mother who gave too much but resented it at the same time? Has an illness or condition impeded your progress? Has it simply been unfortunate circumstances, or was it specific people who've held you back? If so, are you still angry or resentful with them?

Here's your first clue: *Self-sabotage comes from repressed anger.*

"I'm not angry anymore," you might say. Yet if you continually sabotage your efforts, then there's a very good chance that you've never dealt with your pain. You tucked it away and made a decision that showing anger was unacceptable (after all, we were all taught to be nice little girls), so instead of lashing out at the world, you've chosen to beat *yourself* up. Buried deep, you create "walls"—layers of protection—so that no one can ever hurt you again. No one can get close enough. It feels safer this way. But soon your protection becomes your captor. You feel stuck and helpless.

Wanting love and needing approval doesn't go away when we reach adulthood, and sometimes it even gets worse. Our fear of not being good enough—or worse, not being loved—is so powerful that we'll do everything we can to avoid it, even if it means sabotaging our life today. Each hurtful experience causes us to doubt ourselves, so we add another layer to protect our spirit. We spend our lives hoping for those *A*'s on our interminable "report card," and then we beat ourselves down when we don't get them.

Unless we've done some serious soul-searching and worked through our anger, other people's opinions really matter. How do you handle it when you don't get the approval you're looking for? Well, for most us nothing comforts better than food. Or we find

Crystal Andrus

temporary solace in shopping, gambling, or new relationships. Some of us numb our pain with alcohol, drugs, or casual sex; and many of us use a combination of escapes. Often these outlets become bad habits. When we feel hurt, upset, or defensive, we harbor resentment that we don't know how to move beyond . . . so we end up self-sabotaging. We numb our pain, convinced that numb at least feels better than pain. Maybe you've stopped allowing yourself to feel because from what you remember, "feeling" felt awful!

This self-destructive need for approval only disappears when we begin approving of *ourselves,* and that can only happen after we face our greatest fears and truths. As I've already mentioned, facing our fears will open the door to truth (we've all heard the saying "The truth will set you free"). Truth opens the door to authenticity, which is the magical ingredient to living with inner peace and self-love. And as scary as it may seem to face your truths, as scary as it may seem to shine light on "what is," I guarantee that it only appears that way on the surface. Once you begin to be honest with yourself about what you feel, why you're stuck, whom you blame, what you use to cope, and what you're afraid of, you'll feel a thousand pounds lifted from you.

In reality, truth is always easy. It's the lies we tell ourselves and the world that weighs us down and keeps us immobilized in fear, convinced that we have no other option. Lies keep us disillusioned. Disillusionment keeps us in denial; thus, addictions are virtually impossible to overcome.

Open your journal and begin the page with this sentence: *The truth is . . .*

See where it leads you.

Step 20: Do Something You Love

I'm certainly not the first, nor will I be the last, to remind you that time is one of the most precious commodities that we all take for granted. When you have a baby, people will stop you everywhere to tell you to enjoy the experience fully because time passes so quickly. Of course you try to do so, but you probably still tend to keep looking forward to your child's next milestone: *I can't wait until she's walking,* or *I wonder what he's going to look like as he gets older.* Before you know it, your "baby" is in the seventh grade and you don't know where the time has gone.

Spend a day with a senior citizen. As she reminisces, she'll impress upon you that not so long ago she was exactly your age. Now, without warning, she feels old, sometimes aching and often alone. Wishing, remembering, and wondering what could have been, all she has now is time.

When I hear a song that I thought was released only a few years ago, only to find out it was actually from the '80s, I feel just like that old woman. It doesn't seem possible, but the older I become, the faster time passes. It will, whether we want it to or not!

We all become so caught up in life that sometimes we forget to really live. We have the illusion that we've got lots of time to do it all, but we're just too busy being busy. All too often, we gobble our meals in front of the television, thinking that there will be plenty of time to light candles, sit at a nicely set table, and really savor our food. Soon, we say, we'll go for a picnic. Once the kids are out of the house or we've paid off the mortgage, then we'll travel. Maybe when we lose 20 pounds or win the lottery, we'll start volunteering. . . .

This week I want you to create a list of things that you liked to do before you got caught up in your busy schedule. Maybe as a child you visited the library and spent hours reading. Did you knit with your grandmother, play the piano, or kick a ball around in the park? Did you write poetry, paint with watercolors, or take ballet lessons? Pick one thing on that list and spend at least an hour this week doing it.

Step 21: Start Eating Green Light Protein

Last week we learned about carbohydrates, so now let's focus on protein. Meat, poultry, fish, eggs, and dairy products are the most obvious sources of protein; but there are also many others, such as seeds, nuts, beans, and lentils. The principal role of protein in your body is to build and repair close to 300 billion cells daily, including muscles, ligaments, and tendons. Although carbohydrates and fats supply you with energy, every cell in your body is constructed from the protein you eat. When protein enters the stomach, it begins to break down into macronutrients called *amino acids*. The human body is unable to produce these essential amino acids, so you must obtain them from the food you eat. Consequently, protein (amino acids) is sent to work building and repairing skin, enzymes, muscles, bones, and hair.

How is this important to weight loss? Well, think of protein as your "muscle protector." The more lean muscle you have on your body, the more calories you'll use all day and all night—even when you're sleeping; however, without protein, you'll have a difficult time making and keeping muscle.

Protein doesn't stimulate insulin production and isn't converted to fat easily. It also helps elevate your resting metabolic rate because it has a high "thermic" response. You see, metabolism is a sequence of hundreds of multistep biochemical reactions that take place in your cells to produce energy and heat. It comes from the fuel you give it: protein, carbs, and fat. Thermogenesis, on the other hand, is how your body burns stored body fat to produce heat. One way to do that is with exercise; another way is to eat a high-protein diet.

All food has a different thermic response. High-fat foods such as butter or oil have virtually no response, and carbohydrates are far less thermic than protein. Since protein has such a high thermic response, when you eat egg whites or a chicken breast, your body works overtime trying to digest the protein into amino acids.

Simply eating a 200-calorie chicken breast could burn up about 60 calories!

A study conducted in Spain found that protein could increase the metabolic rate by 25 to 30 percent, compared to carbs' increase of just 4 percent. Wow, that means we can eat pork chops, hamburgers, and cheese without getting fat, right? Wrong! The protein in that pork chop won't be stored as fat, but the saturated fat *will*. Just like carbohydrates, proteins aren't created equal. This is why you need a list of Red Light, Yellow Light, and Green Light proteins to make sure that you eat the right kind every few hours. (You'll find them in the Traffic Light Food Charts at the back of the book.)

We hear all the time that North Americans eat far too much protein, but I believe that we're simply eating too much saturated fat or Red Light proteins. When most of us go on a calorie-restricted diet for the purposes of fat loss, we either begin to consume higher amounts of carbs—especially the fat-free kind—but we don't take in enough low-fat protein . . . or we eat a high protein, low-carb diet and eat far too much fat. This program will show you how to eat the perfect combination.

Protein combined with exercise builds muscle, as we know, but it's worth repeating: Muscle speeds up our natural metabolic rate and burns body fat.

Ideal sources of proteins are those low in saturated fat, such as fish, skinless chicken breast, and skinless turkey breast; low-fat tofu and tempeh; low-fat dairy products such as yogurt and cottage cheese; protein shakes; and my ideal choice: egg whites. I always say, "When in doubt, eat an egg white!" Boil an entire carton of eggs and just peel and eat them throughout the day. This is a simple way to satisfy hunger, speed your metabolism, and burn body fat. Discard the yolk by feeding it to the birds or your dog. Don't worry about the few cents you may feel you're wasting (you're worth throwing away a yolk!).

Apart from your egg whites, at each meal try to consume roughly 20 to 30 grams of Green Light protein per serving—about the size of your palm—along with your Green Light carbs at every meal. Keep in mind that this is *not* a high-protein diet.

Protein Shakes

There's no getting away from it: Protein supplementation is today's hot nutritional topic. While protein shakes shouldn't become the staple of your diet, they definitely serve an important purpose, especially for those who have a difficult time taking in their daily protein requirements. I recommend using protein shakes when you can't eat a Green Light protein food.

Beware, though: There's no efficient governing body that protects consumers to ensure that protein shakes (or other nutritional supplements) even contain all the ingredients that are listed on their labels. Many companies add fillers and Red Light sweeteners to make their drinks tastier, and some even embellish the amounts of protein in their products. And while whey protein, specifically high alpha-lactalbumin whey isolate, is biologically superior to eggs, cow's milk, beef, or chicken, it's very expensive to manufacture—so many companies mix the isolate with other proteins but claim it's pure. So check labels and stick with a reputable company.

Soy protein has gotten a bad rap lately from the fitness world as being biologically inferior to whey; however, the astounding benefits of soy make its consumption equally important to include in your diet. Soy speeds the metabolism; increases growth-hormone levels; and supplies calcium, folic acid, and iron. Be sure to purchase a soy protein powder in isolate form that is nongenetically enhanced (non-GMO).

The U.S. Food and Drug Administration claims that diets including 25 grams of soy protein a day may reduce the risk of heart disease, and researchers are also studying how soy may reduce the risk of prostate cancer in men and breast cancer in women. Some women do have a hard time digesting soy, so test yourself first by trying a small container of soy milk and watching for bloating, gas, a sore throat, or intestinal discomfort.

Whatever protein shake you decide on, be sure to check the label for fillers, Red Light sweeteners, and excessive and unnecessary ingredients. Remember, it's not the taste that matters most, it's the results!

> **Fat-Burning Secret #11:**
> Eating protein is highly thermogenic and can increase your metabolism by 25 to 30 percent.

Most energy bars are out of the question, for they're filled with empty calories and Red Light carbohydrates. Although low-carb and low-fat *protein* bars will work as an occasional fill-in when you're simply unable to eat the proper food or have a shake, don't get hooked on them. Most protein bars are just too high in calories.

Step 22: Learn to Relax

Close your eyes and take a deep breath through your nose, holding it for three full seconds. Then slowly exhale through your mouth. Now do it again. Can you feel your heart beating? Are you aware of the sounds around you? Do you feel yourself slowing down?

In a world full of deadlines and pressure, we've forgotten how to relax. We're so stressed out and overwhelmed that many of us are like ticking time bombs. What's funny is that even though we know that poorly managed stress is one of the world's great silent killers, many of us are almost proud of our overtaxed schedules, as if they're a sign of success and status.

The minute I begin to experience resentment, anxiousness, impatience, or insomnia, I know that it's time to take a quick personal inventory and reassess my priorities. When I find myself no longer enjoying, but rather enduring, a project, I know that I've allowed stress to overtake me. Since I know firsthand how difficult it can be to de-stress, I want you to understand that by taking just five minutes a day to turn off the outside world so that your mind and body are at rest, you can lower your biological age by up to 12 years and lower your incidence of heart attack and other illness. (Biological age is a concept developed by researchers to quantify how an individual compares with the average of his or her chronological age, and it's determined 15 to 20 percent by our genes and 80 to 85 percent by lifestyle—that is, what we eat, how we exercise, our total stress factor, and our disposition.)

Meditation

There are many different ways to relax—meditation is an ideal form, but some people have a difficult time being still. Try starting out with at least five minutes a day to practice. And keep in mind that prayer is different from meditation: Prayer is talking to God through your thoughts, while meditation is connecting through your body. Both are important for your entire being. Coming from a religious family, I used to think that meditating was somehow wrong or even evil. As I've mentioned, fear and ignorance can be such limiting emotions that they can hold us back from understanding the truth.

Meditation comes in many different forms—you don't have to sit in a white robe in the lotus position and chant to experience the physical, mental, and spiritual benefits of this practice. If you have a difficult time relaxing on your own, please visit me online at: **www.simplywoman.com** to purchase my *Relaxation Therapy* CD, download one of my many healing meditations, or try the following exercise:

- Get comfortable in a quiet and relaxing setting, without any distractions (turn off the ringer on your phone). Try to do your meditation in the dark with one candle lit. Sit facing the candle, focusing on the flame, and lose all your thoughts and worries within its fire. Play beautiful, calming music while you do so, or just enjoy the sound of nothing at all. If it's nice outside, you may want to find a quiet spot under a tree. Just be sure to choose a place where you can be totally comfortable.

- Close your eyes and focus on your breathing. Inhale slowly and deeply through your nose, imagining that each inhalation is a cleansing breath that's permeating every cell in your body. As you exhale, blow away all worries and pain from your body. Take five to ten of these deep, cleansing breaths.

- Next, beginning at your toes, focus on flexing and tensing each muscle. Become aware of the feeling of tension, then release and relax. Work your way up your legs and into your buttocks. Tighten and squeeze the muscle, then relax and release. Feel your legs growing heavy.

- Move into your abdomen and chest, and around to your lower back. Tighten and release. Take it up into your shoulder blades, squeezing your shoulders up and together as tight as you can, then relaxing and releasing them. Notice the difference as the tension leaves your body.

- Work your arms and neck—but spend a little extra time on your neck, as this is where you may hold a lot of stress and tension. Now, go all the way down to your wrists and hands. Squeeze your hands into a tight fist, bend your wrists up and down, then release. Feel the difference.

- Go up to your face and head. Move your lips around, squish up your nose, tighten your eyebrows, and squeeze your eyes tightly closed. Now release every muscle in your face, and feel your brows and eyes relaxing. Sense your body growing heavy.

- Continue to focus on your head—once you reach your crown, imagine a white, pure light that begins to cascade down your body, filling every nook and cranny. This light is healing and cleansing, washing away any pain or illness, and replenishing your body with goodness. Don't worry if your mind occasionally wanders off—this is just your concentration level diminishing. Take another deep breath and continue.

Meditation is a wonderful way to relax when you feel that one of your triggers is being hit. Rather than falling into your normal pattern of excessive eating, drinking, shopping, and so forth, try to adopt this extremely healthy way of releasing your worries and stress.

Stretching

Simple stretching to serene music is incredibly beneficial for reducing tension. Your *Simply . . . Woman! Tight & Toned Workout* DVD incorporates stretching and stress-reduction exercises at the end, so put that segment on if you have a hard time stretching alone.

Now that you've been exercising for a few weeks, extend your stretching time to 10 to 15 minutes at the end of every workout. This will help alleviate muscle soreness, increase flexibility, decrease lower back and neck pain, and elongate and lengthen your muscles. When you exercise, you shorten or contract the muscle belly (the widest part of the muscle), so it's necessary to stretch it back out to give it a longer, leaner look.

Hold your stretches for 20 to 30 seconds, and don't bounce or jerk the muscle. Deep breathing is very important while stretching in order to slow certain physiological responses and promote greater relaxation and range of motion. Proper and effective stretching requires effort with force to reap any lasting benefits.

While you're stretching, visualize the tightness or discomfort you're feeling in a particular muscle as the color red. Then, as you work toward releasing tension, imagine the red fading and a white healing light encompassing that muscle. (Visualization is a useful technique that can actually reduce discomfort.)

Allow this necessary stretching time to do double duty as a stress reliever. Dealing with stress effectively is imperative: After all, it isn't stress that causes premature aging, sickness, muscle atrophy, ulcers, and heart problems—it's how you deal with it. So become mindful of your body's physical reaction to stress. Learn to listen to your body's warning signs, then be aware of changing your reaction to it.

Step 23: Push Yourself to Work Out Harder

Like anything in life, success comes only when you apply yourself with concentrated focus. Certainly there may have been times when you were lucky (or you thought you were), but success is almost guaranteed when you work hard. So imagine pushing your body just a little bit harder than you are right now during your workouts. What do you think would happen if you didn't stop as soon as it got a little tough? What if you didn't give up just because your mind told you to? What would happen if you worked through the burn?

The sad thing is that so many people stop just before having a breakthrough. Thomas Edison attempted to create the lightbulb thousands of times before succeeding—had he given up after 10 or even 20 failed attempts, we'd be sitting in the dark today.

You're about to begin Phase II of the program, so when you're working out, begin to focus mentally rather than physically. *You're stronger than you think:* Your muscles won't rip, and your ligaments won't snap. Push yourself. Feel the power you have untapped within you. With each deep breath, let your mind get past the physical restraints you've put on your body. Use the workout DVD three times this week, and elevate yourself to a new level of intensity. Don't be limited by what's on the DVD: As you get stronger, try variations of the moves. Add walking lunges and push-ups, do the leg workout twice in one day, or double up on abs once a week.

During your jogs or brisk walks, really pick up the pace. You'll only get out what you put in—so if you stay focused and determined, success will be yours!

Step 24: Assess Your Results

It's time to revisit your Success Tracker I. Do your assessment first thing in the morning, before you exercise. Put the date at the top of the third column, sit for a few minutes and relax, and then begin by checking your resting heart rate. Follow down this column, recording your current statistics. In the second column that says "Difference," using a plus (+) or a minus (–), indicate your results so far. In the "Total Inches" column, compare the changes from Week One to now.

Walking/Running
Cold-Weather Safety Tips

During the winter months, you're most likely to injure yourself by slipping on snow- or ice-covered running surfaces. Try to shorten your stride and shuffle when you're on ice, and make sure you run in a relaxed way because tense muscles are more prone to injury.

The secret to keeping warm in the cold is wearing the right clothes in the right combination. Usually three layers work best:

- An inner layer should be fitted and lightweight and consist of a breathable fabric such as polypropylene. It shouldn't absorb your sweat, but remove it from your skin.

- A middle layer should be heavier and fit more loosely so that you can remove it if you become too warm. Go with fabrics that will keep you warm and dry such as fleece or wool. Some runners prefer cotton because it absorbs the moisture away from the inner layer.

- An outer layer should protect you from the wind and repel wet snow or rain. Your biggest enemy isn't the air temperature but rather, the strong winds that can blow away your body heat. (Your legs generate a lot of heat, so usually just one layer here is enough.)

As much as 50 percent of your body heat is lost through your head, so it's critical to keep it covered. Wear a hat, preferably one that covers your ears. I like to put a little bit of cotton in my ears as well to stop the wind from giving me that burning feeling, but you may prefer earmuffs. Fingers and hands are very vulnerable to frostbite, so keep them covered, too. In extreme cold, coat your face with petroleum jelly. If you find that cold air is uncomfortable, a face mask or scarf that covers your nose and mouth will do the trick.

How are you doing: Are you losing inches? Is your dress size smaller? How is your resting heart rate? By now, you should be noticing and feeling much better. If not, get serious with yourself—after all, you have all the tools right here in this program to look and feel your best ever. This journey takes time, perseverance, and consistency, so go back over all the steps from the beginning and make sure that you're still following them all. And stay strong!

※

Summary of Week Four: *Courage*

Body:

- Start eating Green Light protein. Stick with "white-colored" protein such as chicken breast and egg whites, and avoid "dark-colored" protein such as red meat and egg yolks.

- Try a protein shake to supplement your protein requirements.

- Continue with four to five intense cardio sessions each week.

Mind:

- Fill in your Success Tracker I to monitor your progress.

- Check that you're not falling back into your old patterns.

Soul:

- Discover your truth.

- Relinquish the need for approval.

- Do something you love.

Crystal Andrus

Week Five: *Truth*

Congratulations—you've made it through the first month! Now, it's important that you stay focused and don't become discouraged. You may feel like giving up because you've been working so hard, yet the changes may not be significant. That's because you're at the toughest stage now—but the next two months are where it's all going to come together. If you start to scramble now because you don't think that things are happening fast enough, you may lose your driving force. Go back and read your List of Burning Desires, as desire is the starting point of all types of achievement. Wishing won't bring about success, but with a burning desire and a plan, you can accomplish anything.

Step 25: Face Your Fears

Last week I asked that you really get honest with yourself. We all want to better ourselves, yet to do so means that we must admit to our weaknesses. Unfortunately, we spend so much time covering up "who we really are" that our own denial keeps us distracted. In order to ascend to heights unimaginable and to transform our lives on a profound level in body, mind, and spirit, we have to look within. Just as the Buddha said, "Those who have failed to work toward the truth have missed the purpose of living."

Self-acceptance is a critical component of our growth. Most of us have walls so high and layers so deep that we live in an almost numbed state—we've learned how to anesthetize our pain by deadening our awareness. We walk around in a fog of distraction or absentmindedness, making it very difficult to change our pattern of action because we've become so disconnected from ourselves. We've stopped listening.

The first step to moving forward and living your most authentic life is accepting that you're not responsible for someone else's hurtful or neglectful behavior, but you *are* accountable for your reaction to it and how you allow it to affect your life.

**It's not what happens to you.
It's what you do with what happens to you!**

What have you done with the sad stories of your life? What have you made them mean about you? How have you let them drive you, control you, immobilize you, or affect you?

You can't change what's happened in the past, but you can change how you're going to react to things in the future. And you can use trauma and pain as a catalyst for creating the most extraordinary life ever, if you choose to!

You're responsible for all your emotions, whether they're negative ones such as envy, jealousy, insecurity, procrastination, guilt, anger, resentment, or anxiety; and positive ones like patience, forgiveness, compassion, love, strength, understanding, motivation, or empathy. And the truth is, we've all experienced *all* of these feelings at various times. We've all been hurt—some worse than others. We've all felt disappointment, fear, and shame. We've all wondered, *Why me?* We've all wished we looked different, had more, hurt less, and felt happier.

Now, don't get me wrong: Being responsible for your own emotions doesn't mean that you should allow anyone to hurt you or let you down—and if someone unnecessarily and continually mistreats you, you need to set stronger boundaries. Sometimes tough love is the only love we can show. Tough love says, "I love you but not at the expense of myself. I will not compromise my own spirit in order to make you feel better."

In saying that, it's also often the case that we're simply too sensitive. So ask yourself: "Is this my issue or theirs?" If you truly know that it isn't your issue (and you'll only know that once you've embraced all the steps in this program), perhaps you can then dig deep and search for forgiveness and understanding. Realize that

Crystal Andrus

someone's own fears have compelled them to lash out at you—it's not about you. This person is afraid, insecure, and not content within him- or herself, so his or her own fear is manifesting itself as control, aggression, or subtle manipulation.

Anger is simply a fear—a loss of control—and those who easily show rage are desperately fearful people in serious pain. Rather than take it personally or respond with anger yourself, embrace them compassionately (not to own their issues, but rather to forgive and understand them as you'd want someone to do with you). If these individuals continue to abuse you, then you must have the courage to honor yourself and detach from the relationship . . . even just temporarily to regain your own sense of power and nobility.

⁂

I struggled with my own triggers for years. Strangely, I could help others with their relationship problems, but when a family member said something that I perceived as a put-down, my fight-or-flight response immediately took over. My heart would pound, my pulse would quicken, and I wouldn't be able to think about anything else except escaping or defending myself. I couldn't possibly listen to anyone else's opinions about my faults—instead, I took too many things as a personal assault and instantly went into defense mode. While I could understand *why* I was behaving in this way, I couldn't seem to control it.

When you react impulsively, you're only responding to your natural instinct to defend yourself, in the same way that you would if you were being physically attacked. Your body sends you warning signs, so you must immediately find a way to protect yourself. Whether you strike back by becoming defensive or growing silent, or you walk away and gossip, you internalize these attacks and send yourself the unconscious message that "something's wrong with me." Your negative innate beliefs intensify, and another layer goes on your protective shell. Your choices continue to support those beliefs, and without even realizing why, you begin to self-sabotage.

Think about a situation, event, or person that has upset you recently. What physical signs do you experience when someone, or something, pulls your trigger:

- Does your chest constrict, or does your heart pound faster?

- Does your stomach churn, or do you feel butterflies?

- Does your pulse quicken?

- Do you get a lump in your throat, or do you have a hard time speaking?

- Does your mind begin to race, or do you feel temporarily lightheaded?

- Do you want to attack or flee?

Now, compare these symptoms to what happens when you experience real fear. Imagine a situation in which you're truly afraid—hearing a sound in your home late at night while you're alone, for example, or having your car break down on a deserted road where you have no cell-phone service.

The feelings of real fear and those you experience when someone is verbally attacking you are similar. In order for you to understand your triggers, and to change your reaction to them, you must become mindful of your body's warning signs.

Understand that anger, gossip, being controlling, perfectionism, insecurity, jealousy, defensiveness, anxiety, nervousness, and impatience are all feelings that stem from fear. When you're verbally attacked, let down, humiliated, or betrayed by someone you love, you initially feel hurt. That hurt often escalates into bitterness as you begin to justify your pain: *Look at what I do for you and you treat me like this?!* You may feel defensive, which can easily spiral into anger. In either case, you don't like the way you feel around this person and how this has made you feel *about yourself*.

This is where most of us get stuck. And just like a beautiful bottle of champagne that's been agitated for too long, we feel like we're going to "blow." Instead of working through our anger in a healthy and constructive way, we either explode on someone (our husband, boyfriend, kids, or dog) or we stuff it down deep.

It's a natural human condition to alleviate pain in whatever way we know how—when we feel upset, our *learned* coping skills take over. We fall back into our old patterns. You see, few of us were lucky enough to watch our parents calmly and effectively communicate and find resolution to their problems, so we learned to be silent and walk away. Now, our feelings fester and we begin developing resentment. We must find a way to make ourselves not feel the pain, so we:

- Numb it with a tub of ice cream

- Anesthetize it with a bottle of wine

- Distract from it with television, the Internet, e-mails, video games, text messaging, and chat rooms

- Elude it by finding someone new who will love us

- Stay in an unhealthy relationship, desperately trying to convince someone of our worthiness

- Gossip

- Shop beyond our means or gamble away our savings

- Spend days, weeks, months, and even years living
  with anger and resentment, hoping it will go away

But it never does. . . .

Making Peace with Yourself

The only way to make peace with yourself (and your relationships) is to force yourself to look within and face your fears. When
someone can evoke extreme emotions within you, you must realize
that it's *never* about them or the situation you're in. Your defensive
reaction is because the other person has triggered an association to
a past pain, which is a feeling you'd do anything to avoid. He or she
hit a nerve, or a "trigger"—a fear deeply embedded in your psyche.

If you often find yourself upset, let down, or trying to control others (using anger, perfectionism, manipulation, or excessive
pleasing), you need to look at your deepest fears about yourself.
Most fears tend to develop during childhood or the teen years,
while others are hardwired into your DNA as a self-protection
mechanism from thousands of years ago. Regardless of why you're
afraid—learned or evolutionary—you can't let that fear keep you
stuck. As a woman on a quest for self-love and enlightenment, you
must be willing to rise above your past, your triggers, your fears,
and your guilt. Until you do, they'll keep resurfacing and manifesting themselves in your life.

Addictions of all kinds are simply coping mechanisms that you
developed to allay those fears. The numbness may have now sub-
sided, but the reality of why the addiction or bad habit was originally
formed is still buried deep within you. And no matter how much
you want to make changes on the outside, until you do the work
on the inside, you'll eventually fall back into your old habits. Your

outer world is always a reflection of your inner world! So long as you're so afraid of being wrong, of someone seeing your "supposed" flaws, of looking broken or inadequate, you'll spend all your time focused on trying to hide your imperfections from the world . . . and there simply won't be enough energy left over to be who you really are. And you really are amazing . . . *just as you are!*

Embrace your triggers as a gift, and know that people can only upset us when they've triggered something in us that we were taught was unacceptable and that we're still trying to hide. They've shone light on our core beliefs. They've shone light on our unconscious lies! How powerful is that?!

As long as we have attachments and judgments about who we are—who we *wish* we were, or who our parents, mate, children, or self-defeating ego *tell* us we are—we can be triggered. We will continue trying to escape the shame and feelings of inadequacy. It's not about the person we've just encountered; it's about us. They've just linked a neuro-association in our brains to a past pain.

Once you've faced your truth, nothing will have power over you. When you accept that you're solely accountable and completely responsible for all your reactions—and that *no one can make you feel anything*—you can recognize your own "stuff" and deal with it. Once you own your reactions, you can own your choices. Once you own your choices, you'll realize that you're the captain of your ship! You won't keep waiting for someone to come and save you, and you won't keep being tossed around like a willing victim in a stormy sea. You'll see why you developed those fears, and you'll remind yourself that you're worthy no matter who tries to convince you otherwise, and you won't have to prove it to anyone ever again. And you won't keep turning to food or destructive behaviors to escape your fears!

When you feel fear, or those *physical warning signs,* practice feeling it instead of feeding it. First, focus on your breathing by taking controlled deep breaths (such as the ones in the relaxation exercises we did last week), and then ask yourself honestly: "What

SITUATION	YOU FEEL	REAL FEAR	FACING YOURSELF	FACING YOUR FEARS
Your in-laws comment that your house is always messy...	Embarrassed and hurt: "Why don't your parents like me? I try so hard but I'm never good enough for them!"	Inadequacy, unloved	Deep down you fear that you aren't good enough. Are your feelings REALLY about your in-laws or could they have triggered something you feel about yourself?	What beliefs do you have regarding a woman's role as wife and mother? While growing up was cleanliness an indicator of worthiness? Did you feel like no matter what you did you were never good enough?
Your mate is going out on a Friday night with his friends to have a few drinks...	Jealous and suspicious: "Why don't you ever take me out? What are you up to? I hope I can trust you."	Inadequacy, abandonment	You worry that he might meet someone else. You fear that you are not enough. Is this about him or have you been betrayed in the past? Or are you afraid to be hurt and it's causing you to be controlling?	What are your beliefs abut love and fidelity? Are your parents still married? Do they have a wonderful marriage? Have you been betrayed in the past? Have you betrayed someone? Are you afraid of being alone?
An ambitious, hardworking co-worker is getting in tight with your boss...	Worried and envious: "Oh, she is just a brownnoser! The only reason she got this job was that her father knew someone in the company."	Inadequacy, neglect	You fear this person is stealing your spotlight. You fear not being the best. Is this actually about control, and your lack of it? Is your anger really with your co-worker or more that your boss won't need you any longer?	What are your beliefs about employment and social status? Were you rich or poor? Were you constantly compared to others while growing up? Do your parents or peers place a lot of emphasis on money and/or the prestige it brings?
Out one night with a group of friends, the conversation turns to you. They begin making jokes at your expense...	Defensive and humiliated: "My friends are so cruel. All that I do for them and they treat me like this!"	Inadequacy, rejection	You don't like criticism and don't want to be the brunt of their jokes. You fear being disrespected and/or betrayed by those who should love you most. Is this really about your friends' comments or does it trigger a feeling of not being worthy or good enough?	Did your parents/siblings put you down or make fun of you while growing up? Do you doubt yourself and/or your "lovableness"? Did you feel like your accomplishments went unnoticed? Did you feel disregarded? Do you care too much what people think about you?
You are over at your parents' home and they begin chastising you about your past (or current) behaviors...	Angry and hurt: "My parents never let me live down my mistakes. I've never been good enough in their eyes."	Inadequacy, unloved	You fear that you are inadequate in their eyes. You feel unloved. Are you really feeling upset about what they are criticizing you about or does it run deeper, back to your childhood?	What do you believe your parents feel about you? All you've ever wanted is their unconditional love and support. It is time that you face your fears and learn to love yourself NOW the way you always should have been.

DON'T FEED YOUR FEARS...RELEASE THEM

am I most afraid of right now? What fear has this person just triggered in me?"

In the coming weeks, we'll delve much more into fear and the specific ways it manifests in our lives. But right now I want you to get out your journal to answer these questions: What was your childhood like? How loved did you feel as a little girl? How much attention did you get as a teenager? Did your parents like themselves? What beliefs did you learn from them? How did you compare to other families or kids in school? Did you feel healthy enough, thin enough, good enough, loved enough, smart enough, beautiful enough, rich enough . . . worthy enough? What beliefs did you carve into your subconscious?

Step 26: Eat Good Fat to Get Fit

We've spent a lot of time understanding carbohydrates and protein. Since we know that 70 to 80 percent of our

You Have to Laugh!

For most of my adult life, I took myself (and all my problems) far too seriously. Although I joked around a lot about silly things, when the conversation focused on my life or me, I became defensive.

When a business associate disagreed with my opinion, for instance, I felt the need to convince him or her otherwise; if a family member put me down, I wanted to run for the door.

I now realize how ridiculous it was to believe that I could have ever changed anyone's point of view while I was in defense mode. I had to learn to lighten up, so I began to laugh about things—including myself— and it was extremely freeing.

If I was scatterbrained or late at times, rather than trying to justify myself, I'd try to laugh at myself. Most often, my "accuser" would laugh, too, and it defused many difficult situations. Once I decided to stop butting heads with every know-it-all who challenged me, it got much easier to chuckle at their comments. Soon I was learning to relax, realizing that I didn't have to prove my opinions to everyone. If the criticism I'd received was logical, I'd keep an open mind and try to learn something; and if it wasn't, I'd simply let it go in one ear and out the other, telling the other parties that we could agree to disagree (although I'm sure they thought I was actually agreeing with them).

I've always found the best people to be around are the ones who laugh the most. They laugh about their problems, they laugh about their past mistakes, and they laugh when they're wrong, adding, "Oh well, who cares?" What's most appealing is that they laugh when they're right! They don't say, "I told you so"—instead, they just smile and say, "Maybe I got lucky." These people know that life doesn't have to be so serious.

Our little ol' egos are sometimes our worst enemies. It's hard when someone disagrees with us or puts us down, even if they do it half-jokingly. We want to be liked and respected, and we don't like being the brunt of anyone's criticism. So the next time you feel like screaming, try throwing your arms up in the air and just *laugh*: Laugh at your problems, your past, or at the silly things you sometimes do or say. Laugh at how crazy you acted at your sister's wedding or how angry you were with that driver in the car ahead of you. Laugh at how stubborn or defensive you sometimes get, or at something naughty your child has done. Laugh with your mate, your parents, your siblings, and your friends—but most of all, just laugh at how serious you sometimes get!

And, finally, keep in mind that the average child smiles 400 times a day, while we're lucky to squeeze out 12!

diet should be composed of these nutrients, the balance must come from fat. Yes, fat! Contrary to popular belief, the body does need fat. The average woman looking to lose weight needs to keep her daily fat intake to approximately 20 to 30 percent of her calories, which means roughly 25 to 45 grams depending on her weight.

Just like carbs and protein, fats are not created equal, and the majority must come from a healthy source. I've developed Red Light and Yellow Light fat charts, but there are no Green Light ones here, since even healthy fats must be eaten in moderation.

Next, I'll explain the different types of fat.

Saturated Fat

All saturated fats (or as one of my trainers calls them, "Fatu-rated Fats") are Red Light fats because they're lethal. They clog our arteries, slow our metabolism, and raise blood cholesterol; and they contribute to obesity, heart disease, cancer, diabetes, and arthritis. The majority of saturated fats come from animal sources such as beef, pork, lamb, egg yolks, whole milk, cream, butter, and cheese; but also from coconut oil, palm kernel oil, and shorten-ing. (A rule of thumb is that saturated fat becomes solid at room temperature.)

Saturated fat is everywhere. To give you an example, one Big Mac has 32 grams of fat, a half cup of ice cream has 18, and a pound of spare ribs has 54—most of which is saturated. You want to keep your saturated-fat intake below ten grams per day, but aim to eliminate it altogether. Start asking for nutrition guides at all fast-food restaurants and make smart low-saturated-fat choices. If you really love your red meat or pork, try to choose lean cuts from the Green Light protein list.

Unsaturated Fat

Unsaturated fat is further broken down into polyunsaturated and monounsaturated fats.

Polyunsaturated fat remains liquid even when frozen, whereas **monounsaturated** fat is liquid at room temperature but turns solid in the freezer. There are healthy and unhealthy unsaturated fats, but even the healthiest are still very calorie dense, and when we're trying to maintain a certain daily caloric intake, eating too much of them can make us fat. We know that one gram of carbohy-drates has four calories, but one gram of fat has *nine* calories. With this in mind, one would think that eating a fat-free diet would be the best way to go. Wrong! Unfortunately, the majority of fat-free products are crammed with sugar, preservatives, and other fillers to give food satiety. The only fat-free products I recommend are plain organic yogurt, skim milk, and fat-free or one percent cottage cheese.

Let's discuss unsaturated fat in a little more detail.

1. Polyunsaturated Fat

Sometimes referred to as "vitamin F," polyunsaturated fat is where we find those much-discussed omega-3 and omega-6 fatty acids. Although our body can make fat from any food, it can't produce the healthy essential fatty acids (EFAs) on its own.

EFAs are responsible for our brain function, central nervous system and cardiovascular health, and for relieving depression and arthritis. We're also discovering that the perfect amount of these essential fatty acids may also help us burn our stored body fat. Hormonally, fat has no direct effect on insulin, but it does help reduce the rate of carbohydrate digestion, thus cutting down on insulin production.

Omega-3 is creating a big buzz in nutrition. Many people are talking about it, but there are a lot of misunderstandings about it and how it affects the body. Alpha-linolenic acid (ALA) is the main dietary omega-3 EFA. But ALA goes through a series of enzymatic reactions to create docosahexaenoic acid (DHA) and eicosapentaenoic acid (EPA), which can improve many disorders such as cardiovascular disease, eczema, and psoriasis. These acids reduce blood pressure, aid in the prevention of arthritis, lower cholesterol and triglyceride levels, and cut down on the risk of blood-clot formation.

DHA and EPA comprise up to 50 percent of the total fat in the brain and central nervous system. A deficiency of them can impair learning and memory and seriously affect children's behavior. A study at the University of Indiana showed that low levels of omega-3s were associated with behavioral problems, sleep problems, and temper tantrums in boys aged 6 to 12. There's also some evidence linking low DHA levels to mental disorders such as schizophrenia, bipolar disorder, and even postpartum depression. Fish oils high in DHA and EPA are used to treat children with attention deficit disorder, and new claims have recently suggested that people with bipolar disorder are also responding dramatically to high doses of DHA and EPA.

The best sources of omega-3 are cold-water fish, such as salmon, sardines, tuna, mackerel, and trout (cod-liver oil also works), as it takes much less work for the body to convert them into DHA than it does good but secondary choices such as soy products, flax and hemp seeds and oil; and then green, leafy vegetables. Yet, despite the well-documented health benefits of fish consumption, research shows that an increasing amount of fish is contaminated with environmental toxins. Because of this, Health Canada and the Food and Drug Administration (FDA) have issued advisories to limit the consumption of salmon, tuna, swordfish, king mackerel (not to be confused with small Atlantic and Spanish mackerel), shark, and tilefish. FDA research has also found that bluefish, sea trout, orange roughy, and grouper all have significantly more mercury than tilefish. I suggest that you limit your intake of these fishes until more research determines a safe amount—instead, add an enteric-coated fish-oil supplement to your diet every day.

꽃

There are two types of omega-6 fatty acids: One is a healthy essential fatty acid called linoleic acid (LA). Much like the alpha-linolenic acid found in omega-3, LA is the main omega-6 EFA. It too goes through a series of enzymatic reactions to create derivatives. One is gamma-linolenic acid (GLA), which has been shown to help burn stored body fat; reverse the effects of aging; relieve symptoms of arthritis, PMS, depression, and violent behavior; and is showing promise in the treatment of multiple sclerosis.

The ideal sources of healthy omega-6 fatty acid come from borage oil, evening primrose oil, hemp oil, pumpkin oil, canola oil, safflower oil, sunflower oil, and sesame oil. However, because so much of our food has omega-6 fatty acids already present, supplementation is rarely necessary. We need to try to regain our ancestors' ratio 1:1 of omega-6:3 by supplementing with only an omega-3 fatty acid.

The second type of omega-6 is a Red Light fat called hydrogenated fat, which is not an EFA and should be avoided at all costs. Hydrogenated fats are in almost all prepackaged and processed foods, and they're all too prevalent in most North American diets. Hydrogenated fats, such as those found in fried food; stick margarines; store-bought desserts, cookies, and cakes; microwave popcorn; and crackers, promote the inflammation and deterioration of brain cells and pack on the body fat. Anything containing the words *hydrogenated* or *partially hydrogenated vegetable oil* should be avoided.

2. Monounsaturated Fat

The other type of unsaturated fat is called monounsaturated fat, which is occasionally referred to as "omega-9" fatty acid. Monounsaturated fat has been shown to help fight free radicals in the body. And many Mediterranean cultures (such as the French, Italians, and Greeks) who consume high amounts of olive oil, as well as eat higher amounts of saturated fat than we in North America do, have a much lower reported blood cholesterol level than we do. Monounsaturated fat appears to reduce low-density lipoproteins (LDLs, or the "bad" cholesterol), and doesn't affect the good ones (or the high-density lipoprotein—HDL) in any way.

Good monounsaturated fat sources are olive oil, canola oil, avocados, and certain nuts and seeds such as peanuts, almonds, sunflower seeds, pumpkin seeds, and cashews. Keep in mind, however, that although olive oil and peanuts are good for you, they're still very high in calories: One tablespoon of olive oil has 135 calories; while one ounce of shelled, unroasted peanuts has 160 calories.

Adding a touch of healthy fat to your diet is taking a leap of faith for many women, but I promise that you'll feel and look fabulous. It helps burn body fat, speeds up your metabolism, makes your skin and hair glow, and increases your energy. Avoid saturated fat, but start adding these amazing bioenergetic fatty acids to your diet each day! Try to remember to:

> **Fat-Burning Secret #12:**
> Essential fatty acids will help fool your body into releasing stored body fat, and increase your metabolic rate (as well as do hundreds of other amazing things for your body and mind)!

- Keep your daily intake of fat to between 25 and 45 grams, or approximately 20 percent of your total calories.

- Learn to read food labels and avoid any foods containing saturated fat, hydrogenated fat, and partially hydrogenated fat.

- Take one 1,000 mg **omega-3** capsule three times daily with meals.

- Use refined olive or canola oil for all cooking, and extra-virgin olive oil on salads and vegetables.

Step 27: Eat a Balanced Diet

I've trained for fitness competitions and watched as my mother got ready for countless bodybuilding shows—so I know that the percentages of a typical bodybuilder's diet may look something like 55 percent protein, 30 percent carbohydrates, and 15 percent fat. So, when it came time to design the nutrient percentages in this program, I had a bit of a struggle. I went back and forth trying to decide how many of our daily calories should come from protein, carbs, and fats. If your goal is strictly health (not worrying about how you look), your daily calories may look more like 60 percent carbohydrates, 15 percent protein, and 25 percent fat. But most of us want a program that will ensure weight loss and help us achieve optimal health and energy.

Over the past ten years, I've gotten many people into incredible shape, and one fact always remained the same: If the goal is strictly weight loss, then protein needs to be high and saturated fat and carbs have to be low. Therefore, the weight-loss formula I've settled on is 40 percent protein, 40 percent carbohydrate, and 20 percent fat.

Let's determine the correct amounts for you based on this formula. As you know, one gram of protein has four calories, one gram of carbs has four calories, and one gram of fat has nine calories. Using our earlier formula (see page 102), for someone who weighs 180 pounds, that would mean 180 x 9 = 1,620 calories per day. Here's where those calories should come from:

1,620 x 40% = 648 calories from protein
1,620 x 40% = 648 calories from carbohydrates
1,620 x 20% = 324 calories from fat

Next, let's figure out how many grams this person would need from each of these nutrients each day. Since we know that carbs and protein each have four calories in every gram, let's divide these totals by four. Fat has nine calories in each gram, so we divide the fat amount by nine to determine how many grams they should be consuming each day:

648 calories of protein ÷ 4 = 162 grams of protein
648 calories of carbs ÷ 4 = 162 grams of carbohydrates
324 calories of fat ÷ 9 = 36 grams of fat

Based on your own weight, use the formula above to determine how many grams of protein, carbs, and fats you should consume each day.

Step 28: Stimulate Your Natural Growth Hormone

> **Fat-Burning Secret #13:**
> Get 40 percent of your calories from protein, 40 percent from carbohydrates, and 20 percent from fat.

Human growth hormone (HGH) is what keeps us looking and feeling youthful, vital, and lean, since it increases lean muscle mass, decreases body fat, and boosts the immune system. It's our fountain of youth, and it's released by the pituitary gland in spurts, primarily during deep sleep. This is why getting seven to eight hours of uninterrupted sleep each night is necessary for youth and energy.

Unfortunately, this natural hormone begins to decrease as we age. Basically, we all have a free ride until about the age of 24. From 25 to 35, we start to notice the beginning signs of aging, but we still feel pretty invincible. But by the time we hit 35, we start to notice aches and pains, wrinkles, and body fat. From there, our HGH production begins to decline and continues to wane at a rapid rate—until, by the time we're 60, we have only a fraction of our peak amount.

According to some older adults who have undergone growth-hormone therapy, the results have been astounding. They've experienced an increase in lean muscle mass and a decrease in body fat (the average is about 14 percent), diminished wrinkles, increased flexibility and agility, more restful sleep—and they generally feel and look years younger.

Because HGH therapy is still somewhat new, most physicians won't consider it until a patient is well into their 50s or 60s. However, there are many supplement companies that claim to have the magic pill or powder that will help us release our own natural hormone, but beware. Real growth hormone must be administered by injections, and it's only available from doctors. So, until more conclusive research is given, I don't recommend any of these over-the-counter remedies. (The amino acid L-glutamine, however, is showing great signs of helping to release HGH. So I *do* recommend that you take two to five grams of L-glutamine daily at bedtime. After three weeks, begin to build it up to ten grams nightly.)

A natural booster of HGH is touch. Premature babies who are constantly caressed grow and develop much faster than those who aren't. Touching these infants actually releases more HGH. Since touch stimulates growth-hormone production in premature babies, we can assume that it must also stimulate our own HGH release.

Touch is the strongest of all our sensations, but the sad thing is that we live in a world where people are so afraid to reach out to each other. In fact, many of my older or single clients who are alone too much seem starved for affection. And touch doesn't have to be sexual to be significant: When was the last time you cuddled a baby, had a massage, or embraced your favorite person? Study after study has proven the magic of touch. Stroking your child's hair as you watch TV, petting your cat, or touching shoulders with your best friend as you see a movie together can be that small but vital connection you need.

Most important, therapeutic touching helps reduce the amount of cortisol in the body. Cortisol is a stress hormone released by the adrenal glands, and it plays a hidden role in aging. You see, small, nonlethal doses of cortisol and adrenaline are released every time

Crystal Andrus

we're in a stressful or threatening situation—and they're known to play a role in muscle wasting (called *catabolism*), diabetes, fatigue, osteoporosis, thinning of the skin, redistribution of body fat, fragility of blood vessels, hypertension, fluid retention, suppression of immune functioning, and impaired metal functioning. And if that doesn't point to aging, I don't know what does!

There are some other natural ways to stimulate the release of our natural stored growth hormone and to help reverse the signs of aging. You'll notice that many of them are the very same steps that you've already incorporated into your life over the last few weeks. So, by sticking with the program, you're getting the added bonus of looking and feeling more youthful!

The best ways to naturally increase your HGH are:

- **Exercise.** It stimulates all your anti-aging hormones, including growth hormone and testosterone, which increases lean muscle, decreases fat, and also increases sex drive.

- **Sleep.** Get seven to eight hours of uninterrupted restful sleep in a dark environment. You see, 80 percent of growth hormone is released in surges through the first cycle of deep sleep, so a lack of rest decreases the secretion of this youth hormone.

- **Don't eat after 7:30 P.M. or within three hours of bedtime.** Digesting food is a workout for the body, and sleep should be a time of growth and recuperation. If your body is forced to metabolize food while it should be at rest, the natural release of HGH is compromised.

- **Avoid sugary food, especially in the evening.** We've already talked about the damage that sugar plays on the body. As well as being easily converted to fat, eating sweets at night halts your release of growth hormone because of excess insulin levels.

- **Avoid eating before you exercise.** Exercising on an empty stomach not only forces your body to use more fat for energy, but it also releases more HGH.

- **Take two to five grams of L-glutamine daily at bedtime.** After three weeks, begin to build it up to ten grams nightly.

- **Get a massage.** Not only is it a way to keep you young, but it also relieves stress, helps flush out the lactic acid that causes after-exercise muscle soreness, aids in relaxation, and makes you feel wonderful. If you can't afford a massage with a therapist, is there a special person in your life who, with a little coaxing, would give you a nice rubdown with a little warmed sesame oil? What about offering to exchange massages with a good friend? After you've had one, you'll wonder how you ever lived without it.

> **Fat-Burning Secret #14:**
> Increase your natural growth hormone, which will help keep you lean and feeling young.

Step 29: Change Your Cardio Program to Slow and Steady

How's it coming with your interval jogging? You must be noticing improvements in your cardiovascular fitness and body-fat loss by now.

Crystal Andrus

The Cellulite Solution

Massage might actually help get rid of cellulite—the dimpled, cottage-cheese-like fat that affects up to 90 percent of all women. Some women have more, others less; and although many scientists and doctors insist that there's no such thing as cellulite, for most of us, it's very real! Cellulite isn't actually a type of fat, but rather it's the way our fat sits in the fibrous bands that run from our skin to our deeper fatty tissues. The more fat a person has, the deeper these hills and valleys can become. But a woman of ideal body weight can still have cellulite. Most experts agree that a deep and vigorous massage can effectively break up the bands of tissue that create cellulite. This has been a popular notion in Europe, and it's one of the primary reasons why massage is an integral part of the European spa experience. I've even heard of women using a rolling pin across the backs of their legs and butt. (Hey, whatever works!) Don't waste your money on creams and quick-fix treatments—after all, I'm sure you've heard the saying "If it sounds too good to be true, it usually is."

Even liposuction won't remove that dimpling effect, so your best bet is to exercise, watch your diet, drink lots of water, and get massages to minimize the appearance of cellulite.

Long-distance running is highly effective at burning large amounts of stored body fat. (Have you ever seen a fat marathon runner?) So this week, we're going to change your cardio program. Instead of 4-minute intervals for 20 minutes, you'll do a longer mid-level pace for 30 to 45 minutes. The interval training you've been doing for the past few weeks has been effective in accelerating your body's capacity to utilize more oxygen, pushing yourself past what's called your "anaerobic threshold." We'll be going back to interval training again, but think of this as an active recovery, fat-burning, cardiovascular session.

You'll notice how much more endurance you have, and how much stronger you'll be when you go back to the intervals. If 45 minutes is impossible for you, do the best you can. Having a running partner is extremely helpful if you find these workouts difficult to stick with. If you find you can go longer than 45 minutes the first time out, increase your speed during your next session. You don't need to go longer than 45 minutes to effectively burn body fat.

I also want you to try to increase the number of times per week you perform your aerobic or cardio training. Although three to four days a week will still bring about changes, five to seven times is best. I recommend alternating your workout video with your cardio sessions. But if you do your cardio on the same day as your weights, do your weight workout first. You want to have as much glycogen (stored energy) as possible for strength and energy for the tough workouts. Once depleted of glycogen, you'll tap into your fat stores for energy more quickly during your cardio workout. Don't forget to try doing your cardio first thing in the morning, or at least on an empty stomach, as this will greatly increase your fat burning.

Always push yourself as hard as possible so that you burn the maximum amount of calories you can during your workout. If you normally start your intervals at level 3 on the treadmill and work up to level 7 for your last interval, do your cardio sessions this week at a continuous level 5. Remember to push yourself to a point where you could talk if you had to, but you really don't want to. Every 10 to 15 minutes, take your heart rate, and stay between 60 and 80 percent of your maximum. If you're feeling strong, stay close to 80 percent of your maximum.

Another way to monitor your intensity level and make sure that you're training in the zone is to use Borg's Rating of

Borg's Rating of Perceived Exertion	
0	Nothing at all
0.5	Very, very weak
1	Very weak
2	Weak
3	Moderate
4	Somewhat strong
5	Strong
6	
7	Very Strong
8	
9	
10	Very, Very Strong
10+	Maximal

Walking/Running Hot-Weather Safety Tips

Running in warm weather is often much more enjoyable than in cold, but you've got more to watch out for when you run in the heat. Hot and humid weather can cause muscle cramps, blisters, fatigue, heat exhaustion, and heatstroke. Symptoms that you should be aware of include:

- Headaches
- Dizziness
- Disorientation
- Decrease in perspiration
- Cold, pale skin (I've even noticed goose bumps)

Wear breathable, light-colored, loose clothing. Pour water into and over yourself. Avoid the hottest times of the day—instead, try to run during the cool morning or late evening. Adjust your pace and take walk breaks if you need to keep your temperature down. In hot weather, shorten your running distance—and remember, you still need to warm up and cool down.

Perceived Exertion (RPE). RPE takes into account your perception of exercise fatigue, including psychological, musculoskeletal, and environmental factors. On this RPE Scale, you should be exercising between 3 and 4 (moderate to somewhat strong). This is a long, slow, steady jog.

Ideally, you should use this chart, your talk test, and heart rate together to ensure that you're training in your ideal zone. This longer, steady session will burn lots of calories and stored fat!

⁂

Summary of Week Five: *Truth*

Body:

- Eat a balanced diet with the right amount of healthy fats.

- Stay youthful by stimulating your natural growth hormone.

- Change your cardio session from interval training to a long, slow, steady pace; and increase your frequency.

Mind:

- Become body aware. Identify the physical signs that your body sends you when you're upset.

Soul:

- Send energy to the things that light you up and make you feel wonderful; and stop exerting energy trying to hide, cover up, and justify who you are.

Week Six: *Fearlessness*

Things are moving quickly now, but before we get straight to the nutrition and exercises . . . how are you doing? I know that last week we started some intense emotional work, but now, in order for you to make huge gains over these next two months, you really have to start digging deeper.

Step 30: Let Go of Controlling Perfectionism

We talked last week about taking responsibility for all our reactions, and we're familiar with sayings such as "You must master your emotions" or "You must believe it before you can see it." Although these statements are 100 percent accurate, most of us can't get past our own natural reactive response when someone hits one of our triggers. In hindsight, we know that we should think before we speak or wait to send an angry e-mail, but most often our logical reaction is secondary to our innate reaction. Therefore, to change our patterns and improve our lives, we must become aware of the initial warning signs that our body gives us when we're afraid, insecure, or defensive. I hope that you're allowing yourself to feel those feelings rather than escape them.

You have to feel in order to heal.

The bottom line is that you must believe in yourself. Know who you are and what you want for your life. You're entitled to dress, walk, and talk in any way you choose, regardless of anyone else's opinion. You don't need to explain your choices to anyone. Realize that you alone are enough. You're lovable and deserving of all that life has to offer. We *all* are.

Now that may sound easier said than done. To do it, we'd really have to continue to look at what we've been hiding and discover what we're so afraid of.

Fear has many expressions. For some women, it often manifests as a need to be perfect: They want the perfect home, perfect children, perfect marriage, and perfect body; and they usually want to always appear happy and optimistic. Then, at the other end of the spectrum, are those who self-sabotage in extremely negative ways. They become delinquent, addicted, irresponsible, neglectful, or sexually promiscuous—these are the women whom society ostracizes. We look down on the woman who's in the bar every weekend, or the one who's the opposite of "Suzie Homemaker," such as the exotic dancer or the prostitute. Finally, somewhere in the middle of these two extremes are the women who are simply indifferent. Numb, they live each day without passion or purpose: watching hours of TV, wasting endless time on the telephone, or chatting online with strangers. They distract themselves from their fears by vacating—that is, they self-sabotage by doing nothing at all.

Ironically, I believe that although the behaviors of the perfectionist, the promiscuous woman, and the indifferent individual are contrary, the symptoms all come from the same source: feeling inadequate. Inadequacy drives many people to search for worth and validation. If, as children or young teenagers, they never felt pretty enough, smart enough, rich enough, tall enough, skinny enough, loved enough, or wanted enough, then they may still be carrying that fear deep inside.

Many people will do anything to hide that fear from the world. This is what drives so many of us to become controlling. We think if we can just control our outer world, then our inner world will feel less chaotic and confusing.

This reminds me of when, a few years ago, I was upset and decided to talk to a very wise woman. I was crying and carrying on to her about a situation over which I felt I'd lost total control.

That's when she gently smiled at me and said, "You never had it to begin with."

The enormity of her words didn't hit me at first. But as the day wore on, I realized the magnitude of that simple statement. We really don't have any control over the final outcome of any situation. No matter how diligent we are, there will always be extenuating circumstances. We'll never be able to please everybody and make everyone like us. We won't be able to stop people from gossiping about us if they want to. We can't change our mate, children, or parents. And we'll certainly never be able to stop natural disasters and diseases, so why do we kid ourselves into thinking that we could actually have control over *anything?*

We must let go and choose to exert energy in the only areas that we do have control over: our own attitudes, moods, actions, and energy levels; what we say about others; how we view ourselves; what we put into our mouths; and what we choose to do with our bodies. The beautiful Serenity Prayer is one we should all live by:

> *God, grant me the serenity to*
> *accept the things I cannot change;*
> *courage to change the things I can;*
> *and wisdom to know the difference.*

It takes courage to accept that we don't always have to be right or perfect, or pretend that we're happy when we're not. It takes courage to love ourselves for all our frailties and imperfections—because, although things could be better, they could be worse; and in order for us to learn and grow, things are meant to be just the way they are for now. Besides, it's our supposed flaws that enable us to receive the greatest gift of all: loving ourselves regardless! Life doesn't begin ten pounds from now.

So, what if you made the decision to choose to see things as they are, instead of what you want them to be?

What if you chose to stop trying to manipulate the outcome and allow *what is* to unfold?

What if you realized that maybe you don't have to fix it, change it, force it, know it, or control it? That you simply have to see it for what it is—and ask your spirit "if you need to accept it or let it go?"

Wouldn't that be freedom?

※

So how does food figure into this? Well, for many of us, it eases us through painful times, and loves us when no one else seems to. Yet food also causes us to feel embarrassed, weak, and ashamed.

Many of us learned unhealthy attitudes about eating while growing up. If we were raised by overly strict parents, our meals focused on following rigid rules. We learned that good little girls sat quietly at the table and ate everything on their plates (especially since throwing out leftovers was a waste of money). Mealtimes became power struggles, not celebrations, and soon we forgot how to listen to our bodies. We discovered that by keeping quiet and stuffing our feelings down with our dinner, Mom and Dad stayed happy.

If, on the other hand, we were raised by neglectful parents who were rarely around, we often fended for ourselves and ate whatever we could find. Since meals were rarely planned or eaten together, our parents would use food to deal with their own inadequacies: "I'm sorry I have to go out again tonight, but I'll get you some ice cream and a movie."

The trouble is, when we adults feel pain or are afraid, we still use food to comfort ourselves. We don't always realize what we're doing and don't know how to get off this roller coaster of feeling inadequate, disrespected, lonely (or whatever it might be), then eating our favorite food and feeling immediate comfort and gratification. But as the food starts to digest, we begin to loathe ourselves for not having willpower and being out of control. Unfortunately, the cycle begins again.

Getting Out of the Cycle

One way to break the cycle is by cultivating joy. Joy is different from happiness: It is something you are; happiness is something you search for. Happiness comes from external events or experiences; therefore, you have little control over it. In other words, you can have it swept right out from under your feet. For example, "After my boyfriend dumped me, I was so devastated that I gained 50 pounds," or "I'm upset every time I leave my parents' house because I feel I never can do anything right in their eyes."

Joy can't be bought or sold, and it absolutely can't be found in a pound of chocolate or a tub of ice cream. It doesn't come from someone telling you that you're wonderful or beautiful—it comes from within. It comes from self-love—not looking good for others, making lots of money, or having a perfect body. Self-love comes from acceptance, forgiveness, and faith. It arises when you live in the moment, appreciate all things, give thanks for your blessings, and have faith through good times and bad. Faith that whatever is arising is here for a reason: It is either time to wake up, see things as they really are—perhaps through new lenses—and to make changes, or to accept what is being delivered and allow it to unfold. *This is wisdom, and your soul is the wisest advisor you could ever consult with.*

It's having faith that, *without question,* you alone are enough, you're worthy of love, and you'll be fine with whatever comes your way. It's trusting that you'll take care of yourself no matter what; that you'll always honor your spirit, knowing that as long as you do, the Universe will get behind you. It's the Law of Attraction! For when you honor, trust, and love yourself, you'll attract people, situations, and experiences that affirm that you're honorable, trusting, and lovable. You'll feel like you have God working overtime on your side! Good karma!

I know how difficult this is to achieve all the time, and I'm sure that even the most serene people must occasionally feel anxious when life throws them a curveball, but these people have also mastered accepting those things they can't control or fix. Their internal dialogue continually reinforces that they like who they are, and as long as they stay true to themselves, they'll always be okay. This is authentic power, and it opens the door to joy.

Young children have an inborn faith. They don't question whether things will work out; they know exactly what they want, who they are, and what they like. They never question themselves or doubt that their parents love them. Have you ever seen a two-year-old having a temper tantrum? He doesn't care who's watching! It's poor Mom standing in the grocery store who's embarrassed and worried that people think she's a bad mother. Kids know *exactly* what they think: No one can tell them that their pink polka-dot shirt doesn't match their blue striped skirt, and they don't worry about the designer label inside their jacket or even if their hair is combed. Children haven't yet learned to deny their feelings or to numb them with one of society's coping mechanisms—at least I've never heard of a three-year-old who needs a rum and Coke to calm her nerves or a chocolate bar for stress!

The abundance of energy most kids have is natural and normal. They love to move their bodies—running, jumping, swinging, and climbing . . . feeling alive. But instead, we teach them to sit in front of the TV for hours while we complain about exercise and how much we hate our bodies. They learn these lessons very young—and we learned them, too. It happened just around the time we began searching for acceptance and approval.

We stopped listening to our bodies and doing what we loved around the time we hit puberty. We were growing into women, and the messages we heard from our parents and society were becoming a part our internal dialogue. As we grew, these attitudes intensified, and soon our self-worth was determined by external approval: the size of our bank account, home, or hips; or how popular we were. Still, we search for happiness from these things, oblivious to the fact that it can never come from someone or something outside ourselves. We're constantly tempted by the distractions of the world as we struggle for validation and approval.

Feeling the pain or stress of difficult times can be very hard, but it's the most important lesson you can learn. Of course, it sounds easier said than done, but you must accept that tough times are a part of life. Everybody's on a roller-coaster ride, hoping to be up more than down, but you can't make things go your way by trying to force, control, or fight it.

Tough times can be really hard, but they won't last forever (my favorite line is: "This too shall pass"), and eating a whole bag of potato chips will only make you feel worse. So know that every time you overcome your natural desire to reach for your learned coping mechanism (such as food), you become stronger in all ways: emotionally, physically, mentally, and most important, spiritually. Each time you discover why you're responding defensively, sensitively, or aggressively, you'll find yourself spending less and less time in the valleys, because you've learned how to pick yourself up and listen to your body's true needs. You'll respect and nurture yourself with love, refusing to find comfort in mashed potatoes or cookies. Very soon, you'll climb those mountains of life faster and easier, and you'll realize that food no longer has a hold over you.

꽃*꽃

This week I want you to look back at your journal entry from Week Four, Step 19, when I asked you to make a list of the people or things that you believe have held you back in your life. Looking at each one of those negative experiences now, I want you to discover the gift of your past. First, ask yourself if you can see how you might have reacted differently based on what you know about yourself today. How could a different reaction have changed your life? Even if you were abused, victimized, or betrayed, do you see how you're continuing to hold yourself back by abusing, victimizing, and betraying yourself today? *You've become the captor and captive of your own life!*

I think that one of the biggest realizations I made in my own life was that no one can make an adequate woman feel inadequate, or vice versa. It didn't matter how many times my husband told me I was beautiful or how much he loved me, it was *never* enough.

SITUATION	YOUR INITIAL REACTION	THE TRUTH IS...	FACING YOURSELF	LIVING WITH AUTHENTICITY...
You are out for dinner. When you get up to go to the washroom, a woman at a nearby table gives you a terrible look followed with a half-snicker...	"Oh my God, I knew I shouldn't have worn this outfit. I probably look so fat. I just want to sink into the floor right now..."	She feels insecure or envious. This has nothing to do with you. She isn't feeling good about herself. These are her issues to deal with. You have the right to look or dress any way you want.	Recognize your own fears. Her dirty look has caused you to doubt yourself. Deep down you don't feel confident. Perhaps this comes from feelings of inadequacy. She can't cause you to feel ugly or fat; only you can. Don't own anyone else's garbage and don't give it another thought. You are beautiful!	Don't own her fears. See them as her weaknesses, not yours. Smile as you walk by her and reassure her with your eyes that she has nothing to fear. Your kindness may even cause her to reevaluate her actions. You like who you are and are comfortable within yourself. It is sad that she lives with such insecurities. This is not your issue, so don't make it yours!! Don't go back to the table and order cheesecake to make yourself feel better!
You have spent all afternoon planning a perfect evening with your boyfriend. You've cooked a beautiful meal, set a perfect table, and bought new lingerie. When he gets to your house he gobbles down the food, commenting that there is too much garlic in the sauce and then falls asleep within the hour...	"I'll never cook for him again. He doesn't even appreciate me. And I CAN'T BELIEVE HE FELL ASLEEP. He must not love me. I don't need this jerk."	His actions have nothing to do with you. He has acted in a thoughtless way, probably unknowingly. He is tired and simply didn't realize all the work you had put into the evening. MEN DON'T ALWAYS THINK!	Recognize your own fears. Your reaction may be overly dramatic. Your hurt and anger may stem from past pains. You may not have gotten your parents' approval or were hurt in a past relationship and now your boyfriend's lack of attention has triggered a feeling of inadequacy and neglect. Don't carry old fears around any longer. It's time you approve of yourself! Are you choosing people that let you down because you don't think you are worthy of more or could you be acting too insecure and defensive?	Don't take his thoughtlessness personally. You did a wonderful thing and his actions are about him, not you. Is he normally a great guy? Could he simply be exhausted or have you chosen a jerk? Next time, tell him in advance that you have a special night planned and to "get ready!!" If he still disregards your attempts at romance, you know that "you are an awesome woman and more than enough for any man!" This is not your issue, so don't make it yours! Don't drink the remainder of the wine alone and cry yourself to sleep! It might be time to look at yourself and the choices you are making.

It wasn't until *I realized and claimed my own worth* that I was able to see my true beauty and really love myself.

Even though it feels very difficult sometimes, remember that no one can make you feel worthy or loved . . . authenticity can only come from you.

So, it is time that you *really* get fired up for your life!

Are you ready? Are you ready to face your fears and say, "Oh well, I can't let them hold me back any longer" and go after your wants?

Are you ready to put on your favorite motivating music, such as the theme song from *Rocky,* "Eye of the Tiger"; Aretha Franklin's "Respect"; or the theme song from the movie *Flashdance,* "What a Feeling," and do whatever it takes to tell the Universe . . . to tell your soul . . . that your life matters and that you are back in the game again?

Aren't you worth it? Isn't that little girl inside of you worth it?

To get more momentum on your side, I want you to go back to those words you wrote in Week Two, Step 7. The words that lit you up, and I want you to create a *dream board* based on them.

As you do so, I want you to put on music that motivates you. Go through magazines and cut out words and pictures of things you love, things you want, things that light you up, inspire you, excite you, soothe you, caress you, nourish your soul, and make your heart sing. Paste them onto a collage or a poster and put it up in your office or in your bedroom; somewhere you'll see it every day. You can draw your own pictures as well; add color, sparkles—whatever makes you smile! *And right in the center of your dream board, I want you to put a picture of yourself, as a child.* You can also add pictures of the other people in your life whom you also love—the people you're committed to. . . .

Have fun with this, but don't underestimate the magic you'll begin to conjure up with this very step alone!

Simply . . . Inspirational!

I used to be an overweight, lethargic, depressed person who thought I had nothing great or extraordinary to offer anyone. My life felt boring, and I was stuck in an endless self-sabotaging rut! I constantly compared myself to others, valued my worth by what I owned, and essentially believed that I was a *no*-body—not worth achieving any dreams I may have had. I tried to convince myself that I was meant to be fat, meant to be living a plain and ordinary life, and meant to be living to please and make others happy.

Nevertheless, I couldn't deny the need I felt to be free—the need to live the life I deserved, which would ultimately set me on my path: *to live my destiny.*

I'd like to take you back to the time when I finally decided to listen to my needs and make a change in my life:

It all started when I was celebrating my daughter's first birthday. While indulging in my second helping of chocolate cake, I overheard some guests whispering about how I'd let myself go.

What had I let go? I started thinking. *What's wrong with me? Do I look that terrible?*

I had already eaten two plates of lasagna, some pizza, a bowl of potato salad, and two large pieces of cake, along with some pastries. I put my fork down and went to the washroom teary eyed. I couldn't look at myself in the mirror—*what had I become?* The remainder of the night I felt miserable and ended up missing the joy of my daughter's first birthday party.

It wasn't so much the comment that upset me but the realization that this was not the person I wanted to be, nor the example I wanted to set for my daughter. That evening, I made a promise to myself that I would no longer allow food or negative self-talk to take control of my life. I needed to do it differently, though, as I had failed on every diet in the past. This time I wasn't going to give in to my fears. This time I was going to succeed!

The next day I went to the bookstore and saw *Simply . . . Woman!* Its cover was intoxicating, and I was drawn to it the moment I saw it, among the hundreds of other books. Perhaps there was an energy or light emitting from Crystal's book. Whatever it was, I picked it up. I read through the Introduction with tears in my eyes. I'd finally found what I was looking for. I knew that this was the one, and I knew that I was finally ready to take control of my life.

I started the program and instantly began losing weight. I averaged a total of five to six pounds per week. In total, I've now lost over 50 pounds

Crystal Andrus

and have never felt or looked better in my entire life. I'm wearing clothes I never dreamed I could fit into, and I'm currently preparing for a fitness competition. And on top of it all, I'm a S.W.A.T. facilitator and have begun my own personal-training business! Yes, me—Adele Fridman—the girl who thought she was meant to be fat forever!

Crystal's book, her message forum, workout DVD, radio show, *Tele Course*, wellness retreats, and coaching are an unstoppable force—making this a truly life-changing transformation INSIDE and OUT! She provides you will all the tools you'll ever need to be successful.

All the hard work, dedication, and consistency are paying off, and to think that this is just the beginning for me. I can't wait to see where this journey leads me next . . . and I can't wait to see where it leads you!

Just know that if you follow this program, you'll discover that anything is possible, and by banishing doubt and thinking in "no-limit" ways, you too will clear a space for the power of positive intentions to enter your life! The rest will unfold magically. . . .

— **Adele Fridman,** Thornhill, Ontario

Adele before starting the program.

After 12 weeks on the program.

Now, three years later —Adele looking absolutely gorgeous!

Step 31: Live on the 80/20 Plan

Over the past five weeks, I've given you recommendations on how many carbs, proteins, and fats you should eat daily. Now I want you to understand the bottom line on getting lean and burning stored body fat. Although hormones, energy production, insulin levels, amino acids, essential fatty acids, thermogenesis, and metabolism largely affect the way you burn body fat, *total calories are still what matter most!*

As you know, one pound of fat is equal to 3,500 calories. This means that to lose one pound of fat, you'll need to burn off or use up 3,500 calories. It's like a bank account: If you put more money into your account than you withdraw, your balance will grow. Well, if you eat more calories than you expend in a day, your butt will grow! To lose fat, you need to burn off those calories by exercising (*calories out* or *caloric expenditure*) and by reducing the amount of food you eat (*calories in* or *caloric intake*.)

Regardless of how healthy, low-glycemic, high-protein, or low-fat your food is, if you're eating too much, you won't lose weight. Cutting any one particular food group, like some popular diets do, may cause temporary water or fat loss, but calorie balance is what matters most.

Fat-Burning Secret #15:
Eat less and exercise more!

The problem with calorie cutting is that even though it can help you lose the weight, you can actually create more problems for yourself down the road. If you stop eating or cut too many calories, eventually your metabolism will be so s-l-o-w-e-d down that when you do start to eat (and you will), you'll gain weight *so* easily. This is why you should never let your calories drop below 1,100. Your body will learn to adapt to the most horrendous circumstances, and eventually you'll learn to function on the little amounts of food that you feed yourself. When you do start eating again, those extra calories will be stored as fat. Even worse, you will have lowered your resting metabolic rate. This is why so many diets fail.

Plus, we live in a society where portion sizes are out of control. Agriculture is abundant and inexpensive, and restaurant owners want satisfied customers who feel that they're getting their money's worth. The bigger the better!

Think honestly about the calories you're taking in. Remember that too much of *any* food will make you fat. Start paying attention to how much you're eating: Do you have bread with your meals, or consume plates of pasta for dinner? People are shocked all the time by what the USDA Food Guide Pyramid designates as a "serving size": one slice of bread, half a bagel, one ounce of cereal (the average breakfast bowl holds four to six ounces!), or a half cup of cooked pasta. Get a measuring cup and put a half cup of cooked pasta into it and see how little falls into the center of your plate. You'll realize that you've likely been eating four or five servings at a time.

A Better Way

Watching your caloric intake, monitoring portions, and eating Green Light carbohydrates and protein six days a week works perfectly—then, come Saturday, you can eat, drink, and be merry! One day a week is your "treat day." This is what I call the "80/20 Plan," and it works.

Here's how: Whatever we do the majority of the time is going to prevail. So if obese people have salad just one day a week, they won't lose weight; conversely, if healthy, lean individuals eat junk on their treat day, they're not going to gain weight.

The 80/20 Plan effectively increases weight loss because your body will quickly learn how to balance out any changes you make. If you stop eating, your metabolic rate slows; but if you throw in some fat and Red Light carbohydrates to your diet one day each week, your body gets confused. "What's going on?" it will ask. "I thought she was depriving me, but maybe I'm wrong." It's like throwing a splash of gasoline on your campfire.

Step 32: Become Aware of Food Combining

Do you ever wake up, look in the mirror, and think, *Wow, it's happening—I look great! . . .* only to discover that by evening, you're so bloated that you look three months pregnant? Well, have no fear: Low stomach acid (hydrochloric acid) and poor food combining might just be the culprits.

> **Fat-Burning Secret #16:**
> Follow the 80/20 plan!
> Eat "clean" six days a week,
> and then give yourself
> one treat day to eat
> whatever you want.

Along with bloating, do you also experience:

- Fatigue after meals?
- Excessive gas, belching, or burping after meals?
- Longitudinal striations on fingernails?
- Weak, peeling, or cracked fingernails?
- Acne?
- Undigested food in your stools?
- Halitosis?
- A full feeling after eating meat?
- Nausea after taking supplements?
- Multiple food allergies?
- Constipation, diarrhea, or indigestion?
- Chronic yeast infections?

If you answered *yes* to three or more of the above symptoms, you may have an *underactive stomach,* which produces neither enough enzymes nor hydrochloric acid for the proper digestion of food. It can be caused by many symptoms such as improper food combining, eating fruit with or immediately after a meal, drinking ice-cold drinks at mealtimes, consuming refined and processed foods, ingesting red meat, or even internalizing your stress.

Crystal Andrus

It's easy to confuse the symptoms of an underactive stomach with those of an *overactive stomach,* which might lead you to reach for the Alka-Seltzer. Instead of relying on antacids, I want you to become aware of the food combinations you're eating. Whenever I combine starchy carbohydrates such as potatoes with protein, for example, I feel extremely bloated and heavy afterward. I simply can't digest them together—and I'm not alone. It's essential to eat protein with every meal to slow the rate of carbohydrate absorption, but try to eat protein with salad-type vegetables (which are high in fiber and low in starch), and consider taking a digestive enzyme or a hydrochloric acid capsule with your meals.

I swear by digestive enzymes now, but it took me close to ten years of bloating and discomfort before I began taking them regularly. I recommend papain and bromelain (plant enzymes), pancreatin and pepsin (animal-source enzymes), or an enzyme containing about 600 mg of hydrochloric acid or Bentaine. Start with one tablet just before mealtime and increase to two or more if the meal is heavy.

The other very important factor to consider if you're experiencing the aforementioned symptoms is how and when you consume your fruits. Fruits are important to eat because they contain an abundance of vitamins, fiber, and nutrients; however, even the perfect Green Light fruits digest so quickly (in about 20 minutes) that if you eat them immediately following a protein or starchy meal, which take roughly three to four hours to digest, they sit on top of your food and begin to ferment. That's when you can get gas and digestive upset.

You should wait at least three hours after you've had a meal before eating fruit; or if you eat it on an empty stomach, wait 20 minutes before eating anything else. Try having fruit first thing in the morning, for it will race through your system and activate tons of enzymes that perform a mini "internal cleansing." With the fruit digested so quickly, the remaining enzymes will continue to stay at work, cleaning up any "leftovers" still hanging around from the night before.

Step 33: Drink Green Tea

Tea has been gaining popularity in the United States in recent years, and it's been in the news quite a bit for its health benefits. The biggest buzz is about green tea, which has been reported to have anti-cancer properties and raise levels of antioxidants in the blood that may ward off heart disease. It also contains high amounts of catechin polyphenols (also found in red wine) that provide potent antioxidant action.

In addition, green tea appears to promote weight loss, as it has the ability to lower glucose levels so that starch is absorbed more slowly. (Be clear that we're talking about tea products derived from a plant called *Camellia sinensis* here. While herbal or medicinal teas may be tasty and offer different health benefits, they haven't been the focus of concentrated research in terms of weight loss.)

Another compound that green tea contains, diphenylamine, seems to have a strong sugar-lowering action. It may lower intestinal fat absorption and raise levels of serotonin and dopamine in your brain, which control both the appetite and how satisfied you feel after eating. Catechin polyphenols (namely, EGCG) work with other chemicals to increase levels of thermogenesis, helping your body burn fuel such as fat to create heat.

> **Fat-Burning Secret #17:**
> Green tea and green-tea extract help with weight loss without giving you the "jitters."

For extra fat-burning properties, you can also take the extract of green tea, found in health-food stores. I like **lean+** and **abs+**, which specifically target the abdominal region.

Crystal Andrus

Step 34: Add Calcium and Magnesium to Your Diet

Researchers at the University of Tennessee in Knoxville believe that calcium may be the latest arsenal in the war against excess weight and fat. On top of its many important roles in the body, such as maintaining a regular heartbeat; lowering cholesterol; and preventing cardiovascular disease, osteoporosis, and cancer, calcium is also needed for muscular contraction, growth, and fat metabolism. *Yes, I did say fat metabolism!*

Researchers at the university revealed that mice placed on a high-calcium, low-calorie diet lost roughly 42 percent of their body fat in only six weeks, while their counterparts who followed a low-calcium but still a low-calorie diet lost just 8 percent. That statistic is staggering! The only component that changed in the two groups' diets was calcium, yet the fat loss was more than 500 percent greater in the high-calcium group.

Another study found that

Calcium and PMS

Calcium might also be the answer to relieving premenstrual syndrome (PMS) symptoms. If you're one of the infinitesimal percentage of women who don't endure this often life-altering phenomenon, then you should feel extremely blessed. For the rest of us, this syndrome before our periods can wreak havoc! Symptoms can include food cravings, bloating, weight gain, irritability, oversensitivity, breast tenderness, anxiety, depression, and diminished sex drive. Although doctors are still unsure of the causes for PMS, many have found that a well-balanced diet supplemented with 1,200 mg calcium along with 300 mg magnesium, 400 IUs vitamin E, 100 mg of vitamin B6, and 2,000 mg of omega-3 fatty acids can help relieve it. (Aerobic exercise is also probably one of the best ways to fight the blues you may feel during this time.)

Keeping track on our calendar and planning events and important occasions around this time can be very helpful in avoiding the overwhelming effects of PMS. We all should know our individual cycles and be aware of them during the month, as our moods and energy levels are radically influenced by our hormones: Midmonth when we're ovulating, many of us feel unstoppable, while the day before our periods we can't get out of bed. Rather than trying to pretend that PMS doesn't exist, we need to understand and acknowledge our limitations during this time. For instance, I often look back and realize that I've radically cut my hair, gone on a major shopping spree, or had a whopping fight with my mate during these few days, so now I try not to make major decisions when I'm PMS-ing!

". . . if two adults were randomly chosen (same age/gender), one taking 300mg Calcium and the other 1,300mg Calcium daily . . . the research would project a 17 pound weight difference between the two." [Davies, et al. J Clin Endocrinal Metab 2000]

For premenopausal women, an adequate calcium intake is 1,200 mg per day (excessive calcium can actually be harmful). Postmenopausal women need even more—up to 1,800 mg per day—because their estrogen levels are lower, thus reducing the amount of calcium their bodies absorb and increasing the chance of osteoporosis.

A glass of milk has 300 mg of calcium (but it's not necessarily an ideal choice, as it's too high in phosphorus), and a cup of yogurt has 300 to 400 mg. And, believe it or not, a leafy green salad has about 200 to 300 mg; half a cup of tofu (fortified with calcium sulfate) adds a whopping 434 mg; and salmon, sardines, seafood, broccoli, collard greens, and almonds are also great sources. Try to increase your consumption of these foods rich in calcium.

Calcium and magnesium work best together, usually on a 2:1 ratio. Take 500 mg of calcium twice daily (one in the morning and one at bedtime) along with 300 mg of magnesium (taken just once a day). Make sure you also get a supplement with a small amount of vitamin D, as it ensures better absorption. When taken at night, calcium will also help you get a sound sleep.

Together, these essential minerals will keep your bones, teeth, heart, and nervous system strong and healthy, and they'll burn body fat, too.

Step 35: Make Meals a Celebration

You reach for the fresh basil, garlic, tomatoes, and onions and begin to chop and dice like a chef on her own cooking show. The cutting board is flowing with flavorful juices as you slide the mixture down into a bowl. Carefully, you drizzle a touch of extra virgin olive oil over the colorful bounty, and voilà—your meal is taking form. . . .

> **Fat-Burning Secret #18:**
> Calcium and magnesium are essential for burning fat.

Only those who do it, and I mean really do it, can agree that cooking is an art form. Although I'm not a gourmet cook, I believe that preparing meals can be extremely therapeutic and very relaxing. If the idea of cooking dinner tonight overwhelms or depresses you, then it's time to readjust your thinking. Throw away the notion that it's one of those domestic chores that should be avoided at all costs. Cooking a fabulous meal is simply not the same as cleaning a toilet or vacuuming. It's a celebration of life.

Cooking is very different from baking in that you really can't do it incorrectly. Garlic, parsley, basil, oregano, rosemary, and onions can add pizzazz to almost any dish. Sometimes just a dash of red pepper flakes, cayenne pepper, or Tabasco sauce can create a burst of flavor. A little apple or orange juice can add sweetness; and balsamic, cider, or red raspberry vinegars add sparkle to any salad.

Carrots, broccoli, onions, snow peas, peppers, sun-dried tomatoes, mushrooms, and shrimp can become a delicious dish when sautéed with olive oil and garlic. In no time, boneless chicken breast can be mouthwatering when rolled or stuffed with spinach and fat-free ricotta cheese and baked. Lettuce can transform from boring "rabbit food" to a delectable salad with cider vinegar, sprouts, red onions, mandarin oranges, freshly ground pepper, and a sprinkle of walnuts. Within minutes, chickpeas, lemon juice, garlic and plain fat-free yogurt can be pureed into the most fabulous hummus dip. A baked apple with cinnamon and fat-free vanilla yogurt can become the sweetest low-calorie dessert. See, I've given you four days of dinners in one short paragraph! All it takes is a little imagination and love. Yes, *love.*

Food is one of the greatest pleasures in life, and when you learn how to make it taste scrumptious and still keep it low-fat, low-calorie, and low-glycemic, then you, my friend, have discovered how to have your cake and eat it, too.

However, don't forget that cooking a great meal is only the first step toward making a beautiful dinner. Presentation is everything. No matter whom you're cooking for, even if it's just you, set the table properly and eat only there. Forget about your regular old plates; use your finest dishes and glassware because you and your family are worth it. Light a candle, and play some soft music. Dim your lights (every kitchen or dining room should have a dimmer switch. They're simple to install—even I've done it!). Eat in ambiance, always.

Also remember that the people you eat with, and your state of emotions at the time, are as important as the foods you choose. If you're upset or angry when you're eating, you won't digest your food properly, thus inhibiting optimal nutrient metabolism. Remember to take a few minutes before you dine to give thanks for the food you're about to eat and for all the blessings in your life. And finally, chew slowly and savor the flavor.

Kitchens That Cook

The first secret to getting pleasure from cooking is to enjoy your kitchen. That doesn't mean renovations are in order, but a clean, organized area is a must. And since the kitchen is usually the most used room in the house, why not keep it bright and cheerful? Some herbs growing in a pot on your windowsill and fresh flowers in a vase will liven up even the dullest of rooms.

Crystal Andrus

A weekly trip to the grocery store can save time and help you cut back on unnecessary purchases. Before going shopping, take ten minutes to clean out the refrigerator. Throw out any leftovers that will soon have a life of their own, and wipe down all the shelves and drawers. When you get home, put your fruits and vegetables where you'll see them, and recommit to eating some at each meal.

Always make a shopping list, and *never go grocery shopping on an empty stomach!*

Step 36: Keep Up with Your Cardio and Weight Workouts

This week you'll make no changes to your exercise routine. Just keep doing your three to five cardio and three strength-training workouts. You should already be feeling stronger and tighter. If you're having trouble staying motivated to keep exercising, remember that muscle burns body fat. According to expert nutritionist Brad King, creator of the excellent book *Fat Wars*, one pound of muscle can burn up to 50 calories per day. That works out to 18,200 calories per year.

Imagine if you put on 5 pounds of muscles—that means that just by having that extra-lean body, you could lose 250 calories a day or 25 pounds of fat annually. Conversely, you must realize that as you age, you're naturally going to lose muscle—so every time you lose a pound of muscle, you increase your ability to gain five pounds of fat annually. We must defy the signs of aging!

꙳✳꙳

Summary of Week Six: *Fearlessness*

Body:

- Start eating on the 80/20 plan, and become aware of food combining.

- Increase your calcium, and drink at least one glass of green tea daily.

- Keep up with your intense cardio sessions and weight workouts to make your body healthy, lean, and strong.

Mind:

- Make your meals a celebration.

Soul:

- Discover the permanent weight-loss formula for the controlling perfectionist.

Week Seven: *Joy*

Did you ever think you'd last this long on any program? Congratulations for hanging in there. And stay strong!

Step 37: Set Strong Personal Boundaries

This step follows naturally from the last few weeks on facing fears. Now, without guilt or consent, we must make ourselves a priority and live *our* lives. Many of us are programmed to believe that we're selfish or thoughtless if we take care of our own needs. We struggle with all we have to do, and we're resentful and running on empty most of the time, yet we refuse to do something proactive to change it. Well, one thing that can help is setting reasonable personal boundaries.

Establishing limits is necessary in every relationship: We'll get along better with everyone—including co-workers, friends, and family—when we each acknowledge and respect each other's choices and preferences. Without them, marriages crumble, friendships are ruined, and children become rude and impertinent. And, when we lack personal boundaries, we can wound our spirit by mistreating our bodies with excessive food, drugs, alcohol, or meaningless sex.

I find it funny that, in many respects, we women are no better off now than we used to be . . . which can't be what the feminist movement had in mind. Equality, choice, and freedom of expression were what our mothers and grandmothers fought for—not depletion, depression, and divorce. Many of us forget that it was only 50 years ago that women had absolutely no forum to voice their opinions.

I recently read an article from 1955 that I thought had to be some kind of joke, since it said, "The man is the master of the home. He can come and go as he pleases, and the woman has no right to question his judgment or integrity. She should always know her place." In disbelief, I continued to read this serious essay, which assured women that their goal in life should be to make their homes a place of peace, order, and tranquility, one where their *husbands* could renew themselves in body and spirit. And I was struck by one realization: *Imagine the messages our mothers heard while growing up.*

When I tell women to start making themselves a priority, many feel as though I've added one more task to their already daunting to-do list. However, this one is necessary if we want a joyous and fulfilling life. We have to refuse to be martyrs and victims and stop trying to have it all—all at the same time.

Try the following statements on for size:

- "No, I can't iron your shirt ten minutes before you leave, but later when you have time, I'll teach you how to do it yourself."

- "Sorry that you left your gym shoes at home for the fifth week, but I'm not driving them to you."

- "I'm sorry that you don't like me going to the gym, but I love how it makes me feel. I won't be gone long!"

Instead, too many women live their lives with this mentality:

- "I *should* teach him how to iron, but it's just easier to do it myself."

- "I *should* make you walk home and get your shoes, but what would the teacher think! I'll be there in five minutes. Be ready!"

Crystal Andrus

- "I would love to work out, but I *should* get home. I feel guilty for leaving them as much as I do!"

Oh, the dreaded curse of the "shoulds"!

Shoulds lead to guilt, which leads to sacrifice. Sacrifice creates a willing victim . . . a martyr. Wants lead to choice, which leads to self-respect, and that is the only true pathway to self-love.

You see, it's just like when the mask drops down if oxygen levels get too low on an airplane. You're instructed to put your own mask on first before helping your child. If *you* aren't okay, you're useless to everyone else. If *you* aren't living the life you want, eventually everything else will fall apart anyway.

Are you afraid of losing your job if you say no to working overtime, or of hurting someone's feelings if you tell the truth? Maybe you're actually afraid of being physically abused if you stand up for yourself. Are you afraid to be your own person, with your own opinions? Do you feel in charge of your choices right now? Are you happy with the ones you're making? If you aren't, then you need to realize that only you can improve your life. Only you can decide to set stronger limits.

But we'll only make changes in our lives if we believe those changes will be safe and beneficial. You need to see how much you're losing out on by not respecting your needs. There's no need to blame anyone for your present situation or past circumstances. This isn't about feeling sorry for yourself or being angry at someone who's done you wrong. As the great writer and psychologist Florida Scott-Maxwell wrote at the age of 84: "You need to claim the events in your life to make yourself yours. When you truly possess all you have been and done, which may take some time, you are fierce with reality."

If you can't set stronger boundaries without feeling afraid or resentful, then ask yourself, "Why am I filled with so much guilt? Why am I so afraid to say no? Why do I equate being a martyr with being loved and valuable?"

If you're going to do things for others, do it with a willing spirit! If you can't do it with love and joy, then you're really not helping anyone at all!

Soon you'll happily accept that setting boundaries isn't about negating other people's feelings; rather, it's about understanding their fears and not owning them as yours. It means being strong about your wants and needs, and being firm but loving in the way you execute them.

※

Whenever one of my clients blames her husband for her unhappiness and resentment, I ask her to be totally honest and ask herself: "Is it truthfully my spouse who's held me back, or am I really unhappy with myself? Did he force me to put my dreams on hold, or would he have supported me if I'd just gone ahead and pursued them? Do I honestly think that he would have divorced or abused me, or have I been so afraid to really step it up for my life that I've used him as the excuse for not seizing my potential? What am I *really* afraid of?"

Most often we realize that as long as we can blame someone else, we don't have to be accountable for our own choices. This is the ultimate way we give our power away. Perhaps you thought that you'd appear to be a better woman if you put your family's needs way beyond your own—but in the process, you've repressed yourself. And when you blame your husband for your unhappiness (even if he's controlling), you're really just feeling angry at yourself for not setting stronger boundaries and for not claiming your own life. You set your relationship up to get what you thought you deserved from it. But it's never too late to change! Even if you don't think you can "teach an old dog new tricks," you must try!

I think most of us don't really even give our husbands a chance to know this new version of us. We don't think they could deal with us, and in all truth, many of us are so exhausted and tired of fighting that we're just not prepared to try, so we continue to hide our truths, and in the end we prevent them from growing with us! We then end up robbing ourselves.

Setting boundaries is simply about deciding that you have one life and that you deserve the best. You should be able to express yourself easily and feel a sense of power over your choices, which might mean saying, "I love you, but this is what I have to do in order to feel good about myself. This is who I am." There's only one of you in this world; and no one can tell you how you should live, look, act, or feel.

But there's a catch. Being "who I am" can't become an excuse whenever you don't want to face your responsibilities or live with integrity and values. Don't misinterpret setting boundaries: You can't neglect your duties, run away from your responsibilities, and become selfish and thoughtless. The excuse "This is who I am—too bad!" *isn't* an excuse. Be yourself, but be your very best self. The way to do so is to get to know yourself, which is what you're doing by following this program. To thine own self be true!

This week I want you to think about any conversations your spirit knows you need to have, or maybe a letter you need to write. Are there those whom you've allowed to disrespect, take advantage, or disempower you? Are you willing to explain to them, *with grace, dignity, and firmness*, what you need, want, and won't live without? This isn't about blaming them; it's about honoring yourself. Only *you* can do this for you. They may not like what they hear at first, but I guarantee that when you speak with "I" statements (I am _____, I feel _____, I need _____, I want _____) rather than "You" statements (You are _____, You need _____, You must _____) they will eventually understand that this is about self-respect and love, not about control and blame.

Honor their spirit by honoring yours! In the end, you will all be better people for it! A little tough love can go a long way!

How Do We Maintain Joy When Some Days We Can't Even Smile?

Over the last six weeks, we've been talking about tapping into our internal source of power whenever we feel unsure, afraid, or even "unhappy." Although we all want to live with authentic joy, sometimes it's very difficult to achieve. We've closed our eyes, taken a deep breath, and perhaps even called on God for patience, and we're still ready to scream at the top of our lungs. Angry, frustrated, or maybe insecure, we feel virtually on the edge of "losing it." We wonder why we felt so great yesterday, while today we're in the dumps; or why only last week we thought our body was looking pretty good, but now we feel worse than ever. Three weeks ago we loved our mate more than anyone in the world, and being a mother was the greatest role in life—but suddenly, if we have to make one more meal or tie one more shoe, we feel as if we're going to die.

This is a struggle for all of us— it's part of the human condition. No one is exuberant all the time: We have hormones and a fluctuating chemical makeup. Sometimes we're exhausted, or maybe we've gone too long without eating. Some of us are dealing with

Step 38: Remember the Basics in Your Search for Joy

Needs are very different from wants, and although I've heard of monks and priests who deny themselves basic comforts in the quest for total spiritual enlightenment, most of us need food, sleep, and love before we can even begin the process of living in a state of authentic joy.

Get Enough to Eat

Not many people can be exuberant when they're famished. Whenever I think that maybe food isn't a necessity in our pursuit of joy, I look at what happens to my normally happy children when their little bellies need to be filled.

We all need to eat to feel strong emotionally and physically, and although I do feel that a three-day juice fast once or twice a year is essential for optimal health, consistently going too long between meals can not only lead us to bingeing, but it also leaves us feeling shaky, miserable, and joyless. (Isn't it ironic that too much food can bring us so much misery, yet too little means that we'll die?)

Take inventory this week, and make sure that you're getting your four meals and two snacks every day, and not going more than four hours without eating. If necessary, take another look at a typical day of eating in Week One. Do *your* days tend to look like this?

Get Enough Sleep

Ask any mother with a newborn baby how jubilant she feels after many nights of little or no sleep. I remember when my children were babies, thinking, *I love my kids so much. Why do I feel unhappy?* Well, I was exhausted most of the time! In fact, I think a lack of sleep played a bigger part in my frustrations than postpartum depression did.

The average adult requires seven to eight hours of uninterrupted sleep every night—are

colicky babies, small children, aging parents, or sick loved ones, and that wears us down. We might have financial stress, relationship problems, or health concerns, and gobbling down a greasy hamburger or chugging back a cold beer seems like the best solution.

Working with women for so many years, I've come to realize that although we're certainly complicated creatures, the truth is that life isn't that complicated . . . we just make it that way. I believe that most of our unhappiness comes from within. We exist in a reactive state, allowing everything around us to affect our mood: the traffic, a cranky boss, a demanding child, or a piece of chocolate cake calling out our name. Our attitude determines our state of emotions— we feel bad, so things must be bad. And we don't stop ourselves quickly enough to change our perceptions.

It doesn't matter how far we've come in our journey of self-discovery; it takes daily effort to create an inner dialogue that's unshakable, undeniable, and limitless. Those of us who are successful have trained our minds, in the same way we've trained our bodies, to conquer our fears and feel confidence, joy, and inner peace. This mental training begins by simply deciding that we'll stop reacting to exterior events. It's a choice! No longer will we declare our inadequacy, jealousy, dependency, or fear as though we have no control over it. We must stop overdramatizing. Nothing is ever as bad as it seems.

Whenever I'm in a situation where I feel that I must immediately take action, I try to remember a story I heard a few years ago. In the Mafia, where life-or-death decisions are sometimes made, a three-day waiting period must always be respected before any hit can happen, even if the "godfather" commands it. I don't know if this is really true. I mean, I don't know anyone in the mob, and it sounds sort of funny, but I always try to remember the "three-day waiting rule" when I'm about to call someone or fire off an e-mail at someone who's upset me. Instead, I give myself a cooling-down period—and, inevitably, by thinking it through, I'm relieved that I didn't react hastily.

Things always work out, so why do we put ourselves through so much unnecessary inner turmoil and stress? Why are we so afraid of the outcome of a situation, and why do we keep reaching for the chips or chocolate every time we feel upset?

you getting enough? A lack of sleep will increase your susceptibility to illness, and is frequently linked to car crashes and industrial accidents. It will make you irritable, exhausted, and even depressed. Sleep is also the time that our anti-aging hormone (HGH) is released. Without deep sleep, we're inhibiting our HGH, thus speeding up the aging process.

Some common reasons for not sleeping well may include:

- An uncomfortable bed or pillow
- Noise
- Physical discomfort
- Caffeine or ephedrine
- Alcohol or drugs
- Anxiety or worry
- Fluctuations in our hormones

Before rushing off to the doctor for sleeping pills, make some changes in your nighttime environment and routine. If your bed is uncomfortable, try putting a board under the mattress or adding a piece of soft foam on top of it. Switch your pillow if yours is too hard or too soft. When a noisy neighborhood is your problem, block the outside racket by playing serene music or tapes that mimic ocean waves, waterfalls, or tropical rain. You could even try wearing earplugs for a quiet night's sleep. Cut back on coffee, colas, and chocolate to reduce caffeine; and be aware of anything containing ephedrine, as it will speed up your heart rate. Don't take a hot bath or shower just before bed, as this actually increases alertness. Go to bed and get up at the same time each day and stick to that routine, even on weekends and during vacations.

If you find that it takes you longer than ten minutes to fall asleep once your head hits the pillow, you may have anxiety or excessive worry. Use the relaxation techniques that we talked about earlier (or try my relaxation CD, available at **www.simplywoman. com**). Consult a naturopath about trying the supplement melatonin, or try an herb such as valerian root (which can be found in your local natural-foods store) that can help you fall asleep. Talk to a friend about your concerns, or write in your journal before going to bed to help relax your active mind. If you feel overwhelmed by your workload, take five minutes before you go to bed and make a list of everything you need to get done the next day. Even just reading a good book (like this one!) for 20 minutes before falling asleep can ease your mind.

You can also try sweating yourself to sleep. Many studies have shown that regular aerobic or strength training can help improve the quality of your sleep cycle. You'll get the best effects from exercising in the morning, as I hope you're already doing. In any event, don't do vigorous cardio exercise within two hours of going to bed, as it can have the opposite effect and keep you awake. If you must exercise in the evening, do your stretching then. In addition, you may find that you have trouble sleeping at various times of the month: Progesterone promotes sleep; and levels of this hormone plunge during menstruation, causing insomnia; and rise during ovulation, causing drowsiness.

If a lack of sleep is affecting your daily routine and/or causing depression, please seek help from a medical doctor. You honestly can't feel joyous about life when you're depleted and drained.

Get the Love You Need

Do you have love in your life? Real love? It's one of the most important needs we all have. There's the love of a good friend, the love of our children, the love of our family, God's love, and of course, a lover's love! I had one client tell me that she didn't believe in passionate love. After digging deeper, she revealed to me that although she and her husband got along really well, she couldn't remember the last time they'd made love.

Gerontologists are scientists who predict longevity, and they use a standard by which they can make certain assumptions about how long we'll live. They've discovered that the number one factor that retards aging is a fulfilling, long-term relationship. As well as contributing to our well-being, I honestly believe that love makes life feel magical.

One of the most important decisions you can make—one that will directly impact your long-term happiness and success—is choosing the person you spend your life with. With the right partner at your side, you'll feel stronger and more confident. Those who really love you will want you to be your very best and to live a life true to yourself.

As you continue on your journey this week, I want you to think about the people you love the most. Have you told them lately? Have you hugged them tightly and waited until they let go first? Don't be afraid to show your love. This whole big thing called "life" is really all about the love we give and receive.

Step 39: Cut Back on Alcohol

I know how wonderful a glass of wine can sound at the end of a long, stressful day, but it may actually be your worst enemy. Alcohol is a depressant—not only with respect to your mood and energy level, but also your metabolism. It dehydrates your body, causing water retention; is very aging; and packs on the pounds quickly.

Alcohol depletes your body of vitamins C and B-complex, plus it's deadly to the liver. Women are more likely than men to develop cirrhosis and other liver-related diseases, and because it isn't as socially acceptable, women aren't as likely to reach out for help. Drinking too much alcohol is often an indicator of an emotional issue before it becomes a dependency or abuse problem. However, the Texas Commission on Alcohol and Drug Abuse found that even though nearly as many women are addicted as men, only 28 percent of rehab clients consist of women. We're also more likely than men to use prescription medicines with alcohol, which can be very dangerous, and studies indicate that even moderate drinking can increase the risk of breast cancer.

While alcohol doesn't affect blood-sugar levels, it *is* very calorie dense (having almost twice as many calories per gram as protein and other carbohydrates), so try to drink it only on your treat day. For example, wine has about 70 to 75 calories per 3.5-ounce serving; however, many wineglasses hold about 5 ounces. Just as a rough estimate, if each glass holds 100 calories of wine, and you drank three glasses daily, that would add up to 109,500 calories over a year. Since 3,500 calories equals one pound of fat, that amounts to 31 pounds of fat on your body in a year.

Now, you may not drink three glasses each day, but alcohol calories add up just like any other calories do. Limit alcoholic drinks to no more than one a day—or, better yet, have them only on your treat day. Stick with red wine, as it's the best choice thanks to its benefits for the heart; and avoid wine coolers, creamy cocktails, and sweet liquors that are loaded with sugar and calories. The following chart gives the approximate calorie count of some common drinks.

Type	Serving	Calories
Beer	12 oz.	150
Light beer	12 oz.	100
Wine coolers	12 oz.	220
White wine	3.5 oz.	80
Red wine	3.5 oz.	75
Pina colada	12 oz.	320
Strawberry daiquiri	12 oz.	300
Spirits: gin, vodka, rum	1.5 oz.	100

Fat-Burning Secret #19:
Avoid alcohol! It slows down your metabolism and decreases your willpower (you're more likely to snack during or after drinking). Plus, calories from alcohol add up quickly.

Step 40: Make Smart Choices When Eating in Restaurants

Oh, I know this can be a tough one! But by learning what the best restaurant selections are, you can still maintain your 80/20 plan and enjoy a lunch or dinner out. However, if you're really hungry, eat a little something before going out. (It's just like grocery shopping on an empty stomach—everything looks so appetizing when you're starving.) And this is where Step 39 really comes into play: When you drink in a restaurant, not only are you wasting calories that could go toward your meal, but you're also very likely lowering your willpower. One glass of wine with dinner could turn into two, and when the server offers dessert, it's "Ah, what the heck . . . I'm going for it!"

Crystal Andrus

If you're having appetizers, go for a fresh shrimp cocktail or a basic salad with vinegar or a low-fat dressing on the side. Avoid most house dressings or Caesar salads, as they're loaded with fat. Pass on anything fried or high in carbohydrates, and I also suggest that you ask the waiter to leave the garlic bread or rolls that accompany many appetizers in the kitchen. Having them in front of you is just too tempting. Do ask for water, though, and keep your glass filled up.

When selecting entrees, stick to low-fat protein and vegetables. The best choices are grilled chicken with salad; and baked, broiled, or grilled fish and vegetables. Send word to the chef to avoid using any oil or butter, and to replace potatoes or pasta side dishes with a salad. If you explain that you're on a special diet, most restaurants will accommodate you. If you're intent on having pasta, choose red or marinara sauces rather than creamy, white sauces such as Alfredo.

Remember your portion sizes: Half a cup of pasta is considered one serving, and many restaurant servings can be as much as three cups. So when you know you're going out at night, eat fewer starchy carbohydrates (even the Green Light starches) during the day to accommodate a larger meal at dinner.

When eating in restaurants, you don't have much control over how much fat the restaurant might sneak in while cooking to make your food taste better, so control what you can.

Fast Food

Eating in restaurants usually affords you the opportunity to request variations on what's on the menu, but what about when you want to grab a bite on the go? It's still all about choices.

Let's look at an average meal at McDonald's: A Big Mac contains 600 calories and 33 fat grams (11 of them saturated). Add a large fries for another 520 calories and 25 fat grams (4.5 saturated), a large Coke (310 calories), and an M&M McFlurry, with 630 calories and 23 fat grams (15 saturated) for dessert, and the total comes to 2,060 calories and 81 grams of fat, including more than 30 saturated fat grams, *in one meal*. Normally, I might eat that much saturated fat over the course of two weeks!

How could you do it differently? Well, a McDonald's Grilled Chicken Caesar Salad has 200 calories and only six fat grams (three of them saturated). If you're really craving fries, a small size will add another 220 calories and 11 grams of fat (2 saturated). Add a Diet Coke for zero calories, and for a treat have a Fruit 'n' Yogurt Parfait, with 160 calories and two fat grams (one saturated). Your meal is 580 calories and 19 grams of fat; a difference of almost 1,500 calories and 62 fat grams!

McDonald's is no exception. There are smart and poor choices to be made at almost every fast-food restaurant—so just ask for their nutrition guides. Many establishments also post nutrition guides online, so you can look them up and make your choices before you even get to the restaurant. You can find nutritional guides for many fast-food chains on one Website: **www.dietfacts. com/fastfood.asp**.

Making Trade-Offs

Knowing the bottom line regarding calories in versus calories out also means that if you're planning a night on the town (and it isn't your treat day), you can reduce your calories during that day to allow for more at dinner. A low-calorie breakfast and lunch will leave you extra calories to enjoy a bigger dinner. Taking this further (and this is definitely not from my "healthy-eating archives"), if you're planning to have a few drinks, make up for all these calories by reducing your food intake. But be *very careful,* since two glasses of wine on an empty stomach will affect you quickly! And never do this if you're driving.

Crystal Andrus

Now you may think, *Aha! I could trade off calories all the time and still lose weight.* Wrong! Calories are not created equal, so if you do this too often, you'll begin to shut down your oil-burning furnace (your metabolism), and that big dinner or few glasses of wine will land right on your hips.

Step 41: Take Chromium

More than 90 percent of North Americans are deficient in chromium. What does this mean? Well, if you experience uncontrollable cravings for sweets, have an apple-shaped body (where you tend to gain weight through the middle), or have periods of fatigue or irritability throughout the day, you're probably insulin-resistant, hypoglycemic, and deficient in chromium. You already know about reducing your carbohydrate intake, especially by eliminating sugars and sweets—now give yourself a boost by supplementing your diet with chromium.

This element is commonly used in weight-loss programs because it promotes an increase in lean muscle, and as you know, muscle by its very existence burns body fat. Chromium helps insulin regulate blood-sugar levels, which helps you burn stored body fat and stabilize your appetite between meals. It also improves glucose tolerance by increasing insulin's efficiency.

Chromium is found in oysters, chicken, eggs, apples, parsnips, spinach, and broccoli; it's also available in many effective fat-burning supplements, or you can take it on its own. But be careful, as the body only needs a small amount—an excess may inhibit rather than enhance its wonderful properties.

If you're going to supplement your diet, take an extra 400 mcg of chromium daily. If you're already taking a multivitamin, check the amount of chromium in it, and never exceed more than 1,000 mcg daily.

> **Fat-Burning Secret #20:**
> Regulate your blood-sugar levels, burn stored body fat, and reduce carbohydrate cravings by adding 400 mcg of chromium to your diet each day.

Step 42: Don't Eat Before Bedtime

It's simple: Don't do it! Late-night eating is a bad habit that you've just got to break. Good habits take time to form, just as bad ones are hard to quit. Now, you may have gotten used to the feeling of falling asleep on a full belly, but there's nothing worse for a good night's rest. Eating before bed inhibits the release of your natural anti-aging growth hormone, and you'll end up storing these calories as fat. Your metabolism naturally begins to slow down in the evening to get ready for sleep; therefore, too much food in the evening, even if you haven't eaten much all day, won't be utilized effectively, so this increases your chance of storing it as fat.

Step 43: Discover the Healing Power of Garlic

> **Fat-Burning Secret #21:**
> Don't eat within two to three hours of bedtime.

Medical researchers are finally acknowledging garlic's incredible effects on the heart and arteries, and we now know that its powerful antibiotic and anticancer agents elevate this herb into a league of its own. Garlic lowers blood pressure, cholesterol, and triglycerides (fats) in the blood, raising the protective (HDL) fraction of total cholesterol while reducing the susceptibility of the harmful (LDL) fraction, and it inhibits blood clotting by reducing the tendency of platelets to clump together.

Garlic boosts the immune system, acting like a natural antibiotic; inactivates some of the carcinogens that people ingest; and protects DNA from damage, offering other protection from

Crystal Andrus

cancer as well. It's also a strong antiseptic, counteracting the growth of many kinds of bacteria and fungi that can cause disease. Perhaps the truth behind the lower incidences of coronary disease in Spain and Italy could be due to their high consumption of garlic.

Pills, powders, or other dried forms of garlic aren't nearly effective as the whole, fresh herb, though. I simply suggest that you eat more fresh garlic every day. Try cooking with fresh or freshly bottled, chopped garlic. Adding a clove (or one teaspoon if it's freshly bottled) to many recipes will not only enhance their flavor, but can be just enough to strengthen your immune and cardiovascular systems. If the smell is offensive, try peeling a whole clove and swallowing it with a little flaxseed oil at bedtime.

Simply . . . Tips!

- Eat the majority of your carbs before 3 P.M.

- Have a small, high-protein dinner, and don't eat within three hours of bedtime.

- Drink herbal tea if you get hungry at night.

- Go to bed earlier than normal if it's really tough for you not to eat late at night.

- Give up TV if you snack while you watch.

- Brush your teeth immediately after dinner.

- Don't go in the kitchen late at night if it's too tempting.

- Don't keep snacks or junk food in the house, as this will make it difficult for you to snack when you're feeling weak. (You wouldn't tell an alcoholic to keep booze in the house, right?)

Step 44: *Decrease Your Intake of Artificial Sweeteners*

We haven't talked much about artificial sweeteners yet, but most nutritionists are dead set against the consumption of them because of the chemicals they contain. Although research hasn't provided clear evidence of an association between artificial sweeteners and human cancer, animal studies have linked aspartame (Equal and NutraSweet) with brain tumors and central nervous system cancers, saccharin (Sweet'N Low) with the development of bladder cancer, and sucralose (Splenda) with negative effects on the thymus gland. The FDA has denied these reports, claiming that these artificial sweeteners are safe for humans to consume in "moderate amounts" (the key word being *moderate*).

Here's my take on them: Ingested in high amounts, artificial sweeteners may be lethal for the body; however, large amounts of sugar are seriously harmful, too! The ideal is to eliminate both.

When you're used to consuming junk food and soda, it can be very hard to give up the sweetness that you've become addicted to. I admit that going from regular sweetened yogurt to plain is tough. A little diet Jell-O (sweetened with aspartame or sucralose) can do wonders for a sugar craving in the beginning, while a diet cream soda at night can take away many a dieter's jitters. I understand the need for them as you are making lifestyle changes; however, eliminating them—or anything containing them—is advisable!

Given the option, I'd always choose sucralose (Splenda) over aspartame (Equal), as it appears that the former is the safest artificial sweetener for the body. It seems to present far fewer hazards than aspartame, yet I'd still consider it a Yellow Light food.

There are only three types of Green Light sweeteners: one is stevia, an herb that's 300 times sweeter than sugar, yet it has no calories or glycemic response, and can be found at your local health-food store. The other two, of course, are the naturally occurring sugars *fructose* (not to be confused with harmful high-fructose corn syrup), which comes from fruits (using apple sauce is ideal

Crystal Andrus

for baking!); and *lactose,* which is found in dairy products (many people have an allergy to this sugar, however).

Yellow Light "natural sweeteners" that I recommend in tiny amounts are pure honey, blackstrap molasses, and pure maple syrup.

Two weeks from now, you're going to try an amazing detoxification program that can shed pounds and make you feel lighter physically, mentally, and even emotionally. Part of that detoxing will consist of completely eliminating sugar (sucrose, glucose) and artificial sweeteners. So begin to decrease your intake now, if you haven't already.

Don't get stressed out if you do occasionally consume artificial sweeteners, but, on the other hand, don't fill up on tons of it. Switch to natural sweeteners such as stevia—or even better, eat foods in their natural state and you won't need to worry about sugar or sweeteners at all. You'll be shocked at how wonderful food tastes without all the "stuff" we've been programmed to believe it needs! In no time at all, your *true* tastebuds will wake back up, and processed "anything" will taste acidic and unappetizing!

Step 45: Become a Cardio Queen

Girlfriend, if you're not shedding the pounds, it's time to become a cardio queen!

My client Kelly was shocked after she lost 15 pounds in our first three weeks together. After exercising for more than eight months with weights but not losing a single pound, she decided that it was time to hire a personal trainer. Her old program included about 15 to 20 minutes of moderate-intensity cardio two to three times a week, and I knew we had to increase this immediately. Within our second week together, I'd reduced the time on the weight equipment and boosted her time, intensity, and frequency on the treadmill. The fat started falling off Kelly at a rate of six pounds a week!

Are you doing your optimal amount of cardio? Regardless of how many times you've been doing it up until now, you need to increase it to six times a week from now on, at a hard intensity of 40 to 45 minutes. While you're shaping and sculpting those muscles, you have to burn the fat, too, so cut back on your carbs and increase your cardio. It works!

Summary of Week Seven: *Joy*

Body:

- Reduce body fat by cutting back on alcohol and taking 400 mcg of chromium daily.

- Replace artificial sweeteners with natural sweeteners, and discover the healing power of garlic.

- Become a cardio queen!

Mind:

- Remember the basics—food, sleep, and love—in your search for joy.

- Make smart choices when eating in restaurants.

Soul:

- Set strong personal boundaries.

Week Eight: *Forgiveness*

This is it . . . Week Eight—it's full-speed ahead from here on in! Each day your transformation is taking effect. Buddha taught that attaining happiness and enlightenment depends upon one's own efforts. Effort, in fact, is the root of all achievement. If you want to get to the top of a mountain, just sitting at the foot thinking about it won't get you there. Only by making the effort to actually climb the mountain, step-by-step, will you ever reach the summit.

Step 46: *Let Go of the Past in Order to Move Forward*

If you've been faithfully sticking to this program, congratulations! This is *your* success, and no one can take it away from you. Walk proud. Hold your head high. Tuck your stomach in and

Simply . . . Inspirational!

Yvette came to see me just before she turned 50. After working out in the gym for eight years, she weight 158 pounds—she was frustrated and couldn't understand why she wasn't making more progress. While Yvette didn't lack motivation or willpower, she did have inaccurate information and was eating all the wrong foods. She thought that looking and feeling great was about working *hard*—but she discovered that it was about working *smart*.

Only two weeks into the program, Yvette had lost five pounds and some inches. By the end of the 12 weeks, she'd lost 30 pounds and had gone from a size 12 to a size 5. As she stepped on the scale and saw that her weight had dropped for the first time in years, tears rolled down her face.

More important, today she reports having more energy and confidence than she's ever had before. "My husband and I are like newlyweds, and I have a new excitement for life," she says. And she's more attractive now than she's ever been—in fact, a year after completing the *Simply . . . Woman!* program, she went on a trip to Cuba and sent me a photo of herself on the beach in a bikini!

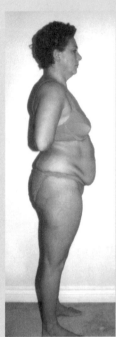 

Yvette before starting the program.

After 12 weeks on the program.

On the beach in Cuba.

throw your shoulders back. Be proud of yourself—don't put a dimmer on your own light or try to downplay how great you feel. This accomplishment is truly your own. You're becoming the woman you've always wanted to be.

Yet, know that this journey will never end: As you reach your goals, new ones will appear. Just when you think you have it all figured out, you'll realize that you have so much more to learn. I'm constantly in search of knowledge, wisdom, and guidance; and I love that moment when I learn something new. I understand that although I've come so far, I still have a long way to go.

As you travel along your own path, may you always be searching for the truth about who you are and what you need to do for yourself. Never allow yourself to feel *less than* anyone else, and never allow anyone to make you feel silly, self-righteous, or even conceited for wanting to be the best you can be. Self-acceptance and love are not about being the best, but rather, being *your* best. It's about knowing that you alone are enough.

Not Doing So Well?

If you're holding on to your weight and are struggling with demanding the most out of yourself, it's time to ask yourself why. Does focusing on your perceived faults distract you from your real problems, *the ones you haven't forced yourself to deal with yet?* Do you not think that you're deserving of an amazing and healthy body? Maybe it's easier to keep the life and body you have because even though you know you aren't completely happy, doing something about it means stepping out of your comfort zone. Perhaps it's easier in your mind to complain and stay complacent than to force yourself to create the life you really want. Maybe you're afraid of what that life might bring.

Exercising and eating healthfully is about so much more than looking better—they're metaphors for life. Going for a walk or a jog is about standing on your own two feet, knowing that no one but you is going to get you where you want to go. Each and every time you work out, you're building your confidence and strength to handle other things that life will deal you. For example, many times when I'm out on a long run, I feel so empowered and strong. As I'm heading back home, I always compare it to any of life's problems. Here I am, all alone, counting on myself, knowing that each small step is bringing me closer to my goal. I always tell myself, "If I can do this, I can do anything."

If you're not making the necessary changes to achieve your goals, you need to figure out why you're holding yourself back. Self-sabotage is your pattern of action when you don't feel worthy of a positive potential outcome. Since feeling let down and disappointed are emotions you've become accustomed to, it becomes "the devil you know is better than the devil you don't know" theory. No matter how discontent you are, you stay in your comfort zone.

Many of us work hard at forgetting and erasing our past, pretending that the tough times we've been through no longer affect us, yet some of us have deep scars that keep us stuck, without even realizing it. Everything we've been through has made us who we are today. Good times and bad are a part of who we are, and we've established beliefs and created patterns based on our experiences.

The past doesn't have to predetermine our future if we can learn from it. It doesn't mean dredging up painful memories to feel awful all over again; instead, we should try to understand and find the wisdom that each experience offers.

What fears have you formed, and how many layers have you built up to protect you? You won't move forward and begin treating yourself with love and respect until you deal with the pain that's keeping you stuck. If, as a child or teenager, you felt the searing pain of abuse, neglect, abandonment, withholding, or any other hurt, you must face it, look within, and discover what fear you've developed and what actions you continue to take to avoid that feeling or

Crystal Andrus

situation ever again. By denying yourself the freedom to enjoy the life or body that you dream of, you're continuing to abuse, neglect, or withhold love from yourself. You're not living at 100 percent of your potential—you're holding yourself back.

Only *you* know what you've gone through, and only you know if you've faced your demons and dealt with them. If your parents caused you pain, where is that manifesting itself? If someone has hurt or abused you, do you blame yourself in any capacity for why or how it happened? Do you fear letting people get close emotionally, or do you discard relationships easily? Do you grow bored easily with jobs or friendships? Are you sensitive and paranoid that others are upset with you, or do you overdramatize situations? These are all signs that you have deep emotional pain tucked away; and until you face it *and release it,* you'll continue to sabotage yourself, your relationships, and your success.

ฯ✻ฯ

I know only too well what it's like to try so hard to get the approval and love we desperately need from our parents. I don't want to hurt my family by sharing all that's gone on in our lives, but to sum it up: I spent too many years in too much pain. I was so smart and could logically make sense of just about anything, yet I could never figure out what was wrong with me.

As I began to face my fears, I discovered that I was terrified of being alone because being alone meant being unlovable. I looked within and uncovered the unconscious messages that I'd been sending myself, and I realized that my core beliefs didn't line up with my logical beliefs. The truth is that I didn't even know what I wanted or what made me happy because I'd spent so much time trying to make others happy, and their happiness made me feel sort of loved . . . sort of important . . . sort of needed . . . sort of worthy. On the surface I looked happy, but deep down I wondered why I couldn't make my own family love me, and no one could fill that void.

Crystal Andrus

Logically, you probably know all this, too, but are you innately embracing that you're truly *not* messed up? Just remember that a weak or unstable woman would never have gotten to Week Eight of this program. I don't know what you've been through in your life—what matters more is that it made you the woman you are today. The searching and struggling you may be going through now means that you're ready to rise above your past.

When I perceive God, I imagine love in its highest, purest form. Some of today's spiritual teachers call this "consciousness." All things are formed from consciousness. We are a part of that consciousness—a part of God. When we realize that God is within all of us, connecting all of our spirits, we discover that we're never alone and that we're absolutely lovable and perfect, even if those who are supposed to love us the most don't realize it.

The greatest gifts parents can give their children are roots and wings: roots to keep us grounded, and wings to let us fly. Maybe the birds have it all figured out. They nurture and feed their chicks until one day Momma bird says, "It's time." She pushes her little chick up to the edge of the nest and nudges him out. She's done all she knows how to do, and now it's time for that bird to fly out into the world. If the chick can't fly, there's nothing else the mother can do. If he's going to make it, it's up to him to soar. That chick can't go back and yell at his mother for not teaching him enough to make it in the world. If he doesn't find the resources to survive, he'll die.

If your parents couldn't show you the love, affection, tenderness, warmth, and role modeling that you desperately needed, understand that it has nothing to do with you. We're all victims of victims, and our parents couldn't possibly teach us things that *they* never received. I mean, if your mother doesn't know how to love herself, how could she teach it to you? Or if your father came from an abusive family, how could he pass down love and high self-esteem to you? Can you think about your parents or anyone that you may feel hurt by as mere children, innocent and young? What messages were they told growing up? What pain did they experience? They only did what they knew, even if they may have made mistakes. They were only human, and no matter how monstrous those mistakes may have been, as an adult, you have no choice but to heal yourself by forgiving them.

Your forgiveness must also carry over into any other hurtful relationship you've had in your life, from boyfriends, spouses, siblings, friends, business associates, in-laws, teachers, grandparents, or anyone you feel has hurt you. Festering pain builds into resentment, which slowly kills you—body, mind, and soul. The only way to move forward in life is to forgive those who have hurt you, stranger or friend. Forgiveness means wiping the slate clean, *deleting the recycle bin permanently.* I know that this is one of the hardest lessons to accept, but forgiveness doesn't mean sweeping things under the carpet and moving on. It means completely releasing the resentment you harbor. (Ah, but isn't this the hardest thing to do?)

Many people simply can't forgive; they won't allow themselves to. They truly believe that their pain is too deep to let go of. Others can forgive but they can't forget. *Both cause deep, decaying resentment.*

The Power of Your Choices

Some women hold on to their pain because it allows them to blame others when they make poor choices; that is, they choose to stay stuck because it gives them justification for their fears. Others love to feel sorry for themselves: "Do you know what I've been through? Do you have any idea how much I've been hurt in my life?" Living in pain becomes their comfort zone, so they thrive on crisis and drama to prevent anyone from getting close enough. In fairness, you may be in terrible pain and your wounds are still raw. The notion of forgiving someone who's just ripped your heart out is something that may even infuriate you, but please stay with me on this one. . . .

Forgiveness isn't intended to mend anyone else or to say, "It's okay to abuse me." Instead, its purpose is to help *you* move forward to find new joy and love. Your "held-on-to pain," no matter how justified, only hurts *you*. Only you know if you're ready to make the choice to live authentically. You can choose to be angry and resentful, or you can choose to be loving and forgiving. It's up to you.

Now, finding forgiveness is very much like facing your fears: It appears much harder than it actually is. I'd like you to get out your journal and make a list of all the people who have hurt you. Begin with the one who has caused you the most pain; the one who comes to mind first. Take out a pen and paper—not your journal—and write this person a letter. Express how you feel, and the feelings of hurt you've experienced. Explain what he or she has done to your ability to trust in the world, *and in yourself.* Write, write, write. And when you're done, burn it. Yes! You must burn it!

As you watch that paper burning, visualize this person standing in front of you and say aloud, "I forgive you, _____ [say his or her name]. I don't understand why you did what you did, but I do know that no one comes into this world with the intent to hurt. I forgive you, in the same way that I hope that those who I've hurt or may unintentionally hurt will forgive me. [Say the person's name again] _____, you did what you did because of some pain or fear inside of you. I haven't walked in your shoes, nor can you ever walk in mine, but holding on to you—holding on to this story . . . this memory—is hurting me too much, and it's time I set myself free. [Say his or her name again] _____, I forgive you, and I set you free."

Throughout the week, become mindful of the power of your choices every time you start drifting back to negative thoughts about this person. Stop yourself, and instead repeat (even just to yourself), "I forgive you, _____ [say the person's name]" ten times; over and over. It might not feel authentic—maybe it will even be futile right now—but that's okay. Remember: *Fake it till you make it!* Your words will begin to change your thoughts, which

Heal Yourself

Take a quiet moment to do the following exercise:

- Close your eyes and try to remember yourself as a little girl. What were you doing, and who was with you? What were you like? How did parents fit into your life? How did they make you feel about yourself? As you see yourself as that little child, do you see the innocence in your eyes, the wonder at the life ahead of you, and the dreams and ideals you had for yourself? You were so special, and so entitled to a wonderful life.

Now pause for a moment . . .

- Close your eyes again, and see yourself now as an adult. Go up to that little girl, put your arms around her, and tell her that you love her and that although she sometimes feels unloved or afraid, everything is going to be all right. Tell her how sad you are when she feels alone or hurt, and that tough times will come, but you'll always be with her, like a guardian angel watching over her. Tell her that she's so beautiful, smart, and wonderful; and her life will work out! She'll be okay, even if no one tells her so.

- As you come back to this present moment, always remember that you're still that child, just grown up. You're still beautiful and sweet, and it's time to start healing any pain you have tucked away. You haven't lost yourself yet because you're reading this book in search of something more. Love that little girl inside you, the way she should have been loved all along. It's time to learn from your past and from your choices, and to forgive those who have done you wrong. Only you can free yourself.

will begin to change your beliefs. Your beliefs will then affect your actions, which in turn will transform your outcome. Living with authenticity will ultimately become effortless.

On the other hand, you may have done some things that you regret, so *you* are the one now living with excessive guilt or shame. These are the burdens that hold you captive in your life—and just as you must forgive those who have trespassed against you, you must also forgive yourself. Wipe your own slate clean, and begin to make smarter choices from this point on. Realize that you were simply responding to the situation the best way you knew how. Don't make things more complicated than they have to be, and don't continue to self-sabotage. Don't stay stuck in a mess simply because you're ashamed of your actions or, even worse, because you fear that others might discover your mistakes. Those who really love you will always forgive you.

If you need to ask someone for forgiveness, then do so. And always ask yourself in any battle, "Do I want to be right, or do I want peace?" What's more important to you now?

Step 47: Avoid Toxins

Sam Graci is the best-selling author of *The Food Connection,* and he's also an incredible man. I met him some years ago at a convention where we were both speaking, and I was overwhelmed by his knowledge and passion for living. That first encounter with Sam changed my life forever because he was a living endorsement that eating well reflected growing young. In his fabulous book, Sam shares that eating food is the most intimate experience you'll ever be involved in. Every mouthful becomes your skin, hair, body weight, muscles, bones, heart, organs, nervous system, brain, immune system, energy, enzymes, and hormones. More important, food can be used to enhance your life. Sam is so right!

The toxins or chemicals from modern technology in our food supply lead to cell damage, resulting in such ailments as fatigue, cloudy thinking, lowered self-esteem, leaky gut syndrome, a bad complexion, weight gain, irritability, and poor digestion. This can then turn into a vicious cycle, creating mood swings, poor concentration, depression, and even PMS.

It's now very clear to me that at least 80 to 85 percent of all our ailments are caused by diet, lifestyle, or environment, while less than 15 to 20 percent are genetically ordained. This means that although we do have a genetic predisposition for certain disease, only 15 to 20 percent of all illnesses are passed on from our parents. In other words, our genetics are *not* our destiny!

This goes back to the old argument of biological versus chronological age (or that we're only as old as our lifestyle). You see, our way of life is a huge factor in determining how old we really are. What and how much we eat and drink; how much we sleep; how we deal with stress; if we exercise and take vitamins; and if we avoid toxins, pollutants, caffeine, sodium, and refined or processed foods all directly affect how old we truly are.

Next week you'll be trying a three-day juice-and-broth fast that can increase your vitality, boost your immune system, cleanse your entire digestive and intestinal tracts, and fight illnesses. It will be like a spring cleaning for your body!

If you experience any of the following, then you need to eliminate toxins from your body (next week's detoxification will greatly benefit you):

- Frequent, unexplained headaches
- Back or joint pain
- Arthritis
- Chronic respiratory problems
- Sinus problems
- Asthma
- Abnormal body odor, bad breath, or a coated tongue
- Food allergies
- Poor digestion or chronic constipation
- Intestinal bloating or gas
- Brittle nails and hair

- Psoriasis or adult acne
- Unexplained weight gain over ten pounds
- Unusually poor memory
- Chronic insomnia
- Depression and/or irritability
- Chronic fatigue
- Environmental sensitivities, especially to odors

Try to get your hands on a juicer, for during the cleanse you'll be concocting some amazing health elixirs that will have you looking and feeling lighter and more alive. To prepare your body gently and naturally for next week's three-day fast, this week eliminate the following (even though you should have already done much of this!):

- Chlorine found in tap water

- Processed food containing preservatives, hydrogenated oil or fat, and artificial flavor and coloring

- Sugar and salt (or sodium)

- Red meat

- Aspartame

- Alcohol and cigarettes

- Aluminum pots and pans

- Pesticides, herbicides, and fungicides found on fruit and vegetables—try always to buy organic (if you use conventionally grown fruit and vegetables, wash them carefully, removing outside leaves and peeling when possible)

Step 48: Make Peace with Your Breasts

As your body is changing on this program, you might be taking a new look at your breasts. Yep, we all have 'em in some shape and size. We hold them in our hands, pushing them together, often imagining more cleavage. Wishing they were higher, firmer, or bigger (and, occasionally, smaller), the one thing many of us can agree on is that we aren't content with our breasts. We condemn the women who have had them surgically enhanced, yet we secretly wonder how we'd look with those perfectly symmetrical but fake ones! We secretly hope all women's breasts look like our own do after pregnancy (kind of saggy and deflated), and we worry about stretch marks.

From the time we're adolescents, these breasts of ours become our passage into womanhood. Few of us naturally have the large, perky ones that are featured so often in movies or girlie magazines. Yes, it can be very intimidating and disheartening, but the fact is that saggy breasts simply don't sell magazines. So how do we make peace with these things sitting (or for some, hanging) on our chests? Is breast augmentation or enhancement surgery a danger and a disgrace? Should we make ourselves look better if it's not hurting anyone else, or are we sending the wrong message to our children—both our daughters and our sons?

There's no getting around it: In our society, breasts are sexual, and most of us want to be considered sexy. Breast augmentation is on the rise, and pads and silicone cups are making their way into every lingerie department—push-up bra sales are at an all-time high. Although confidence and beauty truly do radiate from within, it's hard to just accept our breasts if we aren't happy with the way they look.

Breasts are different from any other part of our body because they aren't muscle that can be toned or firmed (although there *is* muscle under them). They're primarily fat and breast tissue that's composed of glands and ducts; so there really isn't much we can do to change the size, shape, or consistency of them, except through surgery.

This preoccupation with perfection goes back to the distorted body image we talked about in Week Two, and the fear that we aren't good enough. I've been in and out of women's changing rooms all my life, and I want you to know that there's nothing you may see each day in the mirror that millions of other women don't see, too! So where do we go from here?

First of all, appreciate that you're not one of the 185,000 women who fall victim to breast cancer every year, a disease that takes more than 50,000 lives annually. Some factors that contribute to it are a weight gain around the age of 30, being 25 percent above your recommended weight, smoking, and eating high-fat foods such as meat and dairy products; in addition, having a relative with breast or prostate cancer in your father's family doubles your risk. Trans-fatty acids from fried fast foods and commercial snack foods are especially dangerous, and some European studies show that the risk is 40 percent higher in women who have high levels of these fatty acids in their blood. However, exercise, a low-saturated-fat diet, and an increase in soy products all contribute to the fight against this deadly disease.

Become comfortable with your breasts: Examine them, and know what feels normal to you. Each month just after your period, perform the following checkup (if this isn't the right week for you, come back to this step when it is):

- Raise your right arm and put your hand behind your head. Use your left hand to examine your right breast, starting at the armpit.

- Hold your left hand flat, and use the fat pads of your middle three fingers (not the tips) to create circles of ever-increasing pressure—light, medium, and deep— over every inch of your breast tissue, moving up and down vertically at least ten times.

Crystal Andrus

- Repeat with your right hand on your left breast.

Lying down:

- Place a small folded towel or a pillow under your right shoulder.

- With your right hand behind your head, use your left hand to examine your right breast, using the pads of your three middle fingers, moving in small circles with increasing pressure.

- Repeat over your left breast with your right hand.

In the mirror:

- Place your hands at your side, on your hips, then over your head.

- Look for changes in size, shape, contour, dimpling, and skin texture.

- Learn what's normal for you (one breast is usually slightly larger).

Whatever you feel about your breasts, be thankful for the ones you have, and be thoughtful and educated in your choices. Don't judge another woman for whatever she decides to do with her body, but do remember that true beauty comes from within. And remember . . . it's confidence that matters, not perfection!

Tricks of the Trade!

Everybody knows that woman who always seems to look like a million bucks—she's timeless and ageless, and we can't help but admire how great she always looks! Never underestimate the little "tricks of the trade" that some of the most well-put-together women know:

- **Smile an everlasting smile!** A smile lights up your face and tells the world that you're likable! Since your smile gives others a first and lasting impression of you, keep in mind that white teeth are a sign of health, success, and pride. Brush and floss every day; use a whitening toothpaste; and limit coffee, blueberries, and red wine, which stain teeth the worst.

- **Moisturize!** Use a good moisturizer every night before going to bed and every time you get out of the bath or shower (not just on your face, but on your entire body, too). Petroleum jelly can work wonders for the lips and the sensitive skin around the eyes.

- **Wear sunscreen!** Use one with a minimum SPF of 15 every day, winter or summer.

- **Remember that the woman makes the hair, not the other way around!** Your hair should be the frame that surrounds the picture, *not the artwork!* Puffy, teased hair might have looked good in the '80s, but no longer! Styles change, and so should you—don't stay stuck in an era. Have fun with your hair, but remember . . . less is more!

- **Create beautiful eyebrows!** One of the most important tips for enhancing your beauty is creating beautiful brows: If they're plucked too far apart or they're too thin, they can look like a clown's, yet unplucked eyebrows can look just as bad. (If you don't know how to shape them properly, visit a skilled aesthetician.) Finally, lightly shade your brows one tone darker than your hair color, and then apply a light-colored eye shadow directly under your brow and in the inside edge of your eyes, as this will open your eyes and give you a glamorous and polished look!

Crystal Andrus

- **Whether your wardrobe is big or small, treat it with respect!** No matter how little money you spend on your apparel, take the time to keep it looking good! Always iron your clothes, polish your shoes, and keep your jewelry simple and shining. A stylish watch and *one* ring (even if it's costume) on *one* finger of each hand will spiff up an outfit, but always remember that when it comes to jewelry (just like hair and makeup), less is more.

- **Know that a tan hides a million flaws!** Now that I'm in my 30s, I still want the sun-kissed look of a tan without the damage of the ultraviolet rays, so I've become an advocate for self-tanning creams. Years ago, they were awful: We'd coat ourselves before going to bed and wake up orange and streaky. Thankfully, they've come a long way, but there are still a few secrets to applying them. Exfoliate first; and then be very careful around the knees, elbows, and inside of the arms and wrists. Know that blending is everything—it's well worth the extra time!

- **Remember that nails don't have to be long and fake, but they should always be clean and manicured!** Don't go rushing out to get fake ones (especially if you can't afford the upkeep), but clean, manicured nails (and toenails) are the sign of woman who takes care of herself. Apply a light-colored polish or a clear, shiny coat. French manicures are beautiful if you can afford them. And never put decals or designs of any kind on your nails!

Step 49: Spice Up Your Workouts and Your Green Light Foods

Around this time, your interest in working out might be waning a bit. Keep things interesting by trying some new activities. For example, if you're getting bored with walking, jogging, and running, substitute another form of intense cardio—such as a spinning or step-aerobic class or kickboxing—which will maximize your fat-burning sessions! No matter what you try, just be sure to keep up with that cardio.

How are you doing with your strength training? Are you doing your *Simply . . . Woman! Tight & Toned Workout* three to four times each week? Are you able to complete the entire workout yet? I know it's very tough, so just do the best you can. (Visit me at: **www.simplywoman.com** to find out about some of our other workout videos and products.)

Continue to eat from the Green Light food choices. Pay attention to hidden calories in oil—even healthy kinds such as olive and canola oil are very calorie dense. Don't ruin that perfect low-calorie salad with three tablespoons, which contain just over 400 calories! Instead, apple cider and balsamic vinegar are great on salads. Stir-fries don't need lots of oil either—instead, try sautéing your veggies with a touch of water. Use spices, lemons or limes, vinegars, salsa, garlic, and herbs instead of ketchup, BBQ sauce, gravy, and dressings. Freshly squeezed lemon juice is fantastic on fish, chicken cooked with salsa has zest, and cinnamon on a baked apple makes a lovely dessert. (Be sure to check the great low-fat, low-glycemic recipes on our Website as well.)

Step 50: Fill in Your Success Tracker I to Monitor Your Progress

Do your assessment first thing in the morning, before you exercise. Put the date at the top of the fifth column, and sit for a few minutes and relax. Then begin by checking your resting heart rate. Follow down this column, recording your current statistics. In the fourth column that says "Difference," using a plus (+) or a minus (-), indicate your results so far. In the "Total Inches" column, compare the changes from Weeks One and Four to now.

How are you doing? Getting smaller? Is your dress size down? How is your resting heart rate? By now, you should be noticing that you're feeling much better both inside and out. If not, get serious with yourself—you literally have all the tools right here in this program to look and feel your best ever!

Crystal Andrus

This is a journey that takes time, perseverance, and consistency. Go back over all the steps from the beginning and make sure you're still following them all. Stay strong!

☞ ✳ ☜

Summary of Week Eight: *Forgiveness*

Body:

- Continue eating your Green Light foods.
- Do five to seven 45-minute cardio sessions.
- Avoid toxins.

Mind:

- Fill in your Success Tracker I to monitor your progress.
- Learn some tricks of the trade.

Soul:

- Release your resentment and learn to forgive *and forget*.
- Make peace with your breasts.

Week Nine: *Simplicity*

I'm so excited—Week Nine is here! Okay, if you've made it this far, you're ready for an amazing experience: a body/mind/spirit cleansing. Many detoxification programs address the digestive system only; however, since the body, mind, and soul are inseparable, we're going to take a holistic approach to all three in this chapter.

Step 51: Come Alive with Detoxification

Most of us think of toxins as pollutants, such as nicotine and pesticides, which cause our body harm. Although they can indeed be very obvious (and dangerous), toxins also come in many less apparent forms. For example, if we're suffering from indigestion, it could be from a lack of stomach acid or maybe a short esophagus. We may have too much yeast and unfriendly bacteria in our intestines, or perhaps incorrect food combinations are causing us discomfort. Then again, maybe we don't deal with our problems in a healthy way and it's causing us physical pain—after all, a toxic relationship or job can heap serious harm on our immune system and break down the body; and too much stress and lack of relaxation can put us into toxic overload, causing premature aging and endless ailments.

As we begin to eliminate impurities from our diet, it's important that we look at our environment and lifestyle, too. Yes, the body is a miraculous machine that's equipped with self-preserving, healing, and cleansing systems that enable it to adapt to our environment, but it could cause us a great deal of harm in the process.

You see, when toxins enter our digestive system, most are stored in the large intestine. Our bodies try to protect us by coating the intestines with mucus, which often trap the toxins in the organ's membranes. (Some people even carry around up to 15 extra pounds of mucus that harbors this waste!) However, as it reduces the absorption of the poisons in the blood, this gooey substance also decreases the absorption of nutrients.

A simple way to understand this toxic mucus is to compare it to the same stuff that lines our sinuses and throat when we're sick—we know we're getting a cold when we feel it in our sinus cavities. Mucus isn't meant to be present in a healthy individual, so it's important to remove it from all areas of the body. That's where cleansing comes in.

Last week we focused on many different symptoms that can be greatly helped with a good cleanse and by getting our body's bacteria at ideal levels. Those who are overweight or who have eaten excessive sweets or starchy carbs will especially benefit from a good cleansing, which will help rebalance the body. Everything—gas, intestinal irritation, body odor, and bad breath—will diminish. Energy levels will rise as anxiety levels decrease. Cravings for sugar, caffeine, nicotine, alcohol, or drugs will lessen; mental clarity will improve; and our physical, psychological, spiritual, and even sexual aspects will feel more alive. Every part of the body will feel different because actual cell makeup will change.

Almost everyone can benefit from a cleanse—even those who eat in a healthy way. No one is immune to environmental toxins: Most of us occasionally sip on soda pop, alcohol, or even tap water; and we unknowingly digest pesticides and herbicides that are on our fruits and vegetables. Our meat and poultry products are filled with hormones or antibiotics; and we snack on chips, crackers, popcorn, cookies, and other foods containing hydrogenated oils and preservatives. We shake salt on every meal, as we overload on caffeine from chocolate, coffee, colas, and tea. We pop painkillers for headaches, backaches, and menstrual cramps, unaware of their effect on our liver and other organs. We inhale pollutants in our cleaning products, paint fumes, and even hair spray. It's all simply a part of life.

Now, while we can't escape to a remote, uncontaminated habitat, we can give our bodies a little spring cleaning. Yet a good

Crystal Andrus

cleanse includes much more than just eliminating mucus and toxins from our diet: When done properly, it's not a starvation diet— it's a revitalization. It encompasses all aspects of our lives, and it's truly a time to connect with our higher self. Stress reduction, adequate sleep, supplementation, bathing, and meditation are also important. So don't begin this cleanse unless you're prepared to encompass the *entire* experience, which includes three parts: cleansing, rebuilding, and maintaining.

Cleansing

By eliminating mucus and toxins from your intestinal tract and increasing your friendly bacteria, you'll be restoring balance in your alkaline-acidity levels and cleansing your liver, gallbladder, kidneys, blood, and lymphatic and immune systems. This first part of the detox process is quite detailed, so I've laid it out for you step-by-step:

1. Leading into your cleanse, eat plenty of green salads and fresh fruits, and drink lots of water and herbal tea so that the upcoming body-chemistry changes won't be uncomfortable. And avoid caffeine, alcohol, sugar, aspartame, salt, and red meat.

2. Take the first few days of the week to get organized, and then begin your three-day cleanse once you're ready. The only way to follow this detoxification properly is to read this entire section, and then make a list of everything you're going to need.

3. The ideal technique for successful cleansing is to drink fresh, raw fruit and vegetable juices. A good juicer can juice all of a fruit or vegetable—even rinds, stems, peels, and seeds—in order to give you up to 95 percent of the plant's food and nutritive value. So, did you manage to get your hands on one last week? Yes, a juicer

can be expensive, but it can also really boost the nutrient power of your cleansing drinks, and it will be a good investment that you'll continue to take advantage of as you live a healthier life. (Champion, Juiceman, and Acme are good brands that are less expensive than some others found in health-food stores.)

If you can't find or afford a juicer, don't worry—you have some options. For example, fresh-juice bars have sprung up all over the place, so if there's one close to where you live or work, you can get some of your requirements met there. The counter person will likely be able to make any combination you ask for, but be sure to order fresh-juice drinks and not smoothies, which often contain dairy products and sweeteners. In addition, there are several brands of bottled organic juices that you can find in your local health-food store. Juice tends to start oxidizing and loses some of its nutrients after a while, so fresh-squeezed is always the best bet, but as long as you can find some that have been bottled fresh, they'll help with this detox. Your local health-food store may have a wheatgrass press with which they can make fresh wheatgrass juice, and farmers' markets are also good places to find freshly squeezed, organic juices.

There is a wide variety of juices and combinations of juices, each of which has a different effect on the digestive system, so it's important to choose those that are appropriate for your specific needs. For example, if you need a "constipation cleanse," you could juice green cabbage, celery, and carrots. For weight loss, you'd use carrot, apple, and even orange juices sparingly; on the other hand, you can use grapefruit and cucumber juices generously, as they're exceptionally advantageous for weight loss when combined with the juice of a dark, leafy vegetable such as romaine lettuce. Celery, spinach, and cabbage are other great staple juices. And even though fruit and vegetable juices sometimes don't mix, certain combinations are still delicious and healthful.

Look at the recipes in Appendix 2 of this book, and decide which juices you'll use in your detox. Stock up with produce from your health-food store, from the organic section of your grocery store, or from the farmers' market before you start. One note to keep in mind during these three days is to thoroughly wash all fruit and vegetables, and peel those with strong, bitter, or wax-coated rinds.

If sticking to straight juice for three days seems far too difficult for you, try alternating juice with the actual raw fruit or vegetable. You must use *only* organic produce—and don't add any oils, dressings, or salt to them (you can add apple cider vinegar if you make your vegetables into a salad).

You can also cleanse your body with soups or with an incredibly healthy powdered-drink called **greens+.** (This product contains 23 ingredients—including lecithin, organic alfalfa, barley, wheatgrass, beet root, spirulina, apple pectin, chlorella, soy sprouts, bee pollen, ginseng, Nova Scotia dulse, green tea, gingko biloba, and grape extract—and comes from the same line that I've been recommending for other vitamins and supplements. For more information, please visit: **www.simplywoman.com.**)

4. Whichever level of participation you choose, avoid eating all dairy products, protein, and cooked foods during this three-day cleansing, as they're hard to digest. You want to give your system a chance to rest and heal.

5. You'll drink eight glasses of water each day in addition to your juices, so buy plenty of distilled water. *Do not drink unfiltered tap water.* You can replace some of these glasses with decaffeinated herbal teas, such as green tea, licorice tea, or dandelion-root tea.

6. Over the course of the three days, you may find yourself experiencing a little physical discomfort as your body is beginning to purge toxins. Headaches are common, but resist taking a painkiller. Just know that this is a sign that your cleansing is happening. (You may also notice other side effects, such as bad breath.)

7. Continue to take your regular supplements: multivitamin/ mineral, vitamins C and E, essential fatty acids, and calcium/magnesium. Here are some others that I highly recommend you take during this cleansing:

- **A green drink**, which has extracts of chlorophyll-rich foods and green superfoods to help stabilize and preserve the acid/alkaline balance of the body, and autoimmune-building properties. Since chlorophyll has a molecular structure close to our own plasma, drinking it is like getting a mini-transfusion. They especially help clear the skin, cleanse the kidneys, and purify the blood.

- A **natural fiber product** with both soluble and insoluble fiber, which can help remove mucus from the large intestines and toxins from throughout your body. Continue this after the detox.

- **Powdered acidophilus** containing lactobacillus bifidus. There are more than 400 different types of microorganisms that make up our intestinal flora— acidophilus is the friendly bacteria that lives in the intestines and helps fight the unfriendly bacteria that can make us ill. Toxins, antibiotics, refined foods, and chlorine all affect the proper balance of our intestinal flora. Many women have Candida yeast overgrowth, which can cause virtually any disease anywhere in the body. Take a quarter teaspoon before having your juice two to three times throughout the day. This is something else you should continue even after your detox is over.

Crystal Andrus

- **Hydrated bentonite.** This natural clay, which comes from volcanic ash, is another yeast-buster. When taken internally, it helps the intestines eliminate toxins, and it's especially helpful for those with colon disorders, colitis, constipation, and diarrhea. Take one tablespoon in two ounces of aloe vera juice upon rising, just before your cleansing drink.

- **Dandelion root or dandelion leaf,** which is important to efficiently detoxify your liver and gallbladder. Capsules can be found at health-food stores, and the fresh leaves can be used in raw salads. Dandelion-root coffee or tea is also excellent, as it helps alleviate water retention and acts as a mild diuretic. Take one 100-mg capsule two to three times throughout the day, and try drinking the tea first thing in the morning with your master cleansing drink (found on page 317).

- **Milk thistle.** Another great detoxifier, this is also a potent liver-protecting substance. Take one 200-mg capsule three times a day with meals.

8. Once you get the fruits, vegetables, and supplements you're going to need, map out your day in terms of when you'll take what. This is what a sample day will look like.

A sample schedule follows:

TIME	
7:00 a.m.	Take 1 tbsp of bentonite with 2 oz of aloe vera juice.
7:10 a.m.	Drink dandelion root tea with lemon, cayenne pepper, and ginger.
7:30 a.m.	Take 1 tsp satisfibre+ with ¼ tsp of powdered acidophilus in distilled water. • Drink FRUIT juice (your choice). • Take regular vitamins (one multi+complete-, or a regular multivitamin, vitamin E, vitamin C, and calcium/magnesium.)
8:00 a.m.	Drink distilled water with lemon.
9:00 a.m.	Take ¼ tsp of acidophilus, 100 mg capsule of dandelion root, 200 mg capsule of milk thistle, 1 tsp satisfibre+, and an o3mega capsule. • Drink VEGETABLE juice or a serving of greens+.
10:00 a.m.	Have a green tea.
12:00 a.m.	Drink distilled water with lemon.
1:00 p.m.	Take ¼ tsp of acidophilus, 100 mg capsule of dandelion root, 200 mg capsule of milk thistle, 1 tsp satisfibre+, and an o3mega capsule. • Drink FRUIT juice.
2:00 p.m.	Drink dandelion root tea.
3:00 p.m.	Drink VEGETABLE juice such as the weight-loss cleanser or have a large salad with apple cider vinegar.
4:00 p.m.	Drink distilled water with lemon.
5:00 p.m.	Take ¼ tsp of acidophilus, 100 mg capsule of dandelion root, 200 mg capsule of milk thistle, 1 tsp satisfibre+, and an o3mega capsule. • Have LARGE BOWL of soup (your choice).
6:00 p.m.	Drink green tea.
7:00 p.m.	Have one serving of greens+.
9:00 p.m.	Drink valerian root tea to fall asleep.
Bedtime	Take 500 mg of calcium and 250 mg of magnesium and a vitamin C. Sleep well and begin the next day with the stretches at the end of the workout DVD or try the Relaxation CD.

9. Choose three consecutive days that are as stress free as possible. Try to do your cleanse over a weekend—if that's not doable and Tuesday is your favorite TV night, start your cleanse on Wednesday (you'll want to avoid television and focus on activities that will enhance your thinking and relax your body). At least pick days when you can get up and go to bed an hour earlier than normal, since you're going to need plenty of sleep at night and "alone time" in the morning

10. Allow plenty of time to start the day with yoga, stretching, or a relaxing meditation—or you can try my *Simply . . . Woman! Relaxation Therapy* CD. You won't want to do heavy-duty workouts during the week of your cleanse. If you want, you can do a light cardio workout, but avoid any weight training during these three days.

11. Sip on your morning master cleansing drink while you watch the sunrise, or write in your journal. Light some candles and play some soft music while you get ready for work, and give yourself plenty of time to avoid traffic jams or stressful situations. Many religions use fasting as a devout time to purify the soul and achieve a surreal union with God.

12. During these three days, instead of getting caught up in all the misery life can offer, look at your children, your husband, your friends, your parents, your siblings, your co-workers, and strangers through different eyes; and smile at everyone you see. If things at home aren't great, do something each day to make a difference. How can you extend yourself and show love?

One of the most powerful laws of the universe is the Law of Divine Reciprocity: You receive what you give. So if things aren't going the way you'd like them to, change what you're doing. Search for simplicity, and find the joy in all the blessings that surround you. Jot down five things each night before you go to bed for which you're grateful. Do something on that list that you love to do but have never had the time to—maybe write a poem, read an inspirational book, or paint a picture.

13. Finally, try to have a sauna or steam bath, which flush toxins from the skin. Finish off by giving your dry skin a good brushing to exfoliate dead cells, and then take a cold shower to close the pores. Also, make an effort to get a massage or pedicure during these three days.

An Option Worth Considering

I distinctly remember the day, not too long ago, when my extremely talented Cranio-Sacral RMT (Registered Massage Therapist), Shannon, came to my house, all excited about a new nutritional cleansing/detoxing line she was using and selling. My radar instantly went up.

Oh no, Shannon, please don't do this to me, I thought. *I'm not interested. Please, just massage me!*

I tried to appear open, but the truth is that I was totally closed off. Her massage that day wasn't enjoyable—not because Shannon didn't perform her magic on me, but because I was in a full-blown state of resistance—even to receiving a healing and wonderful massage.

It may sound like an excuse, but as a health and fitness expert, I am constantly approached by people and companies asking me to "just take a look" at their products. I simply can't endorse them all and

because of that, my self-protection mode usually kicks in whenever I'm approached.

My massage schedule with Shannon began to dwindle over the next eight months. She'd done nothing wrong—she wasn't pushy and her hands were still magical—I just didn't want to be "sold" something. I totally resisted her and her cleansing program.

Then, one day, after not seeing her for what seemed like forever, I couldn't fight it any longer. I needed one of her amazing massages. When she walked into my home a few days later, I couldn't help but notice how her body had transformed. She was two or three dress sizes smaller and just seemed lighter and happier than I'd ever seen her. She absolutely glowed. I'd forgotten about the vitamins when I asked her what she'd been doing.

"Crystal, you just have to try this stuff. I know you don't want to hear about it, but I've never used anything that makes me feel so amazing, so energized, and so excited about nutrition before."

Ah . . . those damn vitamins again! Was she going to try and sell me again?!

I listened, smiling and nodding my head, while on the inside I could feel my stomach tightening up. I was still totally and utterly closed off.

Nevertheless, after Shannon left that day, I couldn't get over how different she looked and seemed after all these months of not seeing her. There was clearly something going on. . . .

Then the "clincher" came.

A few weeks later, my best friend, Annette, of nearly 20 years called me up, sounding better than I'd heard her sound in a decade. Annette, bless her soul, is the most beautiful human being and I just adore her, but since getting married and having kids, she has always been tired, run down, burnt out, and frustrated. She's a waif of a thing as it is, and gets the shakes if she goes too long without eating. She never has time for herself. No time to work out. No time for self-nurturing. No time for anything except work, kiddies, and husband. And certainly, never a need to spend money on frivolous vitamins! Yet, for the first time in what seemed like an eternity, Annette was sounding like her old self. (The young one, I mean!)

"Crystal, you have to try this cleanse I've just done. I know it sounds ridiculous for me to approach you because you've been trying to tell me this for years, but I can't believe how incredible I feel!"

If I wasn't hearing this from my "true-blue, straight-as-they-come, never-done-anything-remotely shady, good Catholic Italian" friend, I probably wouldn't be sharing this with you now. And, let me tell you, I couldn't believe it, even as I was doing it, but I agreed to give the cleanse a try. Shannon's passion was just too enticing, and Annette was too honest to ever lead me astray. It would have to stay a secret, though! I called Shannon up and placed my order for a 30-day cleanse. (It's actually one cleanse day a week for four weeks, combined with some meals, shakes, vitamins, and minerals on the other days.)

In my first nine days, I was six pounds lighter* (and I don't have much to lose), but much more eye-opening than the six pounds I released was the clarity that I was suddenly experiencing. It was like nothing I could explain! Not to mention my "natural" bloating completely disappeared, and I stopped taking digestive enzymes** (I didn't need them while on the program). I had energy from morning to night, slept like a baby, and my cravings for sugar and coffee were completely and utterly gone. I felt better than ever!

Could it really be the new products I was taking? How could that be? For goodness' sake, I was a health and fitness expert who ate well, exercised, and took a mountain of other supplements.

Once I ran out, I didn't reorder more. Shannon did as she promised and never bothered me about it. She just waited. She knew . . .

What was so shocking to me was that within a few days I felt strangely different. My "natural" bloating came back and my energy level dropped from where it was. Within a week, I was craving my morning cup of coffee again. There was no denying it. Something had changed.

I anxiously called Shannon, sounding like a "junkie needing a fix" and begged her to bring me over some more "stuff." It wasn't available in the stores, and I didn't want to wait for the products to be shipped to me. I asked her if she would drive them over to me immediately. Poor Shannon . . . she was now my new best friend!

Within a day or two, I was "back on track" and very quickly becoming a believer.

Then, within a few weeks, I ran out again. The same thing happened all over.

Two weeks later, I made a decision that I never dreamed I'd ever make. I couldn't keep it a secret any longer. It was now me asking Shannon to come over, with products, along with more information on how I could share them with my clients and friends.

The results for others have been just as stupendous, so here I am, sharing them with you: The line is called **Isagenix**. And, the nice part is that it simply works. What's even more amazing is that if you set yourself up properly, you can not only get your own monthly supply for free, but you can make money selling them yourself if you want to!

If you want more information for either your own personal use and to have someone on my team coach you through your cleanse for free, or to become a part of my team and distribute the products yourself under my guidance, please e-mail me at: **vitamins@crystal andrus.com** or better yet, go directly to: **www.crystalandrus. isagenix.com** to sign up now. This is an option that I highly recommend if following the three-day cleanse that I previously outlined in this program seems difficult or time-consuming. *Isagenix is a company of the highest regard, and this option certainly takes the "thinking" out of it for you!*

Whatever you decide, rest assured that you will not regret your decision to give your body what it needs to be strong, stable, and energized! Once you get your body on track, it's amazing how much clarity you'll have in order to tackle the other stuff!

---

*Results may be greater than or less than those depicted on this Website and can be influenced by factors including your metabolic rate, energy expenditure, and diet. The average weight loss in a recent study was seven pounds in the first nine days using the 9 Day Program. Always consult your physician or health-care professional before starting this or any other health or fitness program. As with any health or fitness program, a sensible eating plan and regular exercise are required in order to achieve long-term weight-loss results.

These statements have not been evaluated by the FDA. Isagenix programs and products are not intended to diagnose, treat, cure, or prevent any disease. Always consult your physician or health-care professional before starting this or any other health or fitness program. If you are under the age of 18, pregnant, lactating, have allergies, or have any other medical condition, please consult a physician before use. Discontinue use if any allergic reaction occurs. **Diabetics: Use only under direct medical supervision. KEEP PRODUCTS OUT OF THE REACH OF CHILDREN.

Rebuilding

With toxins removed, your body is ready to rebuild at optimal levels, so eat only fresh and simply prepared foods during the remainder of the week and into Week Ten. Your diet should be very low in fat, with little dairy (low- or nonfat cottage cheese and yogurt are okay), and no fried foods. Continue to avoid alcohol, caffeine, tobacco, and sugars. Stay away from meats, but seafood is okay. Continue to take your vitamins, essential fatty acids, acidophilus, and fiber (if you're easily constipated).

Maintaining

You've come so far over the past few months that maintaining all the steps is essential. It's natural to fall back into old habits, but you must work hard at maintaining your new ones. Never think that you're stronger than others who have gained their weight back. Continue to eat natural foods, exercise daily, and stretch. Try not to let the toxins you've eliminated sneak back into your diet. And remember that thin thighs are a by-product of healthy living!

> **Fat-Burning Secret #22:**
> Avoid toxins and chemicals, and eat organic food whenever possible. Try a cleansing detox a few times a year.

Simply . . . Inspirational!

Music can stir the soul like nothing else. Imagine *Titanic* without Celine Dion's "My Heart Will Go On." Or what about Sylvester Stallone's *Rocky* without his theme song "Gonna Fly Now"? To this day, if I hear it, I want to run up a flight of steps the way he did and raise my arms in the air like a champion fighter!

For relaxation, the sounds of Enya or other New Age music can help slow your heart rate and induce a feeling of calmness and peace. Music can be very therapeutic, so close your eyes and let the rhythm and melody wash over you. It can be the link that helps connect your body, mind, and soul!

I love cooking a great meal with music playing and a few candles lit in the kitchen. Sometimes opera can inspire me to great gourmet heights. Andrea Bocelli is exhilarating, and not many other things can improve a meal like the soothing sounds of Barbra Streisand or Neil Diamond! Play your favorite music during a bath, while making love, sitting by a fire, reading a good book, cuddling with your kids, or visiting with friends! Music is a small but simple joy in life—if your car radio is always set on a news station or the TV is a constant background noise in your

Step 52: Look at the World Through Rose-Colored Glasses

During this cleanse, focus on all the beauty and goodness that surrounds you. Go on a media fast: Don't read the paper, listen to the radio, or watch the news on TV. Make an effort to protect your eyes, ears, and heart from the evils and horrors of the world. Turn off those tabloid TV shows, and refuse to participate in gossip of any kind. Read at least one book or story that's uplifting or empowering. Elevate yourself to a higher level, and don't worry if it sounds self-righteous. You're simply choosing to eliminate negative, energy-draining things from your life and to surround yourself with enlightenment and positive energy. It feels great! See the world through rose-colored glasses . . . it really is a beautiful place!

Step 53: Get Rid of All the Garbage in Your Life

Over the past nine weeks, you've been cultivating and nurturing your garden, and this week is dedicated to getting rid of the weeds. Weeds are like toxins that will slowly creep in and destroy you . . . which ones do you still need to pull?

Now let's start by thinking about your home: Would you describe it as your sanctuary, your haven of comfort and serenity? Is your bathroom a miniature spa retreat, or is it a room that you rush into and out of and resent cleaning? How about your bedroom closet—do you open the door and see your garments hanging beautifully organized, or do you claw through ten years of old clothes in an assortment of sizes? How about that junk drawer in the kitchen, overflowing with papers; or the hamper in the laundry room that's been filled with mismatched socks for two years? What about your computer—do you use it to better your life, or does it consume your evenings with shallow chatting and energy-depleting e-mails?

As you can see, detoxing is necessary in *all* areas of life; in fact, after a few years on my own *Simply . . . Woman!* journey, I decided to sell everything I owned and to start afresh. I'd collected and saved many things over the years, but I'd grown into a different woman, so all the belongings that had once defined me now meant nothing.

I went through my house selecting certain possessions that were special to me and locked them up in one room, and then I posted signs around my neighborhood and in the newspaper

home, turn it off! It's time to find a melody that soothes your soul and opens your heart.

What were your favorite songs as a teenager? Keep them handy for those low days when you need to feel the reminder and rush of your youth. Music is an expression of yourself, so don't deny this powerful tool to rediscover yourself. Let your home come alive with its magic!

The Healing Scents of Nature

When you smell a wonderful fragrance, it can transport you to another place and time. In your brain, you have neurotransmitters that associate smell with past memories or associations. So the aroma of baking cookies can induce a feeling of happiness if your mother baked when you were young, while your favorite guy's cologne can arouse you sexually. Even smells such as freshly cut grass or coffee can stimulate your senses. Scent has the power to transform your emotions and help heal your body.

Aromatherapy is the art and science of extracting oils from aromatic flowers, herbs, woods, and fibers. The Egyptians and Chinese have records dating back 5,000 years that show the use of more than 300 different plants; and the Greeks, Romans, Indians, and Native Americans all used plant life for medicinal and cosmetic purposes, as well as for preserving food.

Today many therapists still use the remarkable power of this ancient art. The only difference between aromatherapy and a beautifully scented candle is that in the former, the essential oil is taken from plants, while the latter is often a synthetic fragrance. Now, in order to reap the true medicinal benefit, you must use the real thing. Many companies put scents in their bath products, skin lotions, and candles; however, the oils lose their potency if exposed to sunlight. If they're packaged in a clear bottle, the powerful extract is long gone before you ever get it home. You may love the smell, but if your goal is to reap the medicinal benefit, purchase pure essential oil in a small dark bottle with a stopper. (The oil should be used sparingly, with a dropper.) If properly stored, good essential oils will keep for years.

There are many uses of essential oils, such as in baths, compresses, vaporizers, diffusers, and, of course, massage. (Whether you rub the oil on your own skin or have someone else do it for you, always mix it with a carrier oil such as almond or grapeseed.) You may love the smell of lavender, which originally came from France and is undoubtedly the most useful and versatile oil—it relaxes, soothes, and restores balance in your body, mind, and spirit. Excellent as a muscle relaxant, lavender is often used for massage, and a few drops on your pillow or sheets can induce a peaceful night's sleep. It's also a skin conditioner and astringent: Try adding six drops to two teaspoons of almond oil and rub it all over your skin.

While lavender oil is a must-have, there are also hundreds of

Crystal Andrus

announcing an open-house sale. I sold everything from the plates in my cupboards to the art on my walls. The sentimental things were safe, and I was creating space.

These days I realize that this sale was symbolic of me cleaning out the garbage I'd held on to for so many years. I got rid of old letters that made me sad, clothes I never wore, half-full bottles of perfume, and countless containers of red nail polish. I sorted through boxes of old magazines and books I'd never read, and I realized that these possessions had been distractions cluttering my space and occupying my mind. As I shed weight, I also became ready to shed my emotional baggage and to discover the woman I was really meant to be.

Now don't worry: I'm not going to ask you to sell your house, trade in your husband, or move across the country in your search for self. But I do want you to think about the things in your life you could live without and the things you couldn't. In other words, what do you really cherish? Start to take a personal inventory, and consider detoxing yourself of all the things that weigh you down.

⁂

other therapeutic oils out there, from jasmine to juniper berry, coriander to chamomile. Some relax the senses, while others arouse and stimulate. For example, clary sage and sandalwood are great to diffuse into the air at parties, while peppermint can clear your mind; and cinnamon and jasmine are aphrodisiacs, while eucalyptus is useful for clearing congested sinuses when vaporized into your room.

If aromatherapy interests you, many great books and Websites explain the different oils and their benefits. Believe the powerful therapy of this great art, and surround yourself with the healing scents of nature.

Summary of Week Nine: *Simplicity*

Body:

- Do your three-day detoxification, or visit: **www.crystal andrus.isagenix.com** for more information on cleansing products.

Mind:

- Take inventory at home.

Soul:

- Go on a "media fast," and see the world through rose-colored glasses.

Week Ten: *Respect*

I hope that you made it through the cleanse okay. How do you feel? The first day or two are generally the toughest—as your body was removing toxins, you may have felt awful, but now you should be feeling great.

In one year from today, more than 98 percent of your cells will be brand new. What does that mean to your health or future? *Everything!* So in this chapter, we're going to work on rebuilding to optimal levels.

Step 54: Rebuild a New Reality

One evening I was called into the office of the health club where I worked. A 17-year-old guy had rushed off the gym floor, afraid he was having a heart attack. His hands were shaking; his pulse was racing; and he felt dizzy, was tingling, and was slightly disoriented. I asked him if he'd eaten.

"A few hours ago," he replied.

"Have you taken any drug or pill?"

"Just some caffeine," he replied with some embarrassment. "You know, those pills you get at the health-food store."

As I looked at the ingredients on the bottle he showed me, the words *ephedrine* and *guarana extract* jumped out at me. I asked him how many capsules he'd taken.

"Just two. The bottle said you could take up to eight a day."

I explained to him that he'd taken a stimulant. Now, there are actually many different types of stimulants that can excite the nervous system, such as sugar, nicotine, and caffeine; and then you have drugs like ephedrine (or *ephedra*), all the way up to cocaine. Guarana extract is like a concentrated form of caffeine that, when combined with ephedrine, can really crank you up. These pills are also taken for weight loss, and they're highly addictive because they give you so much energy that when you come down from the high, you feel exhausted and irritable. And, as with any stimulant, the higher the high, the harder the crash.

Years before, I'd tried diet pills, so I knew the excitable, high-strung feeling they could cause. I asked the young man, "Do you ever drink coffee or tea?"

"Not really," he responded.

"How about alcohol or cigarettes?"

"Never! I've never smoked or drunk alcohol."

"Well," I said, "your young body is so clean and free of stimulants and toxins that you've had a severe reaction to the caffeine and ephedrine in these pills. Go home and just let it wear off. It will pass in a few hours—if it doesn't, go to the hospital, and don't ever take anything like this again."

The point of this story is that before your three-day cleanse, you may have been so filled with toxins from years of consuming coffee, tea, alcohol, and nicotine, as well as diet pills like these (before beginning to train with me, many of my clients admitted to taking them), that you were unaware of the truly powerful consequence of those toxins on your body.

By continuing to eat fresh, organic foods in their natural state; keeping fats very low; and eliminating toxins such as diet pills,

Diet Pills and Ephedrine

The U.S. government has prohibited the sale of dietary supplements containing ephedrine, and the Olympic governing body has also banned it as a sports-enhancing drug. Keep in mind that this substance can cause dizziness, headaches, decreased appetite, anxiety, restlessness or nervousness, gastrointestinal problems, irregular heartbeat, insomnia, flushing, sweating, high blood pressure, strokes, seizures, psychosis, and even death. Ephedrine is especially dangerous for people suffering from thyroid disease, diabetes, and glaucoma. And you should never take it if you're pregnant or breast-feeding.

alcohol, sodium, preservatives, caffeine, tobacco, sugar, artificial sweeteners, and red meats, you can begin to restore healthy tissues and vital cells and be as unpolluted as that young man. You'll be a new you!

Reality Is Your Perception

In one year from today, you can restructure the very essence of your cellular makeup. Do you believe that, or do you think it's too late to erase the harm you've already done to yourself?

The brain is a fascinating organ. Whatever your mind believes (whether it's true or not) is the truth for you. A belief is more powerful than actuality, which is why I always say, "Reality is your perception." For example, let's look at someone with a phobia: His or her belief about something—whether it's a fear of germs, elevators, spiders, or going outside—is so strong that even the most logical explanation can't override that conviction. So, grounded in fear, not fact, this belief becomes the person's reality.

You may believe that atrophy, deterioration, and even sickness and senility are part of aging because it's what you've seen—so it must be the truth, right? Yet scientists have proven that eating well and exercising into your 70s and beyond can halt and even reverse the signs of aging. In their book *Biomarkers*, Tufts University researchers William Evans and Irwin Rosenberg outlined nine markers for age that are now considered reversible: high blood pressure, blood-sugar tolerance, cholesterol/HDL ratio, bone density, aerobic capacity, body fat, lean muscle mass, metabolic rate, and strength. *Reversible:* meaning you can undo the damage you've done! And you've already started doing that with your cleanse.

How Do You Want to Feel One Year from Now?

The keys to rebuilding a more positive *you* lie in what you do with and to your physical body, and what you believe about yourself and your future. Before you can begin to manifest positive changes in every cell of your body, you must believe that a new you—a stronger, healthier you—is your reality.

Do you remember reading about "programmed audiotapes" in Week Two? Well, are your beliefs so deeply ingrained that your very essence still believes some of your negative, false statements to be fact? Do you embrace the belief that you're an incredibly healthy, fit, beautiful, kind, successful woman who's comfortable in her own skin—who knows where she's been and where she's going? If not, why?

Your success will come only when you step out of your natural set point and rise above any preconceived notions that have been laid out for you. You must erase any negative messages and rerecord positive ones that will carry you toward your wildest dreams.

Don't be like that dog lying on the nail on the farmer's front porch: whining in misery but doing nothing to change the situation. Even if complaining is natural for you—meaning that one or both of your parents probably complained all the time so that's the behavior you saw and adopted—you must change your attitude, as it can be the most powerful self-defeating behavior. If this seems impossible, remember, as I've said before: "Fake it till you make it!"

Rebuild a new reality and dramatically change the very essence of your current cells or your body as you know it by:

- Adding protein back with every meal, choosing primarily fish, egg whites, nonfat or one percent cottage cheese, and protein shakes

- Continuing to eat fresh, fibrous vegetables with each meal

- Cutting back on starchy carbohydrates and sticking with high-fiber carbs such as salads

- Choosing brown rice, pumpernickel bread, or oatmeal (if you do decide to have starch), and eating it before 3 P.M.

- Not drinking distilled water (go back to reverse-osmosis or spring water)

- Continuing to take your vitamins, essential fatty acids, apple cider vinegar, acidophilus, and fiber (if you're easily constipated) every day

I also want you to look back over your "List of Burning Desires": Do they seem more attainable now than they did ten weeks ago? What about your "Self-Proclaiming Declaration" that you wrote in Week Two—has it changed over the past ten weeks? Do you have a new reality of who you truly are and what you really need to be joyous and content? If so, rewrite it and continue to read it every day.

Step 55: Know Your Worth

I remember the day a friend of mine decided that she wanted to reenter the workforce. After raising her children, she was a little nervous about plunging back in, so she decided to refresh herself by taking some courses. Eventually, she finished at the head of her class, but she still felt that she wasn't quite ready—perhaps she needed more education or volunteer work. She'd come up with every possible reason why she wouldn't be hired, or why working would negatively affect her marriage or kids, yet she couldn't shake her desire to pursue a career she loved.

My friend decided that being self-employed was a better bet for her. By having no boss, she could gear her own hours around the kids' schedule and still be there for dinner every night. She set her prices for her services far lower than market value . . . yet months went by, and she had no clients. Figuring that it had to be her price, she decided to drop it to less than half of the going rate, but she still had no business! By this point, her confidence was gone and she even began doubting her capabilities. The idea of subjecting herself to job interviews was more than she could bear, so she gave up.

I tried to explain to my friend that if she didn't think she was worth it, no one else would. Her mother was a stay-at-home mom, so while growing up, my friend never saw a woman make a lot of money—thus, she didn't really believe that women could. Her beliefs became her reality. Sure, she wanted to be out there fulfilling her dreams and making a good living, but she obviously didn't think that she was worth the going rate. By dropping her prices, all she did was tell potential clients that she must not be as good or as competent as her competitors.

※

I often wonder if we really get a better haircut for $65 than we do for $20, or if we just believe we do because the stylist does. Attitude is everything! I mean, we can come up with all kinds of reasons why we'll never feel great or look our absolute best, why we aren't good enough yet, or why our goals seem unattainable. We can even convince ourselves that we really didn't want them in the first place.

This is simply our innate belief that we'll fail eventually, so we sabotage ourselves every step of the way. We're brilliant at manipulating ourselves into believing—especially if we're mothers—that it's safer and less selfish to say that we're taking that art course for enjoyment rather than let anyone believe we really want to be an artist, or that we'd prefer to sing karaoke rather than actually pursuing a singing career. It's much more difficult to really put ourselves out there because it goes against most of our belief systems: What if we're not good enough? What if we try and no one wants us? What if the world thinks we're too old or too young, not educated or smart enough, or too fat or not pretty enough?

These "truths," grounded in fear, aren't true at all. We're great at coming up with all the reasons for why "now isn't the right time, but I'll do it soon!" Well, soon is never going to come, and we'll finally realize that we're so filled with regret that we don't even know how to dream. So begin to change those internal messages *today,* and believe that you can become the woman you were always meant to be.

I've tasted some of the most incredible meals by women who claim that they can't cook, or visited the most beautiful homes decorated by those who say they have no talent. I've seen the most exquisite women who think that they're fat or ugly, and I wonder how they think that the world is ever going to see them differently when they don't see it themselves.

If you don't think you're worth it, no one else will.
Every success begins with an idea.
That idea escalates into a goal.
With a Plan of Action, it becomes a reality.

We've all met people who will tell us that it will never work, or why we're foolish for believing it can. Feel sorry for them—realize that your passion scares them and forces them to look at themselves.

Dreams come in all shapes and sizes: It might be to run a marathon to raise money for research for a deadly disease, or it may be far less serious but equally important to your spirit. Your dream may be to become a stay-at-home mom instead of rushing the kids off to day care every day, or finally applying for that position after years of wondering "What if?" It's *never* too late. More women become highly successful in their 40s than at any other age, probably because they've raised their kids, supported their partners, and taken care of the house, and finally it's quiet enough for them to listen to their own heart. They've stopped asking for permission to be themselves, and they've started living the truth of who they are. Don't wait to do the same!

Step 56: Stand Up Straight and Lose Ten Pounds

Stand in front of a mirror with your stomach hanging out and your shoulders slouching forward. Your chest will go concave and your head will drop forward. Now turn to the side—how do you look?

Turn and face the mirror again, only this time, pull your shoulders back and your tummy in. Imagine a string attached to your head, pulling you up as tall as possible. Align your cheekbones with your collarbones and your ears with your shoulders, and focus on lining your hips directly under your shoulders. Now how do you look? Not just ten pounds smaller, but 100 percent better!

The way you stand and walk says so much about you. A wonderful woman who works for me always remarks on the way I enter a room. (I never really thought about it, but over the years people have commented on that very thing.) She'll beam with a huge smile as she points out my relaxed, confident pace: "Your head is always up, arms hanging comfortably at your side, as you walk with a long, powerful stride." She'll tell me that I command respect and exude strength and poise, and I'll smile back at her knowingly, because *if you don't think it, no one else will.*

Posture is an important aspect of your health. If you sit at a desk all day with incorrect positioning or on the wrong chair, you

Crystal Andrus

can get a backache, headaches, and even digestive problems. After a short period of time, your chest muscles shorten and tighten, and your posture is dominated by a rounded back and jutting head. Muscle imbalances take over, and soon you'll lose all sense of correct postural alignment.

You may have a tendency to attract less attention to your breasts by slouching forward and rounding your back. It looks awful—and very weak—and it can cause chronic back pain. Instead, tighten up the muscles in your upper back and shoulders, while stretching out the muscles of the chest and front shoulder. And try the following exercises:

Exercises for Great Posture

— *Chest and shoulders.* Bend both arms up to a 90-degree angle at shoulder height, with your palms and forearms facing forward. Pull your elbows back, squeezing your shoulder blades together. Tuck your chin in rather than allowing it to jut forward. Feel your chest open up. Now face a corner of the room and place one arm on each wall. Keep both feet back from the wall, and let your body lean into your bent arms. Hold this stretch for 30 seconds without bouncing. As it becomes easier, lift your arms higher on the wall and move your feet farther back, increasing the amount of weight you let fall on your elbows.

— *Rear deltoids (upper back).* Sit on a bench or chair. With a three-pound weight in each hand, lift your arms back up into that 90-degree position, then bend forward supporting your upper body on your thighs. You'll feel your upper back working. Lower your hands together in front of your knees, keeping your elbows bent, and then lift back up. Do this 15 times.

— *Abdominals.* The abdominal wall is composed of five different sections of muscles. Your transverse abdominus is a band of muscle that runs across your lower abs and is mostly responsible for holding your stomach flat. There are a few different exercises you can do to work this muscle, but the first and most important thing you must do at all times is hold your stomach in! Imagine yourself walking onstage in a fitted black dress. By pulling your stomach in and holding it tight, you're doing an isometric contraction that's working those muscles. The more you do this, the more natural it will feel, and soon you'll begin to hold your stomach in unconsciously. Pull it in when you're driving in your car, sitting at your desk, watching TV, or walking around.

Start your ab workout by kneeling on all fours. Inhale and blow your belly all the way out, letting your back slightly sag. Next, pull your abs in as tight as you can. As you pull in, exhale all the air from of your lungs, contracting your abdominals and holding them in this position for as long as possible. Repeat this exercise ten times. (You can also do it sitting, but it's a little harder.)

When strength training your abs, begin with your lower abs first by doing leg lifts, lying pelvic tilts, bench knee raises, hanging knee/leg raises, or reverse crunches. Next, take it into your obliques with cross crunches—but don't yank on your head and neck. Finish off with your upper abdominals. Keep your hands on your temples as you lift your head and shoulders off the floor. Crunches are great to perform on a stability ball (found at most sporting-goods stores).

I always get my clients to "bear down" and hold each crunch, blowing all the air out of their lungs. I tell them to imagine that they're having a baby, driving all their effort into contracting and squeezing down on the abs as tight as possible. Ten proper crunches like this can replace dozens of half-hearted raises. I never add extra weight when working abs, as they build quickly. For the sides of the waist, I concentrate on slimming it by doing standing twists using a broomstick or bar resting on the shoulders. Perform a minimum of 50 twists every day.

— *Lower back*. Lie facedown on the floor, and lift your head and shoulders off the floor. You can gently raise the feet up at the same time. Squeeze your buttocks muscles so as not to strain your lower back. Repeat ten times.

Step 57: Intensify Your Interval Training

Last week you were detoxing, so I recommended that you avoid heavy lifting or strenuous cardio. This week, let's really pick it back up.

> **Fat-Burning Secret #23:**
> Hold your shoulders back, tummy in, and head held high, and look ten pounds lighter.

We're going back to interval training for 45 minutes. These intense sessions are going to shed pounds and really work your cardiovascular system. This is such an important component of losing body fat—if you're *not* doing your cardio with intensity, you're wasting valuable time. So work harder at these sessions than you ever have. Push yourself past your anaerobic threshold, and reap the incredible rewards! I firmly believe that cardio is nature's Prozac, and the ideal fat burner.

Your Interval Training

- Warm up with three to five minutes of regular walking.

- Pick up the pace to a jog or walk briskly enough so that you could only continue for about ten minutes before having to slow down. Jog/walk at this pace for five minutes.

- Take it back down to a walk for two minutes.

- For the next 12 minutes, you'll do three 4-minute speed intervals. The first minute should be a light jog, the second minute should be faster and quite intense, and the third minute should be *all out* as fast you can go. The last minute, drop back to a walk to catch your breath. Repeat this three times. (If you're outside, continue with two more speed intervals.)

- If you have a treadmill, switch to incline intervals. Continue to walk, but raise the incline up to the same number in height as your original walking speed. For example, if you walk at a speed of 3.5, raise your incline to 3.5 for one minute. The next minute, incline the treadmill one level higher. Continue this two more times, progressively increasing the incline height by one level each minute. For example, take it up to 4.5 for one minute, then up to 5.5 for one minute, and finish it off at 6.5 for one minute. *Do not increase your speed during incline intervals.* Drop back down to a regular flat walk, catch your breath, and let the burning dissipate from your legs. Repeat this incline interval once more.

- For the next ten minutes, jog or walk at a comfortable, steady pace.

- Cool down after your intervals by slowing down the last few minutes to a stroll.

- Spend 10 to 15 minutes doing the stretches at the end of the book, or use the last 10 minutes of the workout video. Concentrate on elongating the muscles of your thighs, and remember to stretch your calves and Achilles tendons, as they can shorten and tighten up.

Step 58: Resume Strength Training

We've focused a lot on cardio here; however, without enough lean muscle, you'll never feel strong and have that really tight, toned look. So keep up with your core body strength conditioning and stretching. You want to work your muscles two to three times every week.

⟿❊⟾

Summary of Week Ten: *Respect*

Body:

- Rebuild by eating only fresh and simply prepared foods.

- Stand up straight and lose ten pounds. Focus on exercises to correct your posture.

- Get back to interval training to maximize your fat burning, and keep up with three to four *Tight & Toned Workout* sessions.

Mind:

- Understand the power of perception.

Soul:

- Know your worth.

Week Eleven: *Compassion*

You're making great progress and are getting closer to the end of the journey we've been on for the past 11 weeks. I hope that you've taken the time to discover some things about yourself: Do you still look to food to fill the void when you're tired, sad, or lonely? Are you recognizing that life is about the choices you make each day, and the outcome is based on your *reactions* to each and every situation and not the situation itself? Are you feeling stronger when a crisis hits and not reverting to your old coping mechanism(s)? Do you feel empowered?

Now it's time to take all of this up a level.

Step 59: Be a Candle in the Wind

I'll never forget the night Princess Diana died. In the early-morning hours of August 31, 1997, my mother and I had been sitting in my backyard around a campfire, watching the moon dance on the lake. Although we've had many personal struggles over the years, on this particular night we talked openly, sharing our fears, joys, worries, and dreams—and we shed a few tears and had many laughs. Just after 2 A.M. we headed inside, hoping that we wouldn't wake my sleeping family. My mother, an eternal night owl, slipped into the family room to watch a little TV before going to sleep. I'd just dozed off when she came running down the hallway, crying, "Princess Diana just died!" I jumped out of bed, not quite registering what she'd said. Sitting down with her in front of the TV, we watched for hours as the news played out the events of Diana's last night. I'd never been a big follower of the British royal family, but her death still felt like a personal loss.

Why did this woman's passing affect so many of us? Why did it take my mother two days to climb out of her bed? Few will ever hear Elton John's song "Candle in the Wind" without thinking of this beautiful lady. She epitomized women's struggle to find ourselves. Overcoming so many personal obstacles while searching for truth, Princess Diana gave generously of herself and tried to make the world a better place. She was the people's princess, and although her life was so prematurely and senselessly cut short, she'll live forever in the hearts of women, inspiring us to let our own light shine.

Divine Discontent

Since that night so many years ago, I've asked myself, *What's worse—knowing who you are but not living up to your potential, or being content with mediocrity?*

Perhaps it's those of us who are constantly in search of something more who suffer the most—yet I can't imagine trading off the occasional bout of insomnia, anxiety, or frustration to be content with indifference and apathy. It takes courage to demand the most out of ourselves and life. I don't believe that people who are content with mediocrity are mediocre people; rather, they're afraid to really live. So they put limits on their dreams, believing that success requires too much effort or that dreaming is for fools.

About eight months after losing my excess weight, I was running, and I began to question God. "What's wrong with me?" I asked Him. "Why am I always looking for something new to do or try? Why can't I just be content with my life?"

As I continued running along the long dirt road, I came over the top of the hill and saw an awesome view in the distance. Somehow all my questions were answered: *Life is a journey that should be filled with great adventures and meaningful memories. The feelings I kept having weren't negative thoughts holding me back, but were a deep yearning. I simply knew I wanted a full and abundant life, and I couldn't settle for less. I was experiencing "Divine Discontent."*

I realized that this longing was present because I wasn't following the right path for me, even if it seemed perfect to everyone else. As long as I denied myself, I'd forever feel this discontentment. I needed to sit down with my journal and let my thoughts, feelings, desires, fears, aspirations, worries, and hopes for my future pour out on the pages. I had to ask myself some tough questions with an honest and open heart, without fear that anyone else would ever read my words. Then I needed to become very quiet within and make sense of it all.

It was time to follow my path, whether my family, friends, or colleagues agreed. I knew that I needed to listen to my gut instincts . . . my spirit. It became the beginning of a scary, but necessary, personal journey, as I stepped out into uncharted territory!

I believe that God fills us each with purpose—that is, a specific plan for our life. He then tucks it away into our soul before we're born. We grow from babies to toddlers looking to our parents, our first earthly teachers, to show and guide us. As we continue to age from toddlers to teenagers, we pull away from our parents, trying to discover who we are. For most of us, our 20s are spent searching for someone to love us. Our 30s seem to be about loving everyone else but ourselves, and by the time we hit our 40s and 50s, we finally start to realize that until we love ourselves, we'll never be totally content.

And when we become parents ourselves, we want to encourage and shape confidence, purpose, and love into these little human beings who have been entrusted to us. Most often, we think that we know what's best for them, just as our parents did for us. Yet sometimes we forget that unconditional love means allowing our kids to let their own lights shine . . . to be candles in the wind.

You may be wondering what all this has to do with weight loss. Well, as I've said many times in my seminars and to my clients:

"The *Simply . . . Woman!* woman" is not simple.
She's not defined by the size of her hips.
She's a strong, empowered woman who embraces
all that life has to offer. She makes herself
a priority, yet never forgets about the people
who matter most. She lives with passion
and purpose and demands the most
out of herself and life. She is fearless.

Deciding that you're going to take care of your body and look your very best—even if that sounds shallow—can become the catalyst for taking control of your entire life. You'll feel such tremendous confidence as you begin to own your success and realize that if you can do *this,* you can do anything!

Tap into your soul and discover (or better yet, remember) the plan that's nestled away inside you. You do know exactly where you're meant to be, if you'll just listen to that Divine Discontent within you. You may, in fact, be pleasantly surprised and gently reminded that you're exactly where you need to be. Or you might discover that further changes are needed before you can start living the life you dream of.

This week I want you to get out your journal and start to write. Become very quiet and introspective and ask yourself, *What excites me? What inspires me? Where do I want to be ten years from now?* The answers will come. When you stop trying to force things to happen, and instead allow them to gently unfold, then your life will fall into place. Pretend that you're an interviewer or therapist trying to respond to your own questions. What would you tell this person to do if she or he were in your exact situation? With that in mind, what should *you* do?

Step 60: Seize Your Potential

In each of us is a calling to do great things: to live to our highest potential. We all come to this planet to make the world a better place, not to wait for the world to make it better for us. As President John F. Kennedy once said: "Ask not what your country can do for you—ask what you can do for your country."

When I was living in downtown Vancouver a few years ago, some friends had flown in to visit me. They were out one evening walking in an area of the city where there are many street kids and homeless people. They'd been warned that these people were trouble, always begging and harassing the hardworking folk. As my friends walked along, they noticed a dirty and disheveled old lady talking to a group of homeless teens. She drove a broken-down car, from which she took out some ice-cream cones to give to the kids. Then she opened a bottle of vitamins and gave one to each of them. The youngsters laughed with her for a short while as they gobbled down their cones and swallowed their pills. She moved on, heading farther down the street before stopping at the next group.

Who was this old woman? She looked as poor and grubby as the rest of the people on the street, yet she was giving them all food and vitamins. Was she using her last few dollars to give some source of health and love to these teenage runaways? With curiosity and awe, my friends followed her route and watched as she gave back in such an immensely giving and meaningful way. When they returned to my place, filled with inspiration and humility, they related the evening's events. Then we sat down and began to think of ways in which we could make a difference.

I'd be lying if I said that now I go out and try to save the homeless. I *can* say, however, that I look at all people much differently today. You see, *everybody* has feelings and dreams, so something or someone has made these frightened and lonely people believe that there's no other way. They've lost hope, and to be without hope is to live in total despair. Neglected, abandoned, abused, or even chemically imbalanced, those who sleep on benches, dig through garbage cans, and sit helplessly in doorways are somebody's children. Sadly, most have wandered so far down a lonely and deserted path that they don't have the faintest clue how to find their way back.

We see and hear about pain and poverty every day of our lives. We see it in our cities and on television, radio, and in newspapers; and we shake our heads and say "What a shame!" as we switch the channel away from that starving child. We feel sorry for those victims of war as we turn on the music or weather station. But we all have gifts to give to the world. Although some come in materialistic packages with offerings of money, they also come in small but special ways. Cutting our neighbor's grass; bringing dinner to a senior citizen; reading a story to a neglected child; volunteering one day a month at a hospital, food bank, or soup kitchen; buying coffee for a homeless person on a cold winter's day; or babysitting for a stressed-out friend are only some of the millions of ways in which we can give back to others.

When we give, we receive, and this makes us feel good about ourselves. It validates the hope that we truly are good, pure, and full of love and tenderness, and that we're all connected through our humanity. Imagine if, just for one day, everyone in the world tried to be the best person they could be. What a beautiful wish . . . and it would be absolutely contagious.

Have you ever gone out of your way and done something for someone—not because you had to or were going to get anything in return, but simply because you wanted to? Well, keep in mind that giving is a funny thing: In order to maintain a loving, generous heart, you must also receive. Imagine if all you did was give and never got anything back in return—you'd eventually feel pretty empty. You've got to remember to give back to yourself and take the time to refuel. You also need to ask for help when you need it, without feeling selfish or weak. Success is a combination

Crystal Andrus

of many factors, one of which is knowing when to do things alone and when to ask for help. Others are so willing to lend a hand to those who give easily and selflessly. And remember that it's easy to help those who love us, but the true test of kindness is reaching out to those who don't love us back.

This week I also challenge you to create a list of ways in which you can reach out to your community and begin to make a difference in the lives of others. I promise you, *with a 100 percent guarantee,* that it will enhance your own life and will show you that you don't have to wait to win the lottery to help change someone else's life. Each month from now on, do one thing on that list, and see how enriched your own life will become.

Step 61: Take Inventory

I was at the grocery store one night when I noticed about 20 people in unusual blue uniforms. I asked the checker who they were, and she told me that they were there to do inventory.

As I drove home, I started thinking about the concept of inventory. Stores count every single item to see if it corresponds with what's been sold—and whatever isn't accounted for is considered a loss. If retail stores do this to make sure that they're operating at peak performance, why don't we?

A very wealthy and successful businessman once told me that people need to start managing their lives the way a successful business is managed; that is, with profit-and-loss statements. He said that we should list all our assets and liabilities to determine our net worth, and look at our income versus expenses. If our assets outweigh our liabilities, then we're in the black, thus producing a profit; if not, we're in the red, or over our heads in debt. Too many of us are operating in the red, I'm afraid.

Financial security is something most of us yearn for, yet we don't tend to have it. We work all week to pay the bills and hopefully have a little left over. Then, in an attempt to have everything we want right now, we buy on credit and "don't pay for a year." We want and want, yet we never really feel that we have enough. Our car isn't good enough, and our house is too small. To show our family and friends how great we're doing or how much we love them, we fall deeper and deeper into debt. The more we make, the more we spend. The bigger the house, the higher the bills, and at times it never seems to end. . . .

For comparison, I look at my maternal grandparents, who lived in the same house overlooking Lake Ontario for their entire 50-year marriage. My mother and aunts were all born and raised in this small two-bedroom home. My cousins and I grew up going to visit Grandma and Grandpa, knowing that they'd be there waving at the front door. We knew we'd find the same trees in the yard, the big back window overlooking the lake, and my grandma sitting in her favorite chair.

After Grandpa died, we all wondered why at the age of 87 she still lived there alone. She rode her bike to the grocery store and bank, and cooked and cleaned for herself. "This is my home," she'd say. "This is where all my memories are." Grandma possessed all the ingredients that gerontologists predict are needed for a long and happy life—she'd created a state of inner joy and peace within herself. No, she never had a mansion, but what she had was hers, and it was filled with the people that mattered most.

By the same token, home is where *your* heart is. If these days your home is more like a burden of bills and pressure, then you need to reevaluate your priorities. If you spend more time away from home trying to make enough money to pay *for* it than you do *in* it, then it's time to take stock.

Crystal Andrus

Your Financial Serenity

Have you ever done a personal inventory? First of all, learn where your money goes by keeping an expense journal. When I kept one for a month, meticulously recording every cent I spent, I discovered that I wasted so much money. I soon realized that if I didn't start saying no, I'd never get ahead. So, if those credit-card bills give you a monthly anxiety attack, end it by cutting up your cards today!

On the other hand, reducing expenses isn't always enough. You also need to discover what you're really good at and figure out a way to make as much money from it as possible. For example, if you're a people person, why are you working behind a computer? This reminds me of the saying I heard many years ago: "Do what you love and you'll never work a day in your life!"

I believe that when you do what fills you with a burning desire and passion, you'll always find a way to pay your bills. I've already told you about the Law of Divine Reciprocity, which goes something like this: *Whatever you send out into the Universe comes back to you tenfold.* So if you keep doing what you're doing, you're going to keep getting what you're getting.

Statistics shows that more than 70 percent of people describe their current job as if they're in prison. It shouldn't take scientific studies to tell us that career satisfaction is imperative for a happy and fulfilling life, yet how many of us would ever actually take a leap of faith and quit a job we hated? I know how scary this sounds. We have a mortgage or rent to pay, children to feed and clothe, car payments, credit-card bills, insurance, and old student loans to take care of. We know that job satisfaction is fundamental for personal joy, yet we still keep thinking we can fudge it. We think we can somehow fool the Universe into passing along some financial serenity in exchange for dreary, unrewarding work. We say we're happy, yet we wake up dreading the day ahead. We hate our job, gossip at work, fight with our children, can't remember the last time we told our spouses that we loved them, and then climb into bed hoping for a different outcome the next day. Well, if life is merely a culmination of each day, one building on top of the next, what can we do?

We think that if only we could win the lottery, everything would be great. In fact, I once had a client who would tell me that an extra $30,000 would fix her life. It would pay off her loans and credit cards, and then she'd be able to get back on track. Her marriage was suffering because of the financial pressure, and she truly believed that this amount of money would set things right.

As luck would have it (this is a true story!), a year later she won just over $30,000 and paid off all her debts. For a short time, she was happy: The credit-card balances were nil, the loans were paid off, and she even had enough for some renovations around the house. But her troubles were back within six months—and this time, a divorce also came with the package. She realized that the money didn't change anything, and that the problems she'd had before her win were still there. She still had trouble communicating with her husband, shopped beyond her means, and continued to buy on credit. It wasn't money she needed; it was a change in lifestyle and attitude.

It's not what we *make,* it's what we *keep* that determines our net worth. I've met people with large incomes but even larger debt and, although they *should* feel financially secure, they're even more stressed out than those who earn far less.

✽

The subject of finances is a tough one. Just like the messages you heard in childhood about food and your body, the ones you learned about money affect you just as deeply as you become an adult. If your parents taught you that it's the root of all evil or that it will never make you happy, then your attitude and perception of money will be tainted. If your parents never seemed to have enough of it and fought about it all the time, what innate messages are *you* carrying around about prosperity? Did you learn to make your money work for you by investing it properly? Did you learn that making money is simply a choice?

If you really want to get ahead, the best way is to "pay yourself first"! Take 10 percent off the top of every dollar you earn, and deposit it directly into a savings account or fund that you can't touch. Some financial planners also advise automatically withdrawing 10 percent of your monthly income and investing it in a mutual fund. (A fabulous book that can teach even the most inexperienced investor financial serenity is the all-time Canadian bestseller *The Wealthy Barber* by David Chilton. It's laid out in a fun, easy-to-read, fictional story that can absolutely change your financial future.)

I'm certainly not suggesting that we all quit our jobs and weave baskets in search of serenity, but I am proposing that perhaps each day we could take one step to making our dreams a reality.

For example, as I wrote this book, I juggled, struggled, and sometimes felt very financially overwhelmed. Between teaching aerobic classes, training clients, watching the kids, cleaning the house, cooking dinner, doing laundry, organizing Christmas parties, and fighting the flu, I'd slip into my office, often typing away until all hours of the night trying to tune out the world beyond my keyboard. As I read the pages over now, I still see things that I could have—or maybe should have—changed, but I feel proud that I made my dream a reality. Some days I felt empowered as I wrote; others, I doubted myself completely; but more than anything else I knew that if I didn't do this program, part of my spirit would die, and I most certainly would have been filled with regret.

The only way to manifest our dreams is to incorporate small, significant, daily steps among life's demands. We can't let ourselves become overwhelmed by the big picture: The bills will always be there, as will the grocery shopping, laundry, and evening classes. However, we must work toward trading off our desire for financial security and all the trappings that go with it for financial serenity. I keep holding on to the message from Marsha Sinetar's book *Do What You Love, the Money Will Follow*, and I'm waiting with excited anticipation . . . are you?

Step 62: Be a Smart, Strong, Independent Woman

Okay . . . so you know you can make money if you put in the time to educate and advance yourself, but what do you do

---

Simply . . . Inspirational!

I'm always amazed when I make a breakthrough with a no-nonsense kind of woman.

I grew up playing sports and competing in track-and-field. Another top female athlete in my grade school was the quiet and competitive Roxanne McGregor. We never really talked then, and when we went off to different high schools, I saw her from time to time, but we never spoke a word.

Years later, a woman walked into my office. Her face was familiar, but I couldn't place her. "Crystal?" she asked me in a somewhat gruff voice. "Don't you remember me? Roxanne Bruno—I used to be Roxanne McGregor?"

Wow . . . we sure did grow up. Roxanne, now 40 pounds heavier and 20 years older, told me that she wanted to hire me. I was shocked and slightly intimidated, since I remembered this tough cookie from school. She was different now, though: Age, children, and a little weight had softened her. We began to chat and laugh a little, reminiscing about our school years. I knew that Roxanne was a straightforward woman, and I was a little worried that she might not like my "emotional, psychological approach."

Three months later, I realized that I'd completely misjudged this kind and thoughtful woman all these years. No, tears don't flow easily from Roxanne, and she very rarely complains about anything, but she has the heart of an angel—and holds a special place in mine. One year after finishing my program, Roxanne called to tell me that she'd just played with the Canadian Gold Medal Olympic Women's Hockey team and scored a goal. She was living with passion again.

Crystal Andrus

with it once you've made it? Be smart: Many successful women have lost a lot of cash simply because they didn't protect it. They didn't understand, nor did they want to learn, what to do with their own money, and they thought that avoiding the issue would be easier. (Hmm, do I ever know about this first-hand!) With a savvy lawyer, a good accountant, and a wise financial planner, you can safeguard yourself.

But don't wait to make money to learn how to protect it. The wonderful and brilliant financial expert Suze Orman has published many excellent books that can lead you in the right direction; she also has a regular column in *O* magazine, and television and radio shows broadcast on CNBC. (And for more advice from her, you can always visit: **www.suzeorman. com.**)

If you're self-employed, learn how to read your own financial statement. Keep all your receipts in an organized filing system, invest in a reputable bookkeeper, and don't scrimp on a top-notch

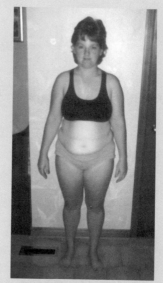

Roxanne before starting the program.

After 12 weeks on the program.

accountant. You may not have a pension plan, so start preparing now for retirement.

If you work for someone else, don't try to save a few bucks by doing your own taxes. Instead, meet with an astute financial advisor and accountant to learn how to maximize your investments, contributions, and write-offs. You may be paying far more tax than you have to.

Take your financial future into your own hands—leave it to no one else. Know your business—and know how much money you have, will have, and should have. Be smart, strong, and independent!

Step 63: Do a Nutrition Check

This week, continue to eat those small portions that your body is becoming used to. I want you to keep limiting (or even avoiding) all cooked, starchy carbohydrates—even the Green Light ones such as sweet potatoes, pasta, rice, and bread. Stay with fresh, frozen, or steamed fibrous vegetables such as lettuce, broccoli, asparagus, spinach, and so forth. Eat no more than two low-glycemic fruits each day, and be sure that they're organic. Completely eliminate sugar and processed items from your diet, and focus on eating foods in their natural state.

The other important area to focus on now is eating protein that's low in saturated fat every few hours. (Remember how highly thermogenic protein is?) Avoid red meat, dark chicken or turkey meat, processed luncheon meat, pork (other than tenderloin), and all dairy products. The best sources are usually the "white" proteins such as egg whites; white chicken and turkey; white fish such as sole, Boston blue, halibut, and tuna; and one percent cottage cheese and fat-free yogurt. Also, supplement your diet with low-carbohydrate, high-protein shakes. As you prepare each meal, visualize a white protein at least the size of your fist; with it, eat two to three handfuls of fresh vegetables. Continue to take your multivitamin, vitamins C and E, your essential fatty acids, and calcium/magnesium.

Step 64: Work Out Your Own Cardio Program

You're getting closer to the end of this program—but certainly not to the end of your own journey. Of course, you'll continue to do cardio workouts after our 12 weeks together are up.

Have you noticed that you're getting better results during long, sustained cardio sessions, or during intense shorter periods? In order to develop your maintenance program, you have to determine what works best for you. Although studies show that intense cardio for 20 minutes burns high amounts of body fat, I've found that nothing works better for me than four to six long early-morning jogs every week (45 to 60 minutes of nonstop, sustained jogging).

This week I want you to vary your cardio workouts, and take notice each day of how you feel. After long, slow-and-steady runs, do you look and feel leaner? Alternatively, do you prefer to maximize your cardio with intense interval sessions? Remember to really pick up the intensity of your cardio if you're doing shorter sessions.

For three days in a row, do highly intense 20-minute interval sessions at a pace where you could *not* maintain a conversation without becoming short of breath quickly. Take a day off; then for the next three days in a row, do sustained 45- to 60-minute cardio sessions (preferably jogging) at a pace where you could maintain a light conversation.

From now on, do whatever style of cardio training is the most effective for your body type for the majority

> **Fat-Burning Secret #24:**
> By varying your cardio training, you'll continue to burn body fat and avoid weight-loss plateaus.

of your cardio sessions, but always interval the opposite style of training once or twice a week to avoid plateaus. Make notes in your journal to track your progress.

⁊❋⁊

Crystal Andrus

Summary of Week Eleven: *Compassion*

Body:

- Eat protein that's low in saturated fat every few hours, and cut right back on starchy carbs to eliminate that last little bit of body fat.

- Discover the right cardio training regimen for you.

Mind:

- Take a personal inventory, and enjoy financial serenity.

- Be a strong, smart, independent woman.

Soul:

- Be a candle in the wind.

- Seize your potential.

Week Twelve: *Love*

You did it! You've come a long way in three months, and this is your success—so own it. Although this journey is really just beginning for you, I want you to pat yourself on the back and take pride in your accomplishments. Do you remember how you felt 12 weeks ago? Doesn't it seem as if that was a lifetime away?

Step 65: Take Time to Appreciate What Matters Most

In our world of deadlines, Little League practices, recitals, housecleaning, laundry, birthday parties, night classes, grocery shopping, overtime, and on and on . . . when is our day of rest, or our holy day?

Although times are changing, and many fathers are becoming more involved in day-to-day family activities, it's still most often we women who set the tone and function as the emotional centers of the home. We're the ones who decide if or when our children will go to ballet practice or soccer, we choose what time they should be in bed at night, and we read them stories. We get dinner ready and make the school lunches; we take the kids to the dentist and we meet their teachers. Most weekends are spent constantly on the move, as we race to activities and occasionally become sidetracked by friends and entertaining.

Unfortunately, we're so distracted by our daily schedules that we're losing our connection to each other. These days, families don't tend to sit together each evening at the dinner table to share the day's events, and couples rarely spend intimate time alone. Each family member has a TV in his or her own room to satisfy different viewing tastes—no longer do we even enjoy a good movie together (half the time we don't even know what our kids are watching!).

If we could learn to relax and slow down, then we, as families, would all probably be a lot better off—instead, we've overscheduled ourselves in the eternal pursuit of having it all. We need to lovingly accept the notion that we *can* have it all . . . just not all at the same time.

I'm tired of hearing women say, "It's not fair—*men* can have it all." Well, I certainly wouldn't want to be a man! I felt very blessed that I was able to stay home while my babies were small, and although many times I felt frustrated that my career was suffering, I look back now and know that I did the best for my children (and myself) because I was connected to them and immersed in their lives. Yes, at times it was terribly draining and sometimes frustrating, but I wouldn't have wanted it any other way. I treasured my middle-of-the-night feedings and being the one to take my girls to the park or hug them when they fell down and scraped their knees.

I feel heartbroken for women who have no choice but to work long hours away from their babies—and I feel even sadder for the women who choose to miss the totality of the greatest blessing they'll ever know. I must stress, however, that I believe every woman has the right to make whatever choice is right for her and her family. But if you're a working mom (as I am), be careful not to get so lost in the demands of work that you miss those cherished moments that you can spend with your kids each day. They grow up so fast, and you can't turn back the clock. A child who doubts his or her mother's love grows up doubting him- or herself.

One night I was bothered by all of this, so I lay down on my kids' beds and asked them, "What's your favorite thing we do together?" I was expecting answers along the lines of "shopping for new clothes" or "going swimming," but both girls pleasantly surprised me. Julia, my youngest, said, "When we kiss," while my older girl Madelaine gently replied, "Just when you're here listening to me read."

Our children won't remember if the windows were spotless or the rugs were always vacuumed, but they *will* remember if we were around. Having a tidy house is necessary for sanity, but keeping an immaculate house will make you crazy!

Think about my friend Cathi, who had everything that the outside world valued: her own business, two brand-new cars, a lovely home, two great kids, and a committed husband. Yet, after reading through this program, she called me one night and said she was miserable. She felt she couldn't do it any longer—yes, she had it all, but she was missing everything in her life.

It hit her one evening when she got in late from work and saw her two little girls' school pictures. Mortified to see them in clothes that didn't match and their hair not combed, Cathi sat down and began to cry. She was never there to see her children before they left for school because she was already working, and she barely got home by the time they went to bed. Weekends were spent trying to catch up on laundry, cleaning, and running the kids around to their different activities. So that night she reevaluated her life and knew that it was time to change her priorities. Even though she'd make far less money, she went ahead and decided to cut her work hours in half and hire someone else for early mornings at the office.

The next weekend she called to tell me that she was out flying a kite with her kids, for the first time ever! She'd always thought that financial success would fulfill her dreams, but it hadn't. Cathi knew that although it was going to be tough—and maybe one of the new cars would have to be traded in for an older model—she could now fall asleep at night without guilt and regret.

I'd also like to share the following story with you (the author is unknown).

An American investment banker was at the pier of a small coastal Mexican village when a little boat with just one fisher-man docked. Inside the boat were several large yellowfin tuna. The American complimented the Mexican on the quality of his fish and asked how long it took to catch them.

The Mexican replied, "Only a little while."

The American then asked, "Why didn't you stay out longer and catch more fish?"

"With this I have more than enough to support my family's needs."

The American asked, "But what do you do with the rest of your time?"

The fisherman said, "I sleep late, play with my children, and take a siesta with my wife, Maria. Then I stroll into the village each evening, where I sip wine and play the guitar with my amigos. I have a full and busy life."

The American scoffed. "I'm a Harvard MBA, and I can help you. You should spend more time fishing, and with the proceeds, buy a bigger boat. With the proceeds from the bigger boat, you could buy several boats—eventually, you'd have a fleet of fishing boats. Instead of selling your catch to a middleman, you'd sell directly to the processor, eventually opening your own cannery. You'd control the product, processing, and distribution. You'd need to leave this village and move to Mexico City, then Los Angeles, and eventually New York, where you'd run your ever-expanding enterprise."

The Mexican fisherman asked, "But how long will all this take?"

To which the American replied, "About 15 to 20 years."

"But what then?"

The American laughed and said, "That's the best part. When the time is right, you'd announce an IPO, sell your company stock to the public, and become very rich. You'd make millions."

"Millions? Then what?"

"Then you'd retire," the American said. "You'd move to a small coastal fishing village, where you'd sleep late, fish a little, play with your kids, take a siesta with your wife, and stroll to the village in the evenings, where you could sip wine and play your guitar with your amigos."

Crystal Andrus

Week Twelve

A Holy Day

A few years ago, I had my kids in lots of activities. Most weekends they'd whine as we drove in the car because they would have rather stayed home to watch Saturday-morning cartoons. One day I'd finally had enough. Why was I stressing myself out to push my kids to be their best and to give them opportunities (as I thought I was doing) when all they wanted to do was play? I now know that kids need relaxation, too. They have enough things to do, and soon enough they'll be adults, doing all the things they *must* do.

I'm concerned that too many kids push themselves hard just to make their parents proud. They see our faces light up when they score that goal or win that contest. They want us to love them, and they feel the immediate adoration we give them when they succeed at something. But they need to feel that love *regardless of their accomplishments.*

I also worry that far too many parents are living vicariously through their children, pushing them into activities either because they couldn't do it themselves as kids, or worse—to compensate for their own regrets of not succeeding in their own lives.

Whatever mistakes our parents may have made—whether they worked too much or yelled too easily—if we never doubted their love for us, we now have an inner confidence that says, *I like who I am.* However, if we doubted our parents' love, whether correctly or not, we must override those wounded feelings now and start giving ourselves the attention and tenderness our parents should have.

We also have a chance to do it differently with our own kids. More than Gap clothes or the latest computer gadgets, our children need our unconditional love and affection. (Mine just want kisses and stories.) And our children need a day of rest . . . as do we adults. All families, no matter their makeup, need at least one day a week together without distractions to do activities they all enjoy— or even nothing at all. Often the best times are the unplanned, lie-on-the-carpet-and-cuddle times. Do whatever works best for your family, but make one day a week *holy.*

Even people who don't have children at home need to take at least one day a week just for themselves. We get so caught up in the big picture that we forget to take time for the little things that can change an overworked, stressed-out woman into a busy but calm and appreciative one. That 24-hour span called a *day* is ours, so we can decide just how we're going to spend it.

> **Fat-Burning Secret #25:**
> When it comes to any success—playing hard is as important as working hard.

If taking one full day of rest and relaxation a week seems impossible, start with just a few hours. Very soon you'll realize the benefits of letting everything else go and relishing the simple joys. This isn't a cleaning day or time to catch up on work—it's time for you to relax and do something you love.

This is your Holy Day, and when God saw it . . . it was good!

Step 66: Appreciate Sex as a Life-Giving Force

We're in our last week together, and if we're really going to embrace this body/mind/spirit connection, we have to tackle this subject! We've talked about the importance of loving ourselves and our kids—now it's time to talk about loving our mate.

For many women, sex has become "the dreaded topic," one they don't want to talk about with their significant other. The idea of passionate and sensuous lovemaking is something many women only want to read about! I wonder why so many women have simply lost their desire. I'm especially bewildered at the surveys in magazines that claim the average couple has sex an average of three times a week. I work with women every day, and certainly don't hear these same statistics coming from them.

For some of us, a low sex drive may stem from a hormonal imbalance, which may be helped with medical intervention. But most often we're just plain tired at the end of the day—we're so stressed out, overwhelmed, resentful, and completely disconnected from our own bodies that we don't even know where to start.

Or maybe we don't allow ourselves the freedom to enjoy a healthy and uninhibited sex life because our own parents demonstrated little affection for each other or, even worse, transferred their sexual hang-ups to us. Because of religious beliefs, some families may have passed down the notion that sex is purely for procreation. Yet even if you're religious, know that in 1 Corinthians 7:4–5, the Bible says: "The wife does not have full rights over her own body; her husband shares them. And the husband does not have full rights over his body; his wife shares them. Do not refuse to give your bodies to each other."

Sadly, for other women, sexual abuse has caused painful memories and, without realizing it, they've allowed their abuser to continue to hold them as victims. By not dealing with the pain of their past, they can't move forward—and by associating negative memories with sex, these women have denied themselves the chance to celebrate their own bodies.

Finally, too many women simply do not see themselves, or their mates, as sexual beings. In fact, just the other day one of my clients told me that once she got married and had kids, being sexual somehow felt rude or unladylike—it just didn't mesh with her new maternal role.

※

Although sex isn't an indicator of intimacy, a sexually secure woman has a certain aura that makes her very intriguing. I'd like you to remember the beginning of your relationship—before kids, stress, boredom, and cellulite took over—when you were excited

Crystal Andrus

to see your mate, planning what to wear, shaving your legs, and making sure you were perfumed. Where did that love go? Have the worries and stresses of life overridden your desire? Are you still making love? If not, maybe the pressure of looking good or the unhappiness you feel about your own body has built up a wall, and it's difficult to let go and relax. Or have you simply lost that chemistry with your partner?

Very often, misplaced aggression manifests itself in the absence of sex, or worse, interest in someone else. I've met many women who have stopped having sex with their husbands, only to seek it outside their marriage. By creating other issues, they then don't have to deal with the real problems that may be going on, or discover their true needs. So they sabotage.

If you're in an unhappy relationship, the idea of a passionate tryst with someone new may sound exciting—you may think that it will leave you feeling desired and even loved. But in reality, once the fling is over, you'll be in need of even more reassurance. The negative energy it takes—that is, the hours of planning, waiting, and rearranging your life for a "phantom man"—is initially thrilling, but it will eventually steal away any bit of self-love and integrity you have left. Imagine if you put the same energy into your marriage, career, or workouts. . . . Just like overeating, excessive shopping, alcoholism, drugs, or gambling, if you have continual meaningless sex, this points to the fact that you're in deep pain, searching for validation and power.

In a committed relationship, though, sex can be a life-giving force that can bond a couple and keep them united in times of adversity. Don't get me wrong: It won't replace friendship or shared values and goals, and it certainly shouldn't come before communication and compromise, which are all necessary qualities in a good relationship. Sex isn't about looking perfect, but rather connecting on a deeper, more spiritual level with someone you love. Making love to someone you care about can take on such an immense meaning and be very empowering. The rush you experience from meaningful sex can make all of life feel so vital!

Crystal Andrus

For example, a friend recently told me that she'd lost interest in sex. Although she loved her husband and they once had a good sex life, it just seemed like a bother now. When he reached out to her, she pulled away. She refused massages for fear they'd lead to something else, and she always wore oversized pajamas to bed and didn't want to kiss him for longer than a few seconds. The longer the two of them went without making love, the less she missed it. I asked her how her husband felt about it.

"Frustrated," she replied.

"Do you love him?" I questioned.

"Definitely," she replied without any hesitation.

"I wonder how it makes him feel about himself," I said.

She thought about it for a minute, and said, "I don't want to make him feel bad about himself. It's really not about him—it's me. I just feel so tired at the end of the day that I can't even think about sex. And when we *do* make love, I find that the whole time I'm worried about what I have to do tomorrow or how fat I feel."

After a lengthy conversation, we agreed that she needed to learn to relax and allow herself to enjoy it in the same way a man does. Her husband didn't have a perfect body, yet that didn't seem to stop him! And he certainly wasn't more worried about the dirty dishes or the sleeping kids.

If we could all think of sex as the ultimate way of reaffirming our love for each other, then perhaps it wouldn't be such a burden. This isn't to suggest that every woman is going to be treated like a princess or that sex should be entirely about pleasing someone else, but I do think that by denying our partners, we're also denying ourselves love and affection. A good sex life can't make a marriage, but a bad one can ruin it!

My friend decided to surprise her husband. The next time we talked, we howled at how much fun she and her husband had both had, and how he strutted around like a peacock the next day!

It's Not All about the Physical Act

I've worked with many women who, once they start feeling great about their appearance, subsequently begin to mistreat their bodies with casual and meaningless sex. Still searching for value and self-worth, their pain just manifests in a different form. These former carbohydrate junkies now use one-night stands to temporarily fill their void.

If you continually have meaningless sex without commitment, then you simply don't feel worthy of true love, and you fear letting anyone get close to you. Nymphomania is really a fear of what you want most: love and intimacy. Deep down inside, you don't believe that your company alone is enough, and unless you give a man what he wants, he might not call the next day. In order to capture his heart or to feel empowered, you're trying to amaze him in bed. You don't realize that it isn't sex you need, it's self-love. Your smile, personality, sense of humor, intelligence, and heart should be sufficient for a man to want to spend time with you—*then* amazing sex can follow.

Meaningless sex may feel good at the time, and it may even make you feel better about yourself temporarily, but the long-term negative side effects can be devastating. Not only are you putting yourself at risk for diseases and unwanted pregnancies, you're killing your self-esteem, emotionally numbing yourself, and making yourself feel even lonelier. Approval was what you were searching for, yet, inevitably, you're left feeling even worse.

As clichéd as it sounds, intimate sex truly is about the body/mind/spirit connection. If you're not in a meaningful relationship, having it with just anyone can bring about more pain and emptiness than the loneliness you may already be feeling.

But keep in mind that sex can be misused in a manipulative and controlling way even within a relationship. When you feel totally disconnected from your partner, or insecure or unloved unless there's constant intercourse, it can be a sign that you're using sex to deal with other issues. This neediness can be an indication of a fear of loss or being alone, or that you're simply not confident in yourself.

⫟✳⫠

For the majority of my ten-year marriage, I used sex to deal with many of the problems between my husband and me. When an issue cropped up or I sensed that my husband was upset with me, having sex was an easy way to fix things. The trouble was that we never actually dealt with any of our issues, either individually or as a couple—so when real problems came along, we didn't have the skills and necessary ingredients to sustain a lifelong commitment. I feared abandonment and his disapproval, so I was unable to have an open, honest friendship and express my truest needs and deepest desires to him. Having sex kept him happy, so I thought I was, too. In the years following my divorce, I discovered that anything that has a hold on us keeps us in bondage. My high sex drive was motivated by control and fear—and intimacy and control can't exist together.

A little abstinence from something that has a hold on you— whether it's food, alcohol, shopping, gambling, drugs, or sex—can be liberating, but be careful of going without sex for too long if you're in a loving relationship. Having sex won't fix your problems any more than eating food will make you happier; conversely, making love once the problems are fixed is an amazing life-giving experience that can be the greatest connection two people can have.

If you're in an unhappy relationship that you feel is beyond repair, it's time to leave it while you still feel okay about yourself. Then, when (or if) you decide to enter into a new relationship, the sex will be about celebrating passion and life, not about making yourself—or even worse, someone else—feel better.

Before you blame your mate or find someone new, look within and ask yourself if it's really your mate you're unhappy with, or is there something else going on? Are you happy with yourself? By developing confidence and finding and following your purpose in life, you won't need anyone else to make you feel good about yourself. Another person can bring a smile to your face and joy to your heart, but self-assurance must come from within.

Try to think of sex in this way: You have one life; and if you're in a committed, long-term, monogamous relationship (and plan on keeping it that way), this is the only person who will touch, kiss, love, and explore you! You deserve a passionate and fulfilling life, and making love is a part of that excitement. You—and your mate—deserve it!

Finally, I want to stress that if you're single, you shouldn't panic and settle for a jerk for fear of being alone. The love of close friends and family can still give a secure and confident woman the companionship and connectedness she needs. However, for the most part, I don't think that any of us can or should totally go it alone forever.

If you're in a relationship and you feel as if things could be improved in the bedroom, try to find out where they broke down and why (this is no different from any other area of your life that isn't working). Do you have some unresolved issues with your mate that are manifesting themselves in your sex life? Are you using intercourse as a power struggle or as a way of exerting control in your relationship? Are you associating sex with negative memories? Is your mate rejecting you? If so, I highly recommend speaking with a professional counselor who can help you work it out.

If you've simply gotten caught up with life, and making love has lost its priority, take it slowly. Start with a date and pretend that it's your first one together. When you do decide to get romantic, a glass of wine and candlelight can certainly enhance the mood. And lingerie doesn't have to be too revealing if you're feeling self-conscious—a pretty nightgown with a touch of lace can do wonders, and it helps remind you that you're still a feminine, beautiful woman!

Step 67: Check Your Results

Complete your Fitness Appraisal for the last time. Look back at your initial scores on your Success Tracker I (on page 37) and compare your results. Did you get smaller? Is your dress size down? How is your resting heart rate? By now you should be feeling much better. I said back in Week One that you might not remember the way you feel in 12 weeks . . . aren't you glad you recorded this journey along the way? Anytime you feel as if you're getting off track, read through your journal and look at your "before" picture. You now know exactly what to do if you ever wander off your path again.

Now it's time to take an "after" picture of yourself. This is very important, as it will become your trophy. Don't feel embarrassed or ashamed to be proud of yourself—let your light shine! I also highly recommend that you spend a few hundred dollars and book an appointment with a professional photographer and makeup artist, since these pictures will be with you for life. When you're an old woman sitting in your rocking chair, you'll be so glad that you took some amazing pictures of yourself. You're worth it, you deserve it, and I want you to do this . . . for you!

Step 68: Look to the Future

Go back to the Goal-Setting Workshop you completed in Week Two, and look at your original goals. Have you accomplished them? Are you ready to set new ones? Your journey has really just begun, so let's look a year down the road and set some realistic and attainable goals that will keep you focused. Whatever your ambitions are, be clear and specific, including setting a date for accomplishing them. Believe that you're going to attain them, because the strength of your beliefs is one of the most important indicators of whether you'll be successful or not. Focus on your dreams with a burning desire: What will these new accomplishments bring to your life? Stay consistent in your actions and persevere, even when you feel frustrated or unsure. Fear of succeeding is one of the top reasons we self-sabotage, but remember that it's just as easy to prosper as it is to fail. It's all in your daily choices!

Goal-Setting Workshop II

Over the next 12 months, your body, mind, and spirit are going to continue grow, develop, and change. Pick three goals that you want to see happen. Remember:

Specific
Measurable
Attainable
Realistic
Time-Bound

Over the next 12 weeks, one goal I really want to accomplish is:

_____

_____

_____

Three of my bad habits or mental roadblocks that could hold me back from reaching that goal are:

1. _____

2. _____

3. _____

Three things I can do to help keep me on track are:

1._____

2._____

3._____

For my second goal, I'd like to:

_____

_____

_____

Three of my self-sabotaging behaviors that could hold me back from reaching that goal are:

1._____

2._____

3._____

Three things I can do to avoid these behaviors are:

1._____

2._____

3._____

The third goal I'd like to accomplish in the next year is:

_____

_____

_____

Three things that could hold me back from reaching that goal are:

1._____

2._____

3._____

Three things that can help me reach that goal are:

1._____

2._____

3._____

Step 69: Develop Your Maintenance Plan

You may be ready to start your maintenance plan, or perhaps you're still working hard and would like more results before you slow things down. Whatever the case, here's the main thing you need to understand about maintaining your success:

If you keep doing what you're doing, you're going to keep getting what you're getting . . . results!

Don't fall back into your old patterns or fool yourself into thinking that you can get away with sneaking three or four "treat days" back into a week. Each person's maintenance plan is very individual: Some find that by staying dedicated with the exercise portion but by taking two days off each week from clean eating, they can still continue to maintain their results, while others prefer to reduce the amount they're exercising but continue on the 80/20 plan, eating clean for six or even seven days a week.

I personally do an 80/20 split each day. Eighty to ninety percent of the foods I eat, especially for breakfast and lunch, are perfect:

low-calorie, low-saturated-fat Green Light Foods. Then I might have a little treat with dinner. However, that also means I don't get a cheat day once a week! I'm pretty much always on track. Some women find that they can begin to adjust their protein, carbohydrate, and fat percentages slightly, allowing for a little less protein and more carbs. Yet I still find that as soon I start noticing the weight creeping back, I readjust my diet to our original ratio.

Watch those wasted calories, and don't fool yourself into thinking that you can begin slipping high-glycemic Red Light Foods or starchy carbohydrates back in. Be aware that change doesn't happen quickly. For example, even if you quit exercising and eat whatever you want for the next six weeks, you'll probably maintain your current success—and this is how most people regain their weight. They start sneaking bread and desserts back in, just a little here and there, and eventually the old weight piles right back on.

For your exercise-maintenance plan, I recommend that you keep up with at least four hours a week, consisting of five 30-minute intense cardio sessions and two or three strength workouts using the DVD. If you want more results, push yourself harder. Your intensity must continue to increase during your workouts for you to keep on making progress. If you maintain your current intensity, you'll maintain your current results.

Continually reassess yourself to stay on track. I want you to do monthly checkups to make sure that you're continually improving. (Use the Success Tracker II provided at the end of this chapter to monitor your progress.)

Finally, I'd love to hear from you. Please contact me at: **crystal@simplywoman.com**, and let me know how you enjoyed this program. Send me your results and a copy of your Success Tracker I. Keep in touch anytime, and send me your testimonial or your "before" and "after" pictures. Just remember: Stay focused and continue to set new goals!

Success Tracker II

For the next 3 months, record your progress at the end of each month.
Take your measurements and then total the number of inches lost at the bottom of each "difference" column.

DATE : _____	12 WEEKS AGO	DIFFERENCE	END OF 4. MONTH	DIFFERENCE	END OF 5. MONTH	DIFFERENCE	END OF 6. MONTH
Resting Heart Rate							
Blood Pressure (if possible)							
Weight lbs/kg							
Push-ups							
Curl-ups							
Measurements:							
Neck							
Chest							
Upper Abs # of inches above B.B							
Waist @ B.B							
Lower Abs # of inches below B.B							
Hips (at widest part)							
Thighs–Upper							
-Lower							
Knee							
Calf # of inches up from floor							
Arm # of inches in from elbow -Relaxed							
-Flexed							
Total Inches =							
"Average" Dress Size							
Body Fat % (if possible)							

Crystal Andrus

Summary of Week Twelve: *Love*

Body:

- Complete your final check-in to see how well you've done. Set some new goals for the next 12 months.

- Develop your maintenance plan.

Mind:

- Stay determined to maintain your results.

Soul:

- Take the time to appreciate the things that matter most. Have fun!

- Appreciate sex with someone you love as a life-giving force.

Our Closing Moments

In our attempt to understand ourselves and the world around us, we often lose sight of the things that matter most—we're so hard on our mates, parents, children, friends . . . and even ourselves. How many times do we get angry with someone for letting us down? Perhaps we're intolerant of the pal who cancelled plans at the last minute, or mad at the husband who forgot a dinner date. We're disappointed that our parents forgot to call us on our birthday, or that our sibling drove two hours to visit us—only to say something that hurt our feelings. We mistakenly focus on people's actions rather than their intentions.

We're determined to hold people to their promises in our attempt to control them: "You offered, now you'd better come through!"

Things can't—and won't—always go our way. Many people have wonderful hearts, filled with goodness, but for reasons of their own, they aren't always able to do what they promised. We must deal with feeling let down: People will sometimes hurt us, not because they don't care about us, but because that's just how life goes. It's the *intention* rather than the *outcome* that matters most.

As I say this, I'm reminded of that famous line "The road to hell is paved with good intentions," and you might be thinking it, too, yet I innately know that when we surrender our attachment to outcomes and look deep into the heart of another, we are able to *live and let live*. We also know that we won't always do it the way others believe we should either; and we embrace the fact that it's not our job, right, or responsibility to impress upon someone else how they should live.

We must discard expectations and not punish ourselves (or others) when someone disappointments us. Disappointments are about judgment. If you believe deep down that your parents, siblings, friends, mates, or even just acquaintances have good hearts, you can accept that they can only give or do what they're able to.

If their actions don't work for you, then surrender to the feeling. Sometimes that even means surrendering the relationship.

Staying with this thought, how about surrendering your attachment to all things, including the idea of who you are and what you expect life to give you? How about surrendering your labels, syndromes, addictions, and disorders? How about if from today forward you discarded your judgments, limitations, and preconceived notions about yourself, and set the intention that all things are not only possible but quite probable, as long as you're an open receptacle to receiving the blessings, abundance, and joy that life has to offer!

Surrendering is powerful, not passive. It is letting go and letting God, trusting that *what is* will always find a way, and that you don't have to make it go your way. *It is what it is. . . .*

We all discover life's lessons at different times and in different ways along our individual journeys: Some of us learn quickly and easily, while others fight the Laws of the Universe; some have an innate ability to understand the soul of a person, while others define another's spirit by their worldly actions. We all make mistakes; we all struggle for love and validation; and we're all more alike than we realize, as we search for understanding, meaning, and purpose. No two people can be at the same place at the same time in their life's journey—so we must relinquish judgment, self-righteousness, and manipulation. Once we begin to live with sincere and pure intentions, we'll be able to live authentically. We resonate with love, true power, and joy; and our bodies become pure conduits of consciousness: We feel incredible, look magnificent, and spread love and light on everyone we meet!

I pray that over these past 12 weeks you've begun to accept, honor, and, most important, *love* yourself. Remember that life will only give you what you ask of it. I hope that you can finally say, "Although I could be better, I could be worse. I'm blessed *as I am*. I am *Simply . . . Woman!*"

Let's summarize the most important steps to living with authenticity:

Crystal Andrus

10 Steps to Living with Authenticity

1. **Honor your temple!** Eat whole foods, drink clean water, cleanse impurities, nourish your brain with EFAs, strengthen your body with resistance training, make your heart and lungs powerful with cardiovascular exercise, breathe, and get your Z's.

2. **Distinguish between the important stuff and the pettiness** that can slow you down, take away your focus, and sabotage your success. Strive to be the very best you can be, but cut yourself some slack and do the same with those you love. Save the drama for the stage.

3. **Discover your passion!** The Universe has a plan for your life that's so much greater than anything you could ever devise. Listen to your gut instincts and follow your inner voice.

4. **Relinquish the need for approval.** Believe in yourself—you're entitled to dress, walk, and talk any way you choose, regardless of anyone else's opinion. Confidence comes from within, so remember: Fake it till you make it!

5. **Be accountable for everything you say and do.** Face your truest fears, and refuse to burden someone else with your issues.

6. **Set strong but loving personal boundaries.** If someone is continually trying to hurt you, control you, or disrespect you, they have issues, and you don't need to own their "garbage."

Crystal Andrus

7. **Detached from outcome.** Change the things you can, and accept the things you can't.

8. **Practice forgiveness.** We're all human and we all make mistakes, so choose to let go of resentment and shame. And love with an open and compassionate heart.

9. **Know your worth**, and honor your values, even if no one else gets it! Refuse to manipulate others for your personal gain. Speak with truth, refrain from gossip, and maintain your integrity.

10. **Have faith in a Higher Power.** No matter how difficult life may seem, every experience is a lesson for growth, so seize the day and make the choice to move forward. Let go and let God!

STOP! STOP! STOP!

CARBOHYDRATE	Glycemic Index	Serving Size	CARB (amount in grams)	FAT
BREAD PRODUCTS				
Bagel	72	1 small	35	2
French Bread	95	4 oz	30	2
Kaiser Roll	73	4 oz	32	2
White Bread	72	1 piece	14	1
Whole-Wheat Bread	72	1 piece	12	1
Millet	71	½ cup	14	1
Stuffing	74	½ cup	21	6
Bread Crumbs	70	½ cup	35	2
CEREALS				
Cheerios	74	½ cup	20	2
Corn Bran	75	½ cup	20	1
Corn Chex	83	½ cup	25	0
Cornflakes	80	½ cup	26	0
Rice Chex	89	½ cup	26	0
Rice Krispies	82	½ cup	26	0
Total	76	½ cup	22	1
Shredded Wheat	83	2 pieces	20	1
CRACKERS				
Graham Crackers	74	8 pieces	18	3
Melba Toast	75	6 pieces	22	0
Stoned Wheat Thins	72	6 pieces	30	2
Ritz	75	10 pieces	20	4
DAIRY PRODUCTS*				
Butter	5	2 tbsp	0	23
		½ cup	0	92
Cheese				
Brie	10	2 oz	0	16
Cheddar	10	2 oz	0	18
Cheddar, shredded	10	¼ cup	0	9
Cream Cheese	10	2 tbsp	1	10
Feta	10	2 oz	2	16
Mozzarella	10	2 oz	2	17
Mozzarella, shredded	10	¼ cup	1	7
Parmesan, shredded	10	¼ cup	1	8
Swiss	10	2 oz	0	16
Ricotta	10	¼ cup	2	8

*These foods may appear lower in glycemic index, but they are too high in calories and/or fat.

Crystal Andrus

RED LIGHT CARBOHYDRATES

STOP! STOP! STOP!

CARBOHYDRATE	Glycemic Index	Serving Size	CARB (amount in grams)	FAT (amount in grams)
DAIRY PRODUCTS* continued				
Half and Half Cream	25	1 cup	10	28
		2 tbsp	2	6
Whipping Cream, regular	30	1 cup	7	88
light	30	1 cup	7	74
Sour Cream, regular	25	2 tbsp	1	7
Ice Cream, regular	61	½ cup	22	18
Milk, homogenized	32	1 cup	11	8
Margarine, regular	10	2 tbsp	0	22
		½ cup	0	91
Yogurt, plain, regular	35	½ cup	12	10
DRINKS				
Power Drinks (i.e., Gatorade)	90	8 oz	15	0
Soda Pop, regular, assorted	70	12 oz	30	0
Lemonade, sweetened	70	8 oz	30	0
Iced Tea, sweetened	70	8 oz	29	0
Fruit Punch	70	8 oz	30	0
Alchoholic Beverages*				
Daiquiri	10	4 oz	42	0
Margarita	10	4 oz	45	0
Piña Colada	10	4 oz	40	0
FRUIT				
Fruits, canned in syrup	79	4 oz	20	0
Figs, dried*	61	10 figs	122	2
LEGUMES				
Fava Beans	80	3 oz	17	0
PASTAS AND RICE				
Instant Rice, white	90	½ cup	21	1
Long Grain Rice, white	72	½ cup	21	0
Jasmine Rice	100	½ cup	21	0
Rice Noodles, white & brown	80 - 92	½ cup	19	0
PROTEIN/POWER BARS				
Power Bar, chocolate	83	1 bar	42	15
MET-Rx Bar, vanilla	74	1 bar	50	2

*These foods may appear lower in glycemic index, but they are too high in calories and/or fat.

RED LIGHT CARBOHYDRATES

STOP! STOP! STOP!

CARBOHYDRATE	Glycemic Index	Serving Size	CARB (amount in grams)	FAT
SNACKS & MISCELLANEOUS				
Corn Chips*	63	20 chips	26	15
Potato Chips*	57	20 chips	25	20
Pretzels, thin	83	30 pieces	20	0
Rice Cakes	85	1 cake	7	0
Candy Bars, examples:				
Mars chocolate bar	68	1.76 oz bar	40	13
Junior Mints	70	1.6 oz	38	4
Candy, examples:				
Skittles	70	45 pieces	45	3
Licorice	80	3 pieces	27	0
Popcorn, plain, microwave	72	1½ cups	11	0
Pizza, cheese & pepperoni	60	¼ pie pie	25	25
Desserts, examples:				
Pie	75	1 piece	50	25
Brownie, with nuts	65	1 brownie	15	6
Carrot Cake	79	1 small piece	48	21
SWEETENERS				
Corn Syrup	80	¼ cup	55	0
Glucose	99	½ cup	10	0
Sugar, white & brown*	65	1 tsp	4	0
	65	½ cup	50	0
VEGETABLES				
Cooked Parsnips	97	1 cup	15	0
Potato, russet, baked	95	1 medium	30	0
Potato, instant mashed	85	½ cup	20	5
Potato, French fried	75	1 large	29	26

SPICES, SAUCES & CONDIMENTS

Gravy, bacon bits, barbeque sauce, ketchup, mayonnaise, cocktail sauce, jam or jelly, marmalade, plum sauce, sweet 'n' sour sauce, teriyaki sauce, honey garlic sauce, salad dressing, butter, margarine, vegetable oil, corn oil.

---

*These foods may appear lower in glycemic index, but they are too high in calories and/or fat.

Crystal Andrus

YELLOW LIGHT CARBOHYDRATES

PROCEED WITH CAUTION!

CARBOHYDRATE	Glycemic Index	Serving Size	CARB (amount in grams)	FAT
BREAD PRODUCTS				
Rye Crispbread	67	1 slice	15	1
Breton Wheat Crackers	67	6 crackers	14	4
CEREALS				
Grape-Nuts	67	½ cup	19	1
Life	66	½ cup	25	1
Oatmeal, quick	66	½ cup	26	1
Cream of Wheat	66	½ cup	26	0
Puffed Wheat	67	½ cup	13	0
Special K	69	½ cup	10	0
Raisin Bran	61	½ cup	23	1
Muesli	66	½ cup	12	2
DAIRY PRODUCTS*				
Yogurt, fat-free with sugar	35	½ cup	17	0
Ice Cream, lowfat with sugar	50	½ cup	22	5
Milk, 2%	32	1 cup	12	5
Sour Cream, light	25	2 tbsp	3	3
Cheese				
Feta, light	10	2 oz	1	7
Cottage, regular	10	2 tbsp	3	3
Ricotta, fat-free	10	¼ cup	12	0
DRINKS				
Wine, red and white	0	3.5 oz	2	0
Beer, light	0	12 oz	4	0
regular	0	12 oz	13	0
Soda Pop, diet[1]	0	12 oz	0	0
Coffee, black	0	8 oz	0	0
FRUITS				
Cantaloupe	65	½ cup	6	0
Pineapple	66	2 slices	10	0
Watermelon	75	½ cup	6	0
Raisins	64	½ cup	44	0
Avocado*	0	½ cup, cubed	18	12
Kiwi	58	1 medium	12	0
Banana	52	1 medium	24	0
Dates, dried*	50	7 dates	40	0

[1] Eat in moderation, as these may increase your susceptibility to some diseases.
*These foods may appear lower in glycemic index, but they are too high in calories and/or fat.

YELLOW LIGHT CARBOHYDRATES

PROCEED WITH CAUTION!

CARBOHYDRATE	Glycemic Index	Serving Size	CARB (amount in grams)	FAT
LEGUMES*				
Split-Pea Soup, canned	66	½ cup	14	2
Baked Beans, canned*	68	½ cup	30	2
PASTA & RICE*				
Basmati Rice	58	½ cup, cooked	17	0
Uncle Ben's, converted, white rice	38	½ cup, cooked	18	1
Pasta, white	40 - 50	½ cup, cooked	22	1
SNACKS & MISCELLANEOUS				
Angel Food Cake	67	1/6 of cake	29	3
Water Crackers	63	5 pieces	18	2
Milk Arrowroot Cookies	69	5 cookies	18	5
Tortilla Chips, baked, lowfat	63	15 chips	24	3
Peanut M&M's*	33	15 pieces	17	13
SWEETENERS				
Honey	58	1 tbsp	18	0
Unprocessed blackstrap molasses	60	1 tbsp	14	0
Organic, grade C maple syrup	55	¼ cup	52	0
Sucralose - Splenda[1]	0	--	0	0
Saccharine - Sweet'N Low[1]	0	--	0	0
Aspartame - Equal, NutraSweet[1]	0	--	0	0
VEGETABLES				
Beets	64	3 oz	7	0
Potato, new, boiled	60	½ cup	15	0

SPICES, SAUCES & CONDIMENTS

Guacamole, fat-free & light mayonnaise, relish, fat-free salad dressing, olive oil, canola oil, peanut butter, soya sauce, horseradish.

---

[1] Eat in moderation, as these may increase your susceptibility to some diseases.
*These foods may appear lower in glycemic index, but they are too high in calories and/or fat.

Crystal Andrus

GREEN LIGHT CARBOHYDRATES

GO! GO! GO!

CARBOHYDRATE	Glycemic Index	Serving Size	CARB (amount in grams)	FAT
BREAD PRODUCTS*				
Pita Bread, whole wheat	57	½ medium	17	2
Sourdough Bread	52	1 piece	16	1
Pumpernickel Bread	50	1 piece	16	1
Seeded Rye Bread	58	1 piece	12	1
CEREALS*				
Kellogg's All-Bran USA	38	½ cup	23	1
Kellogg's All-Bran Canada	50	½ cup	23	1
Kellogg's Bran Buds with Pysllium	47	½ cup	12	0
Old-fashioned Oatmeal	49	½ cup	27	1
DAIRY PRODUCTS				
Milk, skim	32	1 cup	13	0
1%	32	1 cup	12	2.5
Yogurt, fat-free, with sweetener[1]	14	½ cup	7	0
Cheese				
Cottage, 1%	15	½ cup	4	2
Cottage, fat-free	15	½ cup	5	0
Parmesan, fat-free	10	2 tsp	2	0
Cream, fat-free	10	2 tbsp	2	0
Sour Cream, fat-free	10	2 tbsp	6	0
Ice Cream, fat-free, with sweetener[1]	40	½ cup	24	0
Frozen Yogurt, fat-free, with sweetener[1]	25	½ cup	20	0
DRINKS				
Water	0	8 oz	0	0
Apple Juice*	40	8 oz	30	0
Grapefruit Juice	48	8 oz	20	0
Pineapple Juice*	46	8 oz	34	0
Orange Juice	46	8 oz	18	0
Tomato Juice*	38	8 oz	40	0
Carrot Juice	43	8 oz	23	0
Soy Milk, fat-free	44	8 oz	20	2
Perrier	0	8 oz	0	0
Club Soda	0	8 oz	0	0
Tea, herbal	0	8 oz	0	0

[1] Eat in moderation, as these may increase your susceptibility to some diseases.
*These foods are healthy, but are high in glycemic load.

Crystal Andrus

GREEN LIGHT CARBOHYDRATES

GO! GO! GO!

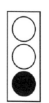

CARBOHYDRATE	Glycemic Index	Serving Size	CARB (amount in grams)	FAT
FRUITS				
Apple	38	1 small	15	0
Apricot, raw	30	3	12	0
Apricot, dried*	30	¼ cup	27	0
Cherries	22	3 oz	12	0
Grapefruit	25	½ medium	17	0
Grapes	48	1 cup	15	0
Mango*	51	½ medium	17	0
Orange	42	1	11	0
Peach	42	1	11	0
Pear	38	1	11	0
Plum	39	1	12	0
Strawberries	20	½ cup	5	0
Blackberries	20	½ cup	8	0
Raspberries	20	½ cup	7	0
Blueberries	20	½ cup	10	0
Cranberries	20	½ cup	6	0
GRAINS*				
Barley, pearled	22	¼ cup, cooked	21	0
Buckwheat (kasha)	54	¼ cup, cooked	15	1
Bulgar	48	¼ cup, cooked	15	1
LEGUMES				
Baked Beans, in tomato sauce	48	¼ cup	4	1
Black Beans	30	¼ cup, boiled	11	5
Green Beans	45	¼ cup, boiled	1	0
Black-Eyed Peas	42	¼ cup, boiled	8	1
Chickpeas*	30	¼ cup, boiled	15	2
Kidney Beans	46	¼ cup, boiled	9	0
Lentils	29	¼ cup, boiled	9	0
Lima	40	¼ cup, boiled	8	0
Pinto Beans	39	¼ cup, boiled	13	0
Split Peas	32	¼ cup, boiled	10	0
PASTA AND RICE* *(please note - a serving is ½ a cup!!!)*				
Pasta, whole wheat*	40	½ cup cooked	22	1
Brown Rice*	50	½ cup cooked	16	1
Wild Rice*	55	½ cup cooked	17	0

*These foods are healthy, but are high in glycemic load.

Crystal Andrus

GREEN LIGHT CARBOHYDRATES

GO! GO! GO!

CARBOHYDRATE	Glycemic Index	Serving Size	CARB (amount in grams)	FAT
SWEETENERS				
Stevia (herb)	0	--	0	0
(Use the herb found at health-food stores, not white crystalline stevia extract)				
VEGETABLES				
Lettuce				
Boston	0	1 head	4	0
Romaine	0	3 cups	4	0
Iceberg	0	3 cups	6	0
Spinach	0	3 cups	4	0
Kale, Swiss Chard	0	½ cup	3	0
Green Peas	45	½ cup	11	0
Asparagus	20	⅔ cup	4	0
Artichokes	0	1 large	6	0
Broccoli	0	½ cup	4	0
Carrots	47	1 whole, 7" long	8	0
Cabbage	0	1 cup	4	0
Celery	0	1 stalk	1	0
Cauliflower	0	½ cup	3	0
Corn*	54	½ cup	21	1
Cucumber	0	½ cup, sliced	1	0
Eggplant	20	½ cup	3	0
Mushrooms	20	½ cup	2	0
Onions	50	½ cup, chopped	7	0
Peppers	0	½ cup, chopped	5	0
Radishes	15	½ cup, sliced	3	0
Sweet Potato (Yam)*	44	½ cup, no skin	28	0
Tomato	15	1 small	6	0
Water Chestnuts	15	½ cup	15	0
Squash	15	½ cup	12	0

SPICES, SAUCES & CONDIMENTS

All spices; basil, oregano, chili powder, thyme, dill, coriander, cumin, cayenne, parsley, rosemary, chives, paprika, mint, etc., Tobasco sauce, lemon & lime juice, garlic, vinegar (balsamic, apple cider, etc.), mustard, hummus, salsa.

*These foods are healthy, but are high in glycemic load.

RED LIGHT PROTEIN

STOP! STOP! STOP!

PROTEIN	Serving Size	PROTEIN	CARB	FAT
		(amount in grams)		
BEEF, broiled, 4 oz				
Porterhouse		28	0	25
Short Ribs		25	0	48
Ground Beef				
Regular		18	0	30
Lean		20	0	23
Extra Lean		21	0	19
Rib Steak		25	0	35
Top Sirloin		31	0	19
T-Bone		28	0	24
Tenderloin		28	0	25
DAIRY PRODUCTS				
Butter	2 tbsp	0	0	23
	½ cup	1	0	92
Cheese				
Brie	2 oz	12	0	16
Cheddar	2 oz	14	0	18
Cheddar, shredded	½ cup	7	0	9
Cream Cheese	2 tbsp	4	1	10
Feta	2 oz	10	2	16
Mozzarella	2 oz	16	2	17
Mozzarella, shredded	½ cup	6	1	7
Parmesan, shredded	½ cup	9	1	8
Swiss	2 oz	16	0	16
Riccotta	½ cup	7	2	8
Half and Half Cream	1 cup	7	10	28
	2 tbsp	0	2	6
Whipping Cream, regular	1 cup	5	7	88
light	1 cup	5	7	74
Sour Cream, regular	½ cup	2	3	12
Ice Cream, regular	½ cup	5	22	18
Milk, homogenized	1 cup	8	11	8
Margarine, regular	2 tbsp	0	0	22
	½ cup	1	0	91
Yogurt, regular, plain	½ cup	9	12	10
DUCK, with skin, domestic	4 oz	22	0	32

RED LIGHT PROTEIN

STOP! STOP! STOP!

PROTEIN	Serving Size	PROTEIN	CARB	FAT
		(amount in grams)		
EXAMPLES OF FAST FOOD				
Wendy's				
Big Bacon Classic		34	45	29
Classic Hamburger, single		24	31	19
McDonald's				
Big Mac		24	47	34
McChicken		17	44	30
Chicken McNuggets	6 nuggets	15	18	20
Swiss Chalet				
¼ Chicken, white, with skin		47	0	22
Double Leg Chicken, meat only		80	0	34
Large Cut Ribs, meat only		118	10	110
Burger King				
Whopper		31	52	43
FISH				
Fish Sticks	5 pieces	10	18	20
HAM, 4 oz, roasted		28	0	24
GOOSE, 4 oz, with skin		29	0	25
LAMB, 4 oz				
Leg, roasted		29	0	19
Rib, broiled		25	0	33
LUNCHEON MEAT				
Bologna	2 slices	7	2	16
Corned Beef	4 oz	21	0	22
Pate	2 oz	9	0	12
Hot Dog	1 wiener	6	5	13
PORK, roasted, *lean and fat*				
Loin, whole	4 oz	31	0	17
Sirloin, without bone	4 oz	31	0	28
with bone	4 oz	30	0	17
Spare Ribs, with bone	1 lb	33	0	34
Bacon	4 slices	10	0	15
Sausages	3 links	8	0	22
VEAL				
Loin	4 oz	34	0	20

Crystal Andrus

YELLOW LIGHT PROTEIN

PROCEED WITH CAUTION!

PROTEIN	Serving Size	PROTEIN	CARB	FAT
		(amount in grams)		
BEEF, 4 oz				
Liver[1]		30	9	9
Flank Steak		30	0	14
Top Round		34	0	12
CHICKEN, 4 oz				
Leg, with skin		30	0	15
Drumstick		14	0	6
Thigh		16	0	10
Wing, with skin		9	0	6
CORNISH HEN, 12 oz, roasted		44	0	24
DAIRY PRODUCTS*				
Yogurt, fat-free with sugar	½ cup	9	17	0
Ice Cream, lowfat with sugar	½ cup	4	19	3
fat-free with sugar	½ cup	4	20	0
Milk, 2%	1 cup	8	12	5
Sour Cream, light	2 tbsp	1	3	3
Cheese				
Feta, light	2 oz	12	1	7
Cottage, regular	½ cup	14	5	5
EGG, whole		6	1	5
yolk only		3	0	5
EXAMPLES OF FAST FOOD				
Wendy's				
Grilled Chicken Sandwich		24	36	6
Chili, small		17	21	6
McDonald's				
Whole-Wheat McGrill		26	39	6
One Chicken Fajita		15	26	6
Burger King				
Santa Fe Grilled Chicken		29	47	5
FISH, 4 oz				
Catfish		18	0	9
Cuttlefish[1]		18	1	1
Shrimp[1]		24	0	2

[1]Although low in fat, these are very high in cholesterol.

YELLOW LIGHT PROTEIN

PROCEED WITH CAUTION!

PROTEIN	Serving Size	PROTEIN	CARB (amount in grams)	FAT
FISH, continued				
Sardines, skinless, canned	3¾ fl oz	12	0	6
In olive oil, drained	¼ cup	13	0	9

(Health Canada & the US Food and Drug Administration have recently issued advisories due to the toxic amounts of mercury and PCB found in many of the larger fishes.)

PROTEIN	Serving Size	PROTEIN	CARB	FAT
Atlantic Salmon	4 oz	25	0	14
Sockeye Salmon	4 oz	31	0	12
Tuna, canned in oil	3 oz	24	0	7
LUNCHEON MEAT				

(It appears to be a Green Light food, but it is filled with preservatives!)

PROTEIN	Serving Size	PROTEIN	CARB	FAT
Roast Beef	3 slices	14	0	4
Ham, Black Forest	3 slices	10	2	2
Turkey	3 slices	10	1	1
NUTS & SEEDS				

(Although seeds and nuts are extremely healthy, due to their high fat calories, I recommend eating them in moderation.)

PROTEIN	Serving Size	PROTEIN	CARB	FAT
Peanuts, dry roasted	½ cup	7	7	13
Peanut Butter	2 tbsp	7	5	15
Almonds	¼ cup	6	6	15
Cashews	¼ cup	5	8	15
Brazil Nuts	6 large	4	4	19
Macadamia Nuts	¼ cup	3	5	25
Pecans	¼ cup	3	2	22
Walnuts	¼ cup	5	0	18
Pistachios	¼ cup	6	4	16
Sunflower Seeds	¼ cup	7	6	17
Sesame Seeds	¼ cup	7	8	20
Soy, milk	1 cup	7	4	4
bean	¼ cup	14	8.5	8
RABBIT				
Domesticated, roasted	4 oz	33	0	9
TOFU, regular, fresh	½ cup	10	2	6
TURKEY				
Dark Meat, no skin	4 oz	32.4	0	8
with skin	4 oz	31.2	0	13
ground	4 oz	20	0	12

Crystal Andrus

GREEN LIGHT PROTEIN

GO! GO! GO!

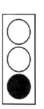

PROTEIN	Serving Size	PROTEIN	CARB	FAT
		(amount in grams)		
BEEF, fat trimmed off				
Eye of Round, lean only	4 oz	33	0	7
CHICKEN, without skin				
Breast	4 oz	33	0	5
Swiss Chalet,				
¼ Chicken, white		40	0	8
DAIRY PRODUCTS				
Milk, skim	1 cup	9	13	0
1%	1 cup	8	12	2.5
Yogurt, fat-free, with sweetener[1]	1 cup	10	15	0
Cheese				
Cottage, 1%	½ cup	14	4	2
Cottage, fat-free	½ cup	13	5	0
Parmesan, fat-free	2 tbsp	2	2	0
Cream, fat-free	2 tbsp	2	2	0
Sour Cream, fat-free	2 tbsp	2	6	0
Ice Cream, fat-free, with sweetener[1]	½ cup	3	19	0
Frozen Yogurt, fat-free, sugar-free[1]	½ cup	4	21	0
EGG WHITE	1 large	3.5	0	0
FISH & SHELLFISH, 4 oz - unless otherwise noted				
Atlantic Cod		20	0	1
Pacific Cod		20	0	1
Clams	9 large or 20 small	14.5	4.5	1
King Crab		21	0	1
Flounder		21.4	0	1
Haddock		21.5	0	1
Halibut		24	0	3
Lobster		21	.5	1
Mussels (boiled or steamed, blue, meat only)		27	8.5	5
Octopus		34	5	3
Oyster	6 oz (12 oysters)	12	6	4
Pike		22	0	1
Scallops	4 large or 10 small	10	1.5	1

GO! GO! GO!

PROTEIN	Serving Size	PROTEIN	CARB	FAT
		(amount in grams)		

FISH & SHELLFISH, continued, 4 oz - unless otherwise noted

(Although the following fish are ideal for weight loss, Health Canada & the US Food and Drug Administration have recently issued advisories due to the toxic amounts of mercury and PCB found in many of the larger fishes.)

		PROTEIN	CARB	FAT
Tuna				
Blue Fin		34	0	7
Yellow Fin		34	0	1
canned in water		34	0	1
Mackerel, King		23	0	2
GOAT	4 oz	31	0	3.5
NUTS AND SEEDS				
Pumpkin Seeds	¼ cup	5	6	5.5
PORK, lean only				
Tenderloin	4 oz	32.5	0	5.5
SNACKS & MISCELLANEOUS				
Protein Shake, proteins+ by ehn-inc		24	.2	2
TOFU				
Lowfat	½ cup	10	2	2
TURKEY				
Breast, without skin	4 oz	34	0	4
VEAL				
Leg	4 oz	41	0	7

RED LIGHT FATS

SOME EXAMPLES OF FOODS WE WANT TO AVOID EATING

SATURATED FATS

Found in:

beef
pork
lamb
dark cuts of poultry
egg yolks
whole or 2% milk
ice cream, regular
cream
butter
cheese

UNSATURATED VEGETABLE OILS
(1 tbsp = 15 grams of fat)

Found in:

coconut oil
palm kernel oil
vegetable shortening
corn oil
peanut oil
cottonseed oil

HYDROGENATED FAT or "PARTIALLY HYDROGENATED VEGETABLE OIL"

Found in:

fried food
stick margarine
store-bought desserts
cookies
cakes
microwave popcorn
crackers

YELLOW LIGHT FATS

YELLOW LIGHT FATS

SOME EXAMPLES OF FOODS WE WANT TO EAT IN MODERATION

Although the following fats are healthy, they are still considered
"YELLOW LIGHT FAT" because they are calorie dense.
Eat in moderation.

UNSATURATED OILS
(1 tbsp = 15 grams of fat)

Found in:

olive oil
canola oil
flax oil
hemp oil
cod liver oil
borage oil
evening primrose oil
pumpkin oil
safflower oil
sunflower oil
sesame oil

AVOCADOS

LEGUMES

soybeans

**MARGARINE
NON-HYDROGENATED**
(still has many chemicals—
use sparingly)

ALL NUTS AND SEEDS

Examples:

peanuts
almonds
walnuts
cashews
sunflower seeds

FISH

Found in:

salmon
sardines
mackerel
trout

Crystal Andrus

GREEN LIGHT FATS

GREEN LIGHT FATS

GO, GO, GO!

There are NO Green Light fats...
All fats, even the healthy ones, must be eaten in moderation!

Tasty Egg-White Omelette

This is my own favorite breakfast staple. You can substitute any other vegetables you like.

Makes 1 serving

¼ cup each: chopped onions, green peppers, tomatoes
4 egg whites
½ cup low- or nonfat cottage cheese
½ teaspoon dried parsley flakes
¼ cup salsa

Sauté veggies in a skillet sprayed with olive oil cooking spray. Remove from pan and set aside. Whisk together egg whites, cottage cheese, and parsley flakes; pour into the skillet and cook over medium heat. Tilt pan to cook egg mixture. When cooked to your liking, add vegetables to one side of omelette. Flip the other side over. Slide on to a plate and serve with salsa.

Baked Chicken Breasts

Make these on Sunday, and have them handy for lunches all week.

Makes 12 servings

12 skinless, boneless chicken breasts
1 cup water
¼ cup balsamic vinegar
1 teaspoon crushed garlic
1 teaspoon each: dried parsley flakes and oregano
1 teaspoon onion powder
Salt and pepper to taste

Crystal Andrus

Preheat oven to 325° F. Place the chicken in a large baking dish. In a separate bowl, combine water, vinegar, garlic, parsley, oregano, onion powder, salt, and pepper; and pour over chicken. Cover with foil and bake for 40 minutes. Remove from oven and set aside to thoroughly cool. Once cooled, pack chicken breasts individually in sandwich bags, and store them in the freezer.

RICH CLEANSING BROTH*

This clear broth is a very satisfying form of nutrition during a cleansing fast. Taken hot or cold, it provides a means of "eating" and being with others at mealtime without going off a liquid detox program.

Makes 6 servings

1½ quarts distilled water
1 large onion, chopped
5 medium carrots, sliced
2 medium potatoes, cubed
1 cup fresh parsley, chopped
4 stalks celery, diced

Place all ingredients in a large soup pot. Bring to a boil; reduce heat and simmer for 30 minutes. Strain and drink the broth.

ONION AND MISO BROTH*

This is a therapeutic broth with antibiotic and immune-enhancing properties. You can have this during your detox.

Makes 6 servings

1 medium onion, chopped
½ teaspoon sesame oil
1 celery stalk with leaves, diced
1 quart distilled water
4 tablespoons miso
2 green onions with tops

In a skillet, sauté onion in sesame oil for 5 minutes. Add celery, and sauté for 2 minutes more. Add water; cover and simmer for 10 minutes. Add miso and green onions with tops. Remove from heat, and liquefy in a blender.

DETOXIFICATION JUICES

Cleansing and reenergizing:

Makes 1 drink

One tablespoon of **greens+**
One cup of pure water or your favorite unsweetened vegetable or fruit juice

Weight-loss cleanser:

Makes 1 drink

2 peeled cucumbers
1 large head romaine lettuce

Weight-loss tonic:

Makes 1 drink

2 grapefruits

Skin-cleansing tonic:*

Makes 1 drink

1 cucumber
½ bunch fresh parsley
One 4-ounce tub alfalfa sprouts
3 to 4 sprigs fresh mint

Allergy cleanser:*

Makes 2 drinks

1 inch fresh ginger root
1 lemon
6 carrots
1 apple, seeded

Constipation cleanser:*

Makes 1 drink

1 papaya
¼ inch fresh ginger root
1 pear

Acne fighter:*

Makes 1 drink

2 slices pineapple, with skin
½ a cucumber
½ an apple
¼ inch fresh ginger root

Sinus cleanser:

Makes 1 drink

2 large apples, seeded
½ teaspoon grated fresh horseradish

*Recipes adapted from *Detoxification: All You Need to Know to Recharge, Renew and Rejuvenate Your Body, Mind and Spirit* by Linda Page, N.D., Ph.D.

Stretching is often overlooked, especially by runners and weight lifters. However, flexibility is an essential component of this program. There are many different ways to stretch and to increase flexibility. The following pictures present an overview of the stretches you should do every day.

We'll be doing static stretching. Static stretching is a slow, deliberate stretch that's held for 30 seconds with no bounce or jerk.

Put on some relaxing music and be aware of your body as you're trying the different poses. Do only what you feel capable of doing. Perform each exercise in a pain-free range only.

MODIFIED STANDING HAMSTRING STRETCH

Extend the right leg, putting the right heel down on floor. Pull the toes back toward the body. Put your hands on your left thigh for support. Lean forward from the hips until a stretch is felt in the back of the right leg. Hold for 30 seconds without bouncing. Repeat on left side.

FULL HAMSTRING STRETCH

Stand with legs straight. Bend forward at the hips until a stretch is felt in the back of both legs. Hold for 30 seconds without bouncing.

SITTING HAMSTRING STRETCH

Sit down on a chair or step. Extend the right leg. Reach forward toward the toes until a stretch is felt in the back of the right leg. Keep the back straight and neck in neutral position. Hold for 30 seconds without bouncing. Repeat on left side.

Crystal Andrus

STANDING QUADRICEP STRETCH

Using a chair or wall as support, bend the right leg up toward the gluteus. Reach back and grasp the right ankle (if this is too difficult, wrap a towel under your foot and hold the ends of the towel instead of your ankle). Pull the foot toward the gluteus until a stretch is felt in the front of the right thigh. Be sure the hips are forward and knees are together. Hold for 30 seconds without bouncing. Repeat on left side.

RUNNER'S STRETCH

Cross the right foot in front of the left foot. Bending the left knee, drop the right hip out to the side of the body, feeling a stretch in the right hip. Support the upper body by placing the hands on the thighs. Hold for 30 seconds without bouncing. Repeat on left side.

STANDING CALF STRETCH

Using a wall or chair for support, place the right foot, behind the left. The farther back the foot, the deeper the stretch. With the front knee slightly bent, drive the back heel down toward the floor and lean forward. Hold for 30 seconds without bouncing. Repeat on left side.

HIP STRETCH

Sit on a chair with the right leg crossed over the left knee. Keeping the right knee down, gently place the hands on the right leg and lean forward until a stretch is felt in the outer right hip. Hold for 30 seconds without bouncing. Repeat on left side.

INNER THIGH STRETCH

Sit erect with soles of the feet together. Gently pull the heels toward the groin. Place elbows on knees and gently push the knees toward the floor until a stretch is felt in the inner thigh. Hold for 30 seconds without bouncing.

UPPER BACK STRETCH

Take the right hand over the left wrist. Rounding out the upper back, pull gently on the right arm until a stretch is felt in the upper back. Hold stomach tight. Hold for 30 seconds without bouncing. Repeat on left side.

Crystal Andrus

STANDING CHEST AND FRONT SHOULDER STRETCH

Clasp hands together behind the back. Gently raise them, feeling the stretch in your chest and shoulders. Hold for 30 seconds without bouncing.

SHOULDER STRETCH

With shoulders down and relaxed, bring the left arm across the chest, parallel to the floor. Place the right hand on the upper arm and gently pull toward the body. Repeat on right side.

TRICEP STRETCH

Raise the right arm above the head. Bending the right elbow, let the hand drop behind the head. Take the left hand and gently pull back on the right elbow until a stretch is felt behind the right arm. Hold for 30 seconds without bouncing. Repeat on left side.

LYING HAMSTRING STRETCH

Lying on back, extend both legs. Raise right leg and place hands behind the calves, keeping the left foot on the floor. Pull the right leg gently toward body until stretch is felt in back of right leg. Hold for 30 seconds without bouncing. Repeat on left side.

LOWER BACK STRETCH—
"CAT STRETCH" (Part A)

On hands and knees, let lower back sag.

LOWER BACK STRETCH—
"CAT STRETCH" (Part B)

Arch back and lower the head.

LYING CHEST AND FRONT SHOULDER STRETCH

Sitting on bent knees, gently clasp the hands behind the back. Leaning forward until the forehead touches the ground, raise arms toward ceiling.

LYING QUADRICEP STRETCH

On stomach, reach behind and grasp the right ankle, pulling the foot toward the gluteus, until a stretch is felt in the front of the right thigh. Keep the hips down and knees adjacent to each other. Hold for 30 seconds without bouncing. Repeat on left side.

ABDOMINALS and LOWER BACK—"COBRA"

A popular yoga pose; lie on stomach, place hands just under shoulders as if to do a push-up. Push away from the floor by raising the head and then upper body off of floor. Keep hips and legs down on floor. Perform this exercise in a pain-free range only.

ADVANCED CALF STRETCH

On hands and feet, bend the left knee slightly. Drive the right heel toward the floor until a stretch is felt in the lower right leg. Push away from the floor and do not let the shoulders sag. Keep tummy tight. Hold for 30 seconds without bouncing. Repeat on left side.

FULL BODY STRETCH—"DOWNWARD DOG"

Position your body in a push-up position. Push the upper body away from the floor, raising gluteus toward the ceiling. Drive the heels into the floor. Don't allow the shoulders to drop into the arms. Keep the abdominals tight.

Crystal Andrus

Acknowledgments

I believe that no one enters our life by coincidence. The duration of the relationship is irrelevant, as some of the shortest encounters have taught me the most, and some have taught me more about myself and who I am simply because of the challenges they've brought me. I value them all. So many incredible people have touched some piece of my soul, and without them I wouldn't be who I am today. Knowing them does my heart good. A special thank you to a small select group of people who have implicitly influenced my life in a powerful way:

My daughters, Madelaine and Julia. My angels in disguise, you've blessed my life with the purest love and joy. I am in awe of both of you! Shine bright—the world needs you!

Aaron James Morissette: You woke me up—in the same way a light gets turned on at dusk. I had no idea how dull life had become. You are "authenticity" to the core. Let's set the world on fire and live every day like it was our last. I completely and utterly adore you!

Tiffany Andrus-Robertson: My baby sister and best friend. I've loved you like my own child since the day you were born; and now to see you as this beautiful, brilliant, amazing woman, mother, wife, sister, and friend is a complete joy! Thank you for all your support and encouragement over the years.

Annette Doose: My best friend. You are the gentlest, sweetest woman I've ever known. I'm so blessed to have you in my life.

Tammy Mair: Loyal, dedicated, and honest. Thank you for always supporting me. I honor you.

Julie and Kamen Nikolov: Your talent amazes me, and your loving spirit and dedication reinforces that there are truly beautiful people in the world.

Michael Webb: What a partner you've proven to be. You are a man of uncompromising integrity.

Shannon Doran-Fisher: Thank you for introducing me to Isagenix, and for your vision, tenacity, ambition, drive, and intense love and support for me and our entire Isagenix team!

Crystal Andrus

You're making such a difference in the lives of many! Bravo to you, Shannon!

Amanda Welde: The love, guidance, and support that you've brought to my children has been incredible. We love you like family.

Violet Viglasky: Home is home! Over the years we've come in and out of each other's lives—always with divine timing. I love you!

Adele Fridman, Helen Valenzuela, Wendy Cowles, Marg Gilbert, Netta Polak, Jessica Boaman, Nitha Nagubody, Jennifer Dent, Roseann Heinrich, Wendy Fleet, Mary Kim Harper, Yvette Lantiegne, Roxanne Bruno, Laura Crisci, Janet Grills, Trudy Wood, Angela Cassibo, Paula Evans, Jeannie Fazio, Lisa Fusco, Gail Gutierrez, Valerie Turck, Dana Theriault, and all the other incredible women who've come to my retreats, volunteered at my events, participated in my *Tele*Course, gotten coaching with me, posted on our message forum, and helped me to share the gift of great health and nutrition—thank you for your support, passion, purpose, and courage! You are candles in the wind!

And finally, the most profound and sincere thank you to Pamela Lee: You saw me speak in Orlando in October 2006. You took a chance, followed your instincts, spoke up, pushed hard, and because of your courage, you have set *our* lives into motion. I am eternally grateful to you! Let's move some mountains!

Last, it goes without saying: to the entire team at Hay House, especially Louise Hay and Reid Tracy—thank you from the deepest recesses of my heart. I am eternally grateful and feel blessed beyond words to be a part of your family.

Stay true to your dreams, goals, and passion for life!

Love,
Crystal

ळ्ळ्ळ् ळ्ळ्ळ्

About the Author

Dedicated to helping women worldwide feel beautiful, feminine, healthy, and empowered—in body, mind, and spirit, **Crystal Andrus** is a leader in the field of self-discovery and personal transformation. A former 200-pound stay-at-home mother of two turned best-selling author, radio host, life coach, fitness expert, and nutritionist, Crystal has woven the tumultuous and triumphant stories of her own life into a courageous journey of healing, health, and ultimate self-empowerment that has inspired thousands. A personal coach to people from all walks of life—including celebrities, medical doctors, artists, musicians, scientists, psychologists, other best-selling authors and coaches, as well as to ordinary people in need—Crystal's passion is to get down "in the trenches" and help those who are ready and willing to become the heroes of their own lives.

She began her journey as a single mom, with little money, but had the courage to invest in herself and follow her dream. Less than 90 days after self-publishing her first book, a journal, an 8-CD Listening Collection, and workout video, she was contacted by two international publishing houses with book offers. Momentum has been a colossal force ever since!

Host of her own weekly radio show on **HayHouseRadio.com**®, she speaks extensively at conventions and conferences worldwide and is always a crowd favorite. Certified by the American College of Sports Medicine and Canadian School of Natural Nutrition, Crystal is working towards her Ph.D. in Holistic Nutrition.

Websites: **www.simplywoman.com** and
www.crystalandrus.com

ʕ◔ʔ ʕ◔ʔ

NOTES

NOTES

NOTES

NOTES

NOTES

NOTES

NOTES

NOTES

NOTES

NOTES

NOTES

NOTES

NOTES

NOTES

NOTES

NOTES

❀✳❀

We hope you enjoyed this Hay House book.
If you'd like to receive a free catalog featuring additional
Hay House books and products, or if you'd like information
about the Hay Foundation, please contact:

Hay House, Inc.
P.O. Box 5100
Carlsbad, CA 92018-5100

(760) 431-7695 or **(800) 654-5126**
(760) 431-6948 (fax) or **(800) 650-5115 (fax)**
www.hayhouse.com® • **www.hayfoundation.org**

❀✳❀

Published and distributed in Australia by: Hay House Australia Pty. Ltd.,
18/36 Ralph St., Alexandria NSW 2015 • *Phone:* 612-9669-4299
Fax: 612-9669-4144 • www.hayhouse.com.au

Published and distributed in the United Kingdom by: Hay House UK, Ltd.,
292B Kensal Rd., London W10 5BE • *Phone:* 44-20-8962-1230
Fax: 44-20-8962-1239 • www.hayhouse.co.uk

Published and distributed in the Republic of South Africa by:
Hay House SA (Pty), Ltd., P.O. Box 990, Witkoppen 2068 • *Phone/Fax:*
27-11-467-8904 • orders@psdprom.co.za • www.hayhouse.co.za

Published in India by: Hay House Publishers India, Muskaan Complex,
Plot No. 3, B-2, Vasant Kunj, New Delhi 110 070 • *Phone:* 91-11-4176-1620
Fax: 91-11-4176-1630 • www.hayhouse.co.in

Distributed in Canada by: Raincoast, 9050 Shaughnessy St., Vancouver, B.C.
V6P 6E5 • *Phone:* (604) 323-7100 • *Fax:* (604) 323-2600 • www.raincoast.com

❀✳❀

Tune in to **HayHouseRadio.com®** for the best in inspirational
talk radio featuring top Hay House authors! And, sign up via the
Hay House USA Website to receive the Hay House online newsletter
and stay informed about what's going on with your favorite authors.
You'll receive bimonthly announcements about Discounts and Offers,
Special Events, Product Highlights, Free Excerpts, Giveaways, and more!
www.hayhouse.com®